Higher National in Business

Higher National in Business

Compiled from:

Marketing: Principles and Practice 4th Edition
by Dennis Adcock, Al Halborg and Caroline Ross

Accounting for Non-Accounting Students 6th Edition
by J. R. Dyson

Management and Organisational Behaviour
7th Edition
by Laurie J. Mullins

Business Economics 2nd Edition
by Win Hornby, Bob Gammie and Stuart Wall

Contract Law 4th Edition
by Catherine Elliott and Frances Quinn

Essential Business Statistics
by Joanne Smailes and Angela McGrane

Exploring Corporate Strategy: Text and Cases
6th Edition
by Gerry Johnson and Kevan Scholes

Research Methods for Business Students 3rd Edition
by Mark Saunders, Philip Lewis and Adrian Thornhill

PEARSON
Custom
Publishing

Pearson Education Limited
Edinburgh Gate
Harlow
Essex CM20 2JE

And associated companies throughout the world

Visit us on the World Wide Web at:
www.pearsoned.co.uk

First published 2005

This Custom Book Edition © 2005 Published by Pearson Education Limited

Compiled from:

Marketing: Principles and Practice 4ᵗʰ Edition
by Dennis Adcock, Al Halborg and Caroline Ross
ISBN 0 273 64677 X
Copyright © Dennis Adcock, Ray Bradfield, Al Halborg, Caroline Ross, 2001

Accounting for Non-Accounting Students 6ᵗʰ Edition
by J. R. Dyson
ISBN 0 273 68385 3
Copyright © Pearson Professional Limited 1987, 1991, 1994, 1997
Copyright © Pearson Education Limited 2001, 2004

Management and Organisational Behaviour 7ᵗʰ Edition
by Laurie J. Mullins
ISBN 0 273 68876 6
Copyright © Laurie J. Mullins 1985, 1989, 1993, 1996, 1999, 2002, 2005

Business Economics 2ⁿᵈ Edition
by Win Hornby, Bob Gammie and Stuart Wall
ISBN 0 273 64603 6
Copyright © Pearson Education Limited 2001

Contract Law 4ᵗʰ Edition
by Catherine Elliott and Frances Quinn
ISBN 0 582 47330 6
Copyright © Pearson Education Limited 1996, 2003

Essential Business Statistics
by Joanne Smailes and Angela McGrane
ISBN 0 273 64333 9
Copyright © Pearson Education Limited 2000

Exploring Corporate Strategy: Text and Cases 6ᵗʰ Edition
by Gerry Johnson and Kevan Scholes
ISBN 0 273 65112 9
Copyright © Prentice Hall Europe 1984, 1988, 1993, 1997, 1999
Copyright © Pearson Education Limited 2002

Research Methods for Business Students 3ʳᵈ Edition
by Mark Saunders, Philip Lewis and Adrian Thornhill
ISBN 0 273 65804 2
Copyright © Pearson Professional Limited 1997
Copyright © Pearson Education Limited 2000, 2003

ISBN 1 84479 244 7

Printed and bound in Great Britain by Hobbs the Printers Limited, Totton, Hants

Contents

Unit 1: Marketing

Learning hours: **60**

NQF level 4:   **BTEC Higher National — H1**

Content Selected: **Adcock, Halborg and Ross, Marketing: Principles and Practices 4th Edition, Chapter 1**

Introduction from the Qualifications Leader

This unit looks at fundamental concepts and principles that underpin the marketing process. The first chapter of Adcock has been selected as an introduction to the unit and as background reading suitable for those with no background or knowledge of marketing.

Description of unit

This unit aims to provide learners with an introduction to the fundamental concepts and principles that underpin the marketing process. In addition, it examines the role and practice of marketing within the changing business environment. This broad-based unit will provide all learners with a concise and contemporary overview of marketing, and give them the knowledge and skills to underpin further study in the specialist field of marketing.

Summary of learning outcomes

To achieve this unit a learner must:

1   Investigate the **concept and process of marketing**

2   Explore the concepts of **segmentation, targeting and positioning**

3   Identify and analyse the individual elements of the **extended marketing mix**

4   Apply the extended marketing mix to **different marketing segments and contexts**.

Content

---

1 Concept and process of marketing

Definitions: alternative definitions including those of the Chartered Institute of Marketing and the American Marketing Association, satisfying customers' needs and wants, value and satisfaction, exchange relationships, the changing emphasis of marketing

Marketing concept: evolution of marketing, business orientations, societal issues and emergent philosophies, customer and competitor orientation, efficiency and effectiveness, limitations of the marketing concept

Marketing process overview: marketing audit, integrated marketing, environmental analysis, SWOT analysis, marketing objectives, constraints, options, plans to include target markets and marketing mix, scope of marketing

Costs and benefits: benefits of building customer satisfaction, desired quality, service and customer care, relationship marketing, customer retention, customer profitability, costs of too narrow a marketing focus, total quality marketing

2 Segmentation, targeting and positioning

Macro-environment: environmental scanning, political, legal, economic, socio-cultural, ecological and technological factors

Micro-environment: stakeholders (organisation's own employees, suppliers, customers, intermediaries, owners, financiers, local residents, pressure groups and competitors), direct and indirect competitors, Porter's competitive forces

Buyer behaviour: dimensions of buyer behaviour, environmental influences, personal variables – demographic, sociological, psychological – motivation, perception and learning, social factors, physiological stimuli, attitudes, other lifestyle and lifecycle variables, consumer and organisational buying

Segmentation: process of market selection, macro and micro segmentation, bases for segmenting markets ie geographic, demographic, psychographic and behavioural; multivariable segmentation and typologies, benefits of segmentation, evaluation of segments and targeting strategies, positioning, segmenting industrial markets, size, value, standards, industrial classification

3 Extended marketing mix

Product: products and brands – features, advantages and benefits, the total product concept, product mix, product life-cycle and its effect on other elements of the marketing mix, product strategy, new product development, adoption process

Place: customer convenience and availability, definition of channels, types and functions of intermediaries, channel selection, integration and distribution systems, franchising, physical distribution management and logistics, ethical issues

Price: perceived value, pricing context and process, pricing strategies, demand elasticity, competition, costs, psychological, discriminatory, ethical issues

Promotion: awareness and image, effective communication, integrated communication process – (SOSTT + 4Ms), promotional mix elements, push and pull strategies, advertising above and below the line including packaging, public relations and sponsorship, sales promotion, direct marketing and personal selling, branding, internet and online marketing

The shift from the 4Ps to the 7Ps: product-service continuum, concept of the extended marketing mix, the significance of the soft elements of marketing – people, physical evidence and process management

4   **Different marketing segments and contexts**

Consumer markets: fast-moving consumer goods, consumer durables, co-ordinated marketing mix to achieve objectives

Organisational markets: differences from consumer markets, adding value through service; industrial, non-profit making, government, re-seller

Services: nature and characteristics of service products – intangibility, ownership, inseparability, perishability, variability, heterogeneity – the 7Ps, strategies, service quality, elements of physical product marketing, tangible and intangible benefits

International markets: globalisation, standardisation versus adaptation, the EU, benefits and risks, market attractiveness, international marketing mix strategies

Outcomes and assessment criteria

Outcomes	Assessment criteria for pass To achieve each outcome a learner must demonstrate the ability to:
1 Investigate the **concept and process of marketing**	• compare alternative definitions of marketing • identify the main characteristics of a marketing-oriented organisation • explain the various elements of the marketing concept • identify and assess the benefits and costs of a marketing approach
2 Explore the concepts of **segmentation, targeting and positioning**	• identify and explain macro and micro environmental factors which influence marketing decisions • propose segmentation criteria to be used for two products in different markets • outline the factors which influence the choice of targeting strategy • explain how buyer behaviour affects marketing activities in two different buying situations
3 Identify and analyse the individual elements of the **extended marketing mix**	• describe how products are developed to sustain competitive advantage • explain how distribution is arranged to provide customer convenience • explain how prices are set to reflect an organisation's objectives and market conditions • illustrate how promotional activity is integrated to achieve marketing objectives • analyse the additional elements of the extended marketing mix
4 Apply the extended marketing mix to **different marketing segments and contexts**	• recommend marketing mixes for two different segments in consumer markets • explain the differences in marketing products and services to organisations rather than consumers • explain how and why international marketing differs from domestic marketing

What is marketing?

Marketing: the action or business of bringing or sending to market.
Oxford English Dictionary

This marketing of supplies was the beginning ... of its prosperity.
Harper's Magazine (1984)

INTRODUCTION

Marketing is now entering a new era, the dawning of the 21st century has brought with it a dynamic and exciting new dimension for both consumers and companies alike, a radical change in how companies and their customers interact is possible with the new technology now available. This technological revolution for sourcing information will alter the way in which many companies conduct their business. Marketing will change and develop, as e-commerce becomes increasingly more important.

This textbook will help you to understand how marketing theory can be applied and made to work in practice, with regard to both traditional and new approaches to marketing. The first step is to understand exactly what marketing is. Almost everyone that has been asked the question, 'What is marketing?' is usually willing to hazard a guess, even if they do give the incorrect answer of selling and advertising, or companies trying to force consumers to buy products that they do not want. Marketing encompasses so many things, from the design and delivery of products, how they are priced, packaged and promoted, to the business side of segmenting and targeting customers, and then positioning the product using the strategic tools available. Traditionally these tools, which are the factors that a supplier can control, have been known as the 'marketing mix'. The mix is sometimes seen as comprising categories based on the product, price, place and promotion (the '4Ps'), however most successful organisations would say that 'marketing' means keeping the customers happy, so much so that they keep coming back to you, and in doing so keep your business profitable. For this it is necessary to see the 'product' offered to customers in a wider context of everything the customer receives, both goods and every type of service. To accommodate this thinking it is necessary to widen the marketing mix to include the people who serve customers, and the processes involved in any exchange that takes place.

All the aspects outlined above will be discussed in greater depth in the book, but it is important to realise that marketing affects virtually everyone, it is literally all around, seen in the variety of products for sale, the advertisements on television, newspapers and the Internet, etc. Today the success of an organisation may depend on how well it markets itself and its products, making sure its customers are satisfied, not only with the product or service purchased, but also with the service received and the ancillary packages of delivery and finance that are offered.

It is evident therefore that marketing covers a wide range of activities, in fact everything related to what was once described as providing:

The right product, in the right place, at the right price, and at the right time.

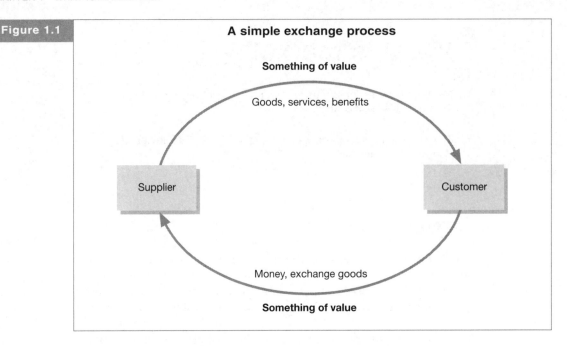

Figure 1.1

A simple exchange process

Something of value

Goods, services, benefits

Supplier

Customer

Money, exchange goods

Something of value

What is 'right'? From the marketing viewpoint it is right if it gets the *desired response* from the required number of potential customers, efficiently and ethically. As customers we expect to have a choice when we spend our money. We can also choose not to spend any money at all by deciding not to buy a product. When we do decide to buy, an exchange takes place. Money is exchanged for the chosen product and hopefully both parties will feel happy with their side of the bargain (Figure 1.1).

Money is not the only form of exchange – for example, companies as well as individuals can exchange products without money actually changing hands. However, in the majority of marketing exchanges, money is used. Usually, in addition to the actual money spent, it is necessary for the purchaser to invest *time* when making the decision to buy. This might involve visiting a shop or other selling outlet, using the Internet, studying catalogues and sometimes discussing the purchase with family or friends.

Inevitably a specific purchase also means the sacrifice of not being able to buy something else with the money spent (the *opportunity cost* of the purchase).

MARKETING DEFINITIONS

It can therefore be seen that Marketing involves an *exchange process*, and this is central to one of the simplest accepted definitions of Marketing which is:

Marketing is the study of exchange processes especially those associated with the provision of goods and services.

While clearly focused and concise, this definition provides no indication of the potential relevance and scope of the subject. It assumes knowledge that money is usually used as the medium for exchange and makes no mention of the objective of the exchange. This aspect is better addressed in the definition proposed by the celebrated American author of marketing textbooks, Philip Kotler:

Marketing is the human activity directed at satisfying needs and wants through an exchange process. (Kotler, 1980)

Since 1980 Kotler's definition has developed:

Marketing is a social and managerial process by which individuals and groups obtain what they need and want through creating and exchanging products and value with others. (Kotler et al., 1999)

An important addition in these definitions is that *needs* and *wants* are to be satisfied. The major addition is the phrase 'of value', and as this is an important aspect of marketing, it will be explored fully in later chapters.

There are many other useful and equally acceptable definitions. The one preferred by the British Chartered Institute of Marketing (CIM) is:

Marketing is the management process responsible for identifying, anticipating and satisfying customers' requirements profitably.

Both Kotler and CIM focus on the profitable exchange being for the supplier. The term 'profitable' is not being used in the strict accounting sense, but rather as an indication of the importance of both parties having to *benefit* from the exchange.

THE EXCHANGE PROCESS

Economic prosperity and progress depends upon the development of ways by which products can be exchanged between individuals and societies. At the simplest level, this would be restricted to direct exchanges with near neighbours. To increase the opportunity to do this, and the variety of goods available, times and meeting places are established so people can gather to make exchanges. Typically these gatherings became known as fairs or markets. These allowed trade to expand over considerable distances as merchants took products from one market to another. Trade involving the direct exchange of goods is known as barter, and depends upon individuals with complementary products finding one another. For an exchange to take place a person who has a pig and wants some wheat needs to find someone with wheat who wants a pig.

This difficulty is significantly reduced once a means of exchange has some general acceptance. This could be a valued product such as salt (paid to Roman soldiers and from which the word 'salary' is derived), tea, precious stones, something made out of precious metal, or the tokens of value that we accept as money. The use of money allows the person to sell the pig on a day when there is someone wanting to buy a pig and buy the wheat on another day when there is someone wanting to sell wheat. It also allows very precise relative values to be placed on different products, depending upon size, availability and demand. Thus, if there are fewer pigs available the person with the pig may find that what he receives in exchange for it will buy several bags of wheat. Alternatively, on another day, the person could find that to buy one bag of wheat it will be necessary to sell two pigs.

The demand and availability for some products such as wheat, or seasonal products such as vegetables, may well depend upon the weather, with the result that the price may vary significantly from month to month. Other products will not be affected in this way, which means that both sellers and buyers can know an accepted price for these products. This makes it unnecessary for a buyer to visit the market, as goods can be purchased at the accepted price through intermediaries or merchants.

As trade increases so does the number of markets and merchants. This provides individuals with opportunities to choose between many more potential suppliers. It also provides suppliers with opportunities to sell to many more potential customers. Inevitably this means that suppliers and customers become increasingly separated: not only by physical distance and time, but also by culture and attitude. This separation is likely to reduce the benefits derived from the exchange. For the supplier this is because eventually income is reduced by the additional costs involved, and for the purchaser as a result of reduced value being received. Marketing, by focusing on the exchange process, provides ways of analysing this process to maximise the benefit both parties gain from an exchange.

WHAT IS MARKETING?

While it could be argued that the definitions and explanations given earlier in this chapter fully answer this question, it is necessary to adopt a different approach to explain the different ways the term 'marketing' is used. This involves recognising that, in practice, the term is used in four different ways. These are as an organisational function, as a management function, as a business concept and as an accepted business philosophy.

Figure 1.2   **The operational functions of marketing**

Marketing as an organisational function

Within all types of organisation it is generally considered good management practice to identify activities and responsibilities and allocate these within specific organisational functional areas such as production or accounting. For most organisations, advertising, sales promotion and marketing research would be considered *core marketing function activities*. Other activities would be dependent upon the type of organisation. For example, within a retail organisation the buying function is likely to be classified as a marketing function whereas, in a manufacturing organisation it would normally be considered a production function. Figure 1.2 shows the wide range of tasks, which can be included within the marketing function. Some of these, like the core activities already mentioned, are sufficiently crucial to the function of marketing to warrant at least an individual chapter in this textbook. Others, such as buying may need more explanation. Within all trading organisations the range of products offered to customers is likely to be of crucial importance to the success of the organisation. As it is the buyers who are responsible for making this selection it is logical to consider this as a marketing function within organisations of this type – for instance, wholesalers, retailers and importers.

It is unusual for organisations to have the responsibility for two of the activities shown specifically assigned to an individual department, and yet both can be of critical importance to an organisation in the marketing context. One of the most important is *risk taking*, as most businesses involve the acceptance of risk. A simple example is the local greengrocer who goes to the market on Friday morning to purchase his stock for the weekend. During the summer it is likely that lettuces, tomatoes and the other salad produce will be purchased. How much of each should be bought? It is important that sufficient is purchased to meet the needs of customers since, if the product is sold out there is always the possibility that a disappointed customer will be a lost customer. Equally the greengrocer does not want to have so much left that some of it will have to be discarded. Since the amount sold in Britain is likely to depend upon the weather, the decision will always involve risk. To reduce this risk it is likely that the weather forecast will be consulted before going to the market.

The second activity for which it is unusual for the responsibility to be allocated specifically is standardisation. At first sight this might be seen as having only a limited relevance to marketing. Yet the introduction of well-promoted standards have significantly contributed to the prosperity of many suppliers. Two very different examples would be the introduction of standardised sizes of eggs by the British Egg Marketing Board and the introduction of quality standards by the Japanese optical industry.

Marketing as a management function

Another aspect of marketing is its crucial role in ensuring that the activities of an organisation are clearly directed towards the principal objective of meeting the needs of customers effectively. This is the *planning* and *co-ordinating* role of marketing. This aspect of marketing was specifically identified in 1974 by the pioneering marketing author T. Levitt, in *Marketing for Business Growth*, in which he stated that marketing is not just a business function, it is a consolidating view of the whole business purpose.

It is useful to separate this management aspect of marketing from the philosophy of marketing and the other functions of marketing, since it involves the allocation of resources as well as the co-ordination of effort and therefore has to be carried out at a higher level within an organisation. It can indeed be argued, that marketing as a management function should always be the central task of the most senior management team, whatever this might be called within any specific organisation.

Marketing as a business concept

This third aspect of the term 'marketing' relates to its use with respect to the insights that have resulted from the exchange process having been studied in detail and from many different points of view. From this study theories have been developed which are used to analyse the process of meeting customers' needs and determining how these may be improved. This has involved developing specific terminology to classify individual components of different types of need and ways that these can be met.

It is now accepted that all types of organisation can effectively use these concepts. These include those that manufacture products and those that provide a service, as well as organisations such as charities like Save the Children Fund. Their product is the feeling you have after making a donation, so that even in this situation a real exchange is taking place between the giver and the charity. Such examples illustrate the relevance of marketing to many activities and products. It is now accepted as being equally relevant to industrial and service industries as well as to the public sector and voluntary organisations.

Marketing as an accepted business philosophy

Marketing as a business philosophy recognises the importance of the customer and that business exists to serve customers rather than manufacture products. To be effective this philosophy must be accepted as being crucial in every part of an organisation. Peter Drucker once wrote, 'There is only one valid definition of business purpose: to create a customer.' If you do not have any customers for the product or service your organisation offers, then there is no reason for its continuing existence.

This was recognised in 1776 by Adam Smith, the father of modern economics, who wrote:

> Consumption is the sole end and purpose of all production and the interests of the product ought to be attended to only so far as it may be necessary for promoting those of the customer.

This is still true today and not dependent on the organisation being a manufacturing firm. An example of how this still applies in today's world is the book selling company Amazon.com.

Example   The philosophy of Amazon.com is that the customer is king. Jeff Bezos, the founder of the company, had several areas of the business which were seen as vital to success. One of these was how to attract and keep customers, customer care was seen as being a vital element and a key growth driver of the company. It will be interesting to chart the future performance of the company and observe whether speedy deliveries, a discount on prices, good selection of books and customised service will continue to attract customers in the years to come.

UNDERSTANDING MARKETING AS A STUDENT

In recognising these four aspects of marketing it can be appreciated that any one of them can be the core theme of a basic text on marketing. A review of these will show that many use 'Marketing as a management function' as the core theme. This approach assumes that marketing is primarily a planning activity and as a result there are a number of disadvantages. This text seeks to avoid these by considering all four aspects of the subject in turn. Initially the philosophy of marketing will be explored in the terms of customers, their context and behaviour. Then the concepts of marketing will be introduced, together with the related functions of marketing and finally the co-ordinating and planning aspects of marketing will be considered.

Before it is possible to fully understand the roles of marketing it is necessary to consider what is a *market*. At its simplest a market is a place where goods and services are offered for sale, and buyers consider those offerings. However the idea of a physical trading place is no longer sufficient to encompass every location where an exchange is possible. There are many points of contact between suppliers and potential buyers and all of these are part of the market. It is, therefore, useful to widen the idea of a market to include the complete *market space* occupied by a group of suppliers and their customers. This could include the so-called *virtual market* that exists when customers are purchasing goods over the Internet. George Day, writing in 1994, suggested that:

Most markets do not have neat boundaries.

And:

Different customers will have different perceptions of the products offered, and suitable substitutes, thus making it difficult to describe a market in an absolute sense.

What should be avoided is the temptation to define a market solely in terms of a specific product that is being offered for sale. Descriptions such as 'the car market' or 'the soft drink market' tend to lead to thinking that revolves around a particular product class rather than around the *benefits* customers desire, and which that product could satisfy. It will be seen that there are often many different ways to achieve the ultimate marketing goal of customer satisfaction and supplier profit.

MARKETS AND MARKET REGULATION

Customers achieve satisfaction through a beneficial exchange with a supplier. The customer receives something they desire and the cost (sacrifice) is considered worth paying. On the other hand the supplier makes a sale and also receives a satisfactory consideration (price) for the goods or services. Historically local customers knew their local suppliers and were able to judge the quality of goods offered. Both buyer and seller obviously want a good deal, but because they know one another they are likely to see the benefit of being fair to the other party. If there was a problem, that could be sorted out locally and it is apparent that dealing with someone who is known involves less risk than dealing with a stranger.

However trade has now grown to a global scale, and beyond. In particular the trade between strangers, customers and suppliers who have no close intimacy has increased with the growth and development of markets. There is an understandable fear that maybe one party is gaining at the expense of the other, and this has required that rules be introduced to protect customers from problems. In particular, those involved in supervising markets have introduced regulations governing how trade should be conducted. These are designed to ensure that those coming to purchase at their market can trust in that market as a whole and thus encourage *'fair'* trading. There are now universally accepted measures of length, weight and volume, and regulations as to the accuracy of the measures used by traders. The penalties for giving short measure became extremely harsh since to do so could significantly undermine the integrity of an established market. To further encourage good practice many of these regulations have become part of nationally administered laws. Whilst such rules and regulations are now a feature of most traditional market places there is still a long way to go to regulate the Internet.

There are three kinds of markets that require discussion:

- Open markets
- Regulated markets
- Unregulated markets.

Open markets

Both of the parties making an exchange are more likely to consider that the exchange has been beneficial when the exchange has been made within the context of what is known as an 'open market'. This is a market that has all of the following characteristics:

1 Single standardised product
2 Many buyers
3 Many sellers
4 Buyers and sellers have equal access to all available information relevant to the market.

An open market can be established and continue only when both buyers and sellers agree to abide by the rules necessary to maintain the four conditions set out above. This means that the product has to be clearly defined, that membership of the market as a buyer or seller has to be regulated and the rules relating to the availability of information are clearly established and regulated. Because the market is formed to trade in a standardised product, there is an overwhelming emphasis on *prices*. In fact, when there is no way to differentiate a product it becomes a commodity and the price becomes the sole determinant of value. Those markets which set the world price for commodities such as gold, oil, orange juice, wheat, coffee or soya beans, as well as the major stock markets, all have rules which are intended to maintain the 'openness' of the markets. The penalties for infringing these rules are inevitably severe.

However, even in these markets there are opportunities for speculation and for product differentiation. Indeed this is often necessary in order for them to continue as effective markets during times of difficulty. Is a product offered for immediate delivery the same as an identical product being sold now, but for delivery in (say) six months time? These are obviously different in that one might benefit a customer with an immediate need, the other offers the benefit of secure supply in order to meet future requirements. Alternatively a supplier who needs to sell immediately might be seen in a different light to one who is able to store stocks and sell when prices are higher due to changes in the balance of supply and demand.

Example | The demand for beer in the UK increases during a hot summer and is significantly depressed if the summer is cold and wet. This would reduce the demand for barley since this is an important ingredient of beer. Furthermore, after a cold wet summer brewers are likely to have unused stocks of the barley purchased in expectation of higher demand. As a result they are likely to postpone purchasing new supplies of barley. The farmer having taken in his crop is likely to need to sell some of it to at least pay for the harvest. If his normal brewer customers are unwilling to buy barley he becomes dependent upon the speculators within the market who will purchase barley believing that because of the poor summer there will be a poor harvest and as a result the price will rise as time passes. Thus, the market is able to function in spite of there being low demand by the actual users of the product.

While there are many examples of open markets, these must be considered exceptions in the context of exchanges normally made by individuals. There are a number of reasons for this:

■ First, products purchased are rarely homogeneous. Even potatoes vary by variety and packaging making comparison by the purchaser difficult, which frustrates the first condition of an open market.
■ Secondly, the numbers of potential buyers and the demand for products is constantly changing, which frustrates the second condition of an open market.
■ Thirdly, the individual purchaser usually has a limited choice of supplier, which frustrates the third condition of the open market.
■ Lastly, purchasers rarely have as much information about the market as does the supplier, which contravenes the fourth condition of an open market.

Because of the special conditions within an *open market* there is less scope for marketing and for the many techniques utilised by marketers to create unique offerings in order to satisfy customers.

Regulated markets

The regulations governing an open market are designed to ensure that it is able to operate with none of the participants having an unfair advantage over the others. Regulated markets recognise that there is a lack of balance between the parties and therefore this type of market has rules that are intended to ensure a degree of fair trading. Such regulations are laid out in the Sale of Goods Act that requires products offered to the general public to be fit for the purpose for which they were intended. Thus, the purchaser of a pair of gloves intended for washing up can expect them to be waterproof and have them replaced should those purchased leak.

All developed societies have similar regulations to regulate legal trade. It is therefore usual for manufacturing and trading organisations to have to comply with such regulations which effectively constitute one aspect of the marketing environment in which an exchange, or trade in general, takes place. Legislation and market regulations are not the only environmental variables affecting marketing. Others involve the economic, social and technological variables in a market place, which are discussed in detail in chapters 3 and 4. Since organisations have little influence over these environmental factors they are generally referred to as 'uncontrollable variables'. They contrast the variables such as product quality, service, additional features and price which can be determined by the organisation supplying a given product and, because

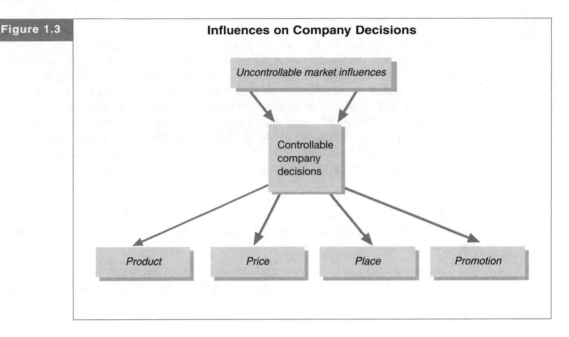

Figure 1.3

Influences on Company Decisions

of this, these marketing activities or variables are known as 'controllable variables'. Figure 1.3 shows the relationship between these two types of variable.

Marketing is involved in developing the controllable variables within the context of the uncontrollable, but regulated market place in order to attract sufficient customers to trade with a specific supply organisation.

Unregulated markets

If there were no regulations then customers would be unprotected and the maxim of 'let the buyer beware' (*caveat emptor*) would apply. There is a distinct difference between an unregulated market and a de-regulated market. In the former the buyer is 'on their own' reacting to offers made such as in a street market or a car boot sale where there is little comeback if products don't perform as expected. De-regulation is the removal of artificial monopoly restrictions in order to encourage free competition and increase customer choice. This has been a feature of a number of markets over recent years, and the results have been dramatic as in the airline sector and now in telecommunications. However the new competitive environment is still regulated, the difference being that those regulations are not restrictive but are based on fair competition.

the Internet is not yet controlled in quite the same way. Because it is international, and the country of origin is not always clear there is still a lack of confidence amongst some customers. Problems persist regarding the reliability of delivery, product quality and the handling of complaints, and the privacy of personal details linked to the possibility of payment fraud. These will be issues that will be the focus of much attention as the Internet grows in importance, and if they are not tackled effectively the growth of e-commerce could be seriously reduced.

Selling and early marketing has traditionally been based on a 'stimulus → response' sequence. In this process the supplier makes an attractive offer (stimulus) in the hope of receiving a positive response (purchase decision) from the customer. This was the basis of much early thinking about marketing, especially in the *fast-moving consumer goods* (fmcg) markets in the middle of the 20th century. It is still relevant in certain markets, and for certain products or services. However the response will depend to a large extent on the confidence a customer has regarding both the product offered and the supplier making the offering. In an unregulated market there is no obvious protection. In such a situation, the marketing role is to promote confidence regarding a supplier so customers are prepared to trade. Many techniques are available, but they all work best in a regulated yet competitive market place. In this type of market the role of marketing is to do more than instil confidence, it is to ensure that an offering is really the best available for a chosen group of customers.

MARKETING TODAY

The four aspects of marketing were earlier described as:

- Marketing as an organisational function
- Marketing as a management function
- Marketing as a business concept
- Marketing as a business philosophy.

Marketing in all these roles has one overriding task – to develop and retain customers for the business and to ensure that satisfactory exchanges take place between the supplier and the chosen customers. There is still a role for marketing in developing offers that customers find irresistible, the use of promotional techniques will always feature strongly in every marketing campaign. However there has been much development regarding the role of marketing over the last few decades. Good marketers understand their customers and base all activities on what can be made acceptable to them. Good marketers work inside their organisations to ensure that the best possible overall offering is developed and that it is supported by all employees of the company. But more importantly, today, good marketers regard customers as *partners* in the exchange process. Customers are not just there to be sold to, but are to be encouraged and developed so that every satisfied customer is an advocate for the supplier, prepared to recommend a favoured company to friends and acquaintances, and willing to purchase again from that organisation. This has led to the development of *relationship marketing*, a concept that focuses on retaining customers not just achieving a sale. Whilst market conditions are not always appropriate for relationship marketing, there are many occasions when such an approach leads to the best marketing option. This aspect of marketing will be discussed further in later chapters.

CONCLUSION

From reading this chapter, you should have grasped a basic understanding of what marketing is. It should also be clear that this involves understanding a number of different aspects of the subject, all of which centre upon the simple basic philosophy that customers are crucial to an organisation's success and this involves interacting with those customers and developing profitable exchanges with them over time. Tom Peters put profit into perspective:

Long-term profit *equals* revenue from continuously happy customer relationships *minus* cost.

Marketing is therefore as we have seen, much more than selling, although some aspects of persuasion and influence are inevitably present. Satisfying customer needs over time, but not at any cost, is an ideal, but this requires that they are customers of your organisation, not your competitors. The obvious problem is that profit is required in any exchange, or at least a cost-effective use of resources. In addition there are wider ethical and moral issues, which will be discussed later. Suffice it to say that business today is not sales at any cost. A prominent US businessman once suggested:

There is a new bottom line for business – social approval. Without it, economic victory would be pyrrhic indeed.

QUESTIONS

1   *How can marketing benefit organisations?*

2   *Describe how the exchange process functions.*

3   *In what ways do you see marketing developing in the future?*

FURTHER READING

Brabbs, C. (2000) 'Coke in One 2 One link to target teens market', *Marketing*, 3 February.

Brown, R. (1987) 'Marketing – a function and a philosophy', *Quarterly Review of Marketing*.

Davidson, H. (1997) *Even More Offensive Marketing*. Penguin.

Day, G. (1994) 'The capabilities of market driven organisations', *Journal of Marketing*, October.

Drucker, P. (1968) *The Practice of Management*, Pan.

Kotler, P., Armstrong, G., Saunders, J. and Wong, V. (1999) *Principles of Marketing*, 2nd European edn., Prentice-Hall.

Levitt, T. (1960) 'Marketing myopia', *Harvard Business Review*, March–April.

Levitt, T. (1974) *Marketing for Business Growth*.

Murphy, C. (2000) 'Why Coca-Cola is no longer it', *Marketing*, 20 January.

Nakamoto, M. and Kehoe, L. (2000) 'Japan to step up production of semiconductors', *Financial Times*, 14 April.

Saunders, R. (1999) *Business the amazon.com way*. Capstone Publishing.

Smith, A. (1976) *The Wealth of Nations*, Macmillan.

Wilson, T. (2000) 'New media choice/Number 10', *Marketing*, 18 May.

Example

Marketing the virtual way

There are many ways in which organisations can try to get the customer to feel more in tune with them, and so more likely to be loyal customers, and it is not only organisations who try to make this happen but also political parties. To this end the government in Britain has a website www.pm.gov.uk and it is becoming increasingly popular. The prime minister at the time of writing is Tony Blair and he has a new message each Friday for the general public who view the site. Also on the site is a page telling how the government feel they have succeeded in many areas.

Other features of the site include photographs of each of the individual cabinet ministers along with a short biography on each, a virtual tour of 10 Downing St – especially the cabinet room. This part of the tour is very novel and to some most interesting, as it offers the view from Mr. Blair's seat as well as close-ups of the furniture, carpets and curtains.

It will be interesting to see future developments on the site, but there is no doubt a government site is here to stay.

Questions

1 *Do you think that the website will help the government to be seen in a favourable light?*

2 *In what ways do you think the government can market itself?*

3 *In what way could the www. pm.gov.uk site be improved for marketing purposes?*

4 *Which other organisations could benefit from having a website such as this?*

CASE STUDY

The Cola wars

There is aggressive worldwide competition between the major suppliers of cola drinks. The 'weapons' used are all aspects of marketing aimed to make individual brands more desirable than competitors.

Coca-Cola has been winning in the volume sales growth, whilst Pepsi Cola takes second place. In the UK although only 60 per cent of the population actually drink colas there are more men than women consumers, and the percentage of drinkers is much higher for the younger age groups when compared to the older age range. Thus the young are the main target market.

For many years Coca-Cola has been the leading brand, outselling Pepsi-Cola by more than two to one in the UK and by four to one worldwide (although in Scotland, the soft drink Irn-Bru is more popular than Coca-Cola). Diet Coke showed a similar dominance over Diet Pepsi. However, more than a decade ago in the US, Pepsi gained significant market share as a result of the effective marketing campaign featuring the 'Pepsi challenge' which concentrated on the product taste. This led to the well-documented launch of the ill-fated New Coke.

However Coca-Cola has now recovered and one of the secrets of its success is its widespread distribution coverage. Former Coke President Bob Woodward pledged 'to put Coke within an arm's reach of desire'. The emphasis on availability complements other aspects of the way Coke is offered.

More recently it has been Pepsi that has changed the presentation of its product with Pepsi Max and project blue – the re-packaging of the product. However the re-launch was reported as not successful. Pepsi worldwide (excluding the USA) made a loss in the year following the ▶

relaunch. Although Max is now performing well, the losses on the other two products (regular and Diet) have been a problem.

Things however have not been running smoothly for Coca-Cola. They suffered bad publicity and a drop in share price after being accused of mishandling a contamination scare in Belgium. The company was forced to destroy millions of cases of both Coca-Cola and Fanta when hundreds of people in Belgium became ill after drinking the products. The bad publicity was more from the fact that it took the company longer than a week to act on the rumours.

In Europe, PepsiCo and Virgin complained that Coca-Cola was using unfair practices. They alleged that Coke used discounts and rebates to entice wholesalers and retailers to grant them exclusive distribution. Similar problems are facing the company in other parts of the world, and in Russia Coke's plants are operating at levels far below capacity.

Coke is using several measures to fight back. The future will see much more use of the traditional glass bottle with its easy-to-recognise shape. 'Enjoy Coca-Cola' will replace the slogan 'Always Coca-Cola' and prices are likely to increase slightly to improve profit margins. Recent major advertising campaigns in the U.K. have encouraged consumers to collect on pack tokens from Coca-Cola and exchange them for a prepaid mobile phone. The mobile phone has a Coca-Cola fascia, and a ring tone that plays the jingle from the Coke television advert.

Pepsi also offered goods to help promote products, they included Sony Mini-Discs and Technics turntables at discounted prices, in return for a specified number of ring-pulls.

It is interesting to watch how the brands develop and how they compete with each other, but in the UK, the war has not been won completely. Companies such as Virgin who produce a variety of soft drinks and Barr's the makers of Irn-Bru are innovative and hungry for success. The future may yet be orange – the colour of Irn-Bru, it has been a runaway success in Scotland, is catching up in England, is especially popular when mixed with vodka in Russia, and is about to be launched in America. The soft drinks war is not static, it is indeed a tough market to be in.

Questions

1 *Given the facts above, what differences do you identify in the UK market between Coke and its competitors?*

2 *Do you think these are the cause of the 'runner up' position of Pepsi?*

3 *What changes do you think Pepsi could make to strengthen its position? – the answer is not to spend more on advertising, which has been tried, although you could discuss the benefits from association, such as those when Pepsi sponsored various international superstars.*

4 *Compare the competition between the following companies from the marketing viewpoint:*
   – Coca-Cola and Pepsi
   – McDonald's and Burger King
   – British Airways and Virgin Atlantic
   – Unilever and Proctor and Gamble.

Unit 2: Managing Financial Resources and Decisions

Learning hours: 60

NQF level 4: BTEC Higher National — H1

Content Selected: Dyson, Accounting for Non Accounting Students 6th Edition, Chapter 4

Introduction from the Qualifications Leader

This unit is designed to give a broad understanding of the ways in which finance is managed in a business organisation. Outcome 4 requires the understanding of financial statements and accounts, and Chapter 4 deals with these accounts and their construction in respect of sole traders.

Description of unit

This unit is designed to give learners a broad understanding of the ways in which finance is managed within a business organisation. Learners will learn how to evaluate the different sources of finance, compare the ways in which these are used and will learn how to use financial information to make decisions. Included will be consideration of decisions relating to pricing and investment, as well as budgeting. Finally, learners will learn techniques for the evaluation of financial performance.

Summary of learning outcomes

To achieve this unit a learner must:

1   Explore the **sources of finance** available to a business

2   Analyse the implications of **finance as a resource** within a business

3   Make **financial decisions** based on financial information

4   Analyse and evaluate the **financial performance** of a business.

Content

1 **Sources of finance**

Range of sources: sources for different businesses, long term such as share capital, retained earnings, loans, third-party investment, short/medium term such as hire purchase and leasing, working capital stock control, cash management, debtor factoring

Implications of choices: legal, financial and dilution of control implications, bankruptcy

Choosing a source: advantages and disadvantages of different sources, suitability for purpose eg matching of term of finance to term of project

2 **Finance as a resource**

Finance costs: tangible costs eg interest, dividends; opportunity costs eg loss of alternative projects when using retained earnings; tax effects

Financial planning: the need to identify shortages and surpluses eg cash budgeting; implications of failure to finance adequately, overtrading

Decision making: information needs of different decision makers

Accounting for finance: how different types of finance and their costs appear in the financial statements of a business, the interaction of assets and liabilities on the balance sheet

3 **Financial decisions**

Budgeting decisions: analysis and monitoring of cash and other budgets

Costing and pricing decisions: calculation of unit costs, use within pricing decisions, sensitivity analysis

Investment appraisal: payback period, accounting rate of return, discounted cashflow techniques ie net present value, internal rate of return

Nature of long-term decisions: nature of investment importance of true value of money, cash flow, assumptions in capital investment decisions, advantages and disadvantages of each method

4 **Financial performance**

Terminology: introduction to debit, credit, books of prime entry, accounts and ledgers, trial balance, final accounts

Financial statements: basic form, structure and purpose of main financial statements ie balance sheet, profit and loss account, cashflow statement, notes, preparation not required; distinctions between different types of business ie limited company, partnership, sole trader

Interpretation: use of key accounting ratios for profitability, liquidity, efficiency, and investment, comparison both external ie other companies, industry standards and internal ie previous periods, budgets

Outcomes and assessment criteria

Outcomes	Assessment criteria for pass **To achieve each outcome a learner must demonstrate the ability to:**
1 Explore the **sources of finance** available to a business	• identify the sources of finance available to a business • assess the implications of the different sources • select appropriate sources of finance for a business project
2 Analyse the implications of **finance as a resource** within a business	• assess and compare the costs of different sources of finance • explain the importance of financial planning • describe the information needs of different decision makers • describe the impact of finance on the financial statements
3 Make **financial decisions** based on financial information	• analyse budgets and make appropriate decisions • calculate unit costs and make pricing decisions using relevant information • assess the viability of a project using investment appraisal techniques
4 Analyse and evaluate the **financial performance** of a business	• explain the purpose of the main financial statements • describe the differences between the formats of financial statements for different types of business • analyse financial statements using appropriate ratios and comparisons, both internal and external

Contracting companies particularly need to be prudent . . .

Conservative accounting policies

Following much discussion about the accounting policies used by support services groups, especially those involved with the public sector, Capita went out of its way in its six month results to 30 June 2002 to stress how conservative its accounting policies are.

Executive chairman Rod Aldridge pointed out that Capita consistently applied more conservative accounting than required by the relevant accounting standards, had a simple corporate structure, no special purpose financing vehicles, no associated companies and no long term Private Finance Initiative (PFI) contracts.

The directors of Capita have noted the recent comments regarding accounting policies adopted by companies in the support services sector, particularly with regard to accounting for contract costs.

The relevant accounting standards for contract costs are SSAP 9 Stocks and Long-Term Contracts; FRS 15 Tangible Fixed Assets; and UITF 34 Pre-contract Costs. Capita claims that it has consistently exceeded the requirements of these accounting standards.

The directors consider that Capita's policies are robust, appropriate and consistently more conservative than those required by the relevant accounting standards. The directors have always adopted this approach and they are committed to continuing to follow this prudent policy in the future.

The effect of complying with UITF 34 is, because only of deferral of success fees, to reduce previously reported net, assets at 31 March 2001 by a cumulative £1.8m and net assets at 31 March 2002 by £0.9m.

Profit before tax cumulative to 31 March 2001 is lower by £2.9m and profit before tax for year ended 31 March 2002 by £1.3m.

The results of W S Atkins for the year ended 31 March 2002 were after charging £8.9m (v £6.1m) on PFI bidding, including the Metronet bid for London Underground and the bid for the Colchester Garrison.

The group capitalises its PFI bidding costs in compliance with UITF 34 from the point at which its consortium is appointed sole preferred bidder and when such costs may be foreseen with virtual certainty as recoverable at financial close. W S Atkins capitalised no costs at 31 March 2002 (v £0.1m).

Accountancy, September 2002.

Questions relating to this news story may be found on page 42 ▸▸

About this chapter

Before you can begin to play any card or board game you normally have to learn the rules laid down by the inventor. You could devise your own rules. It might take some time and the game that you play might not be as enjoyable as it would be if you adopted the inventor's rules. Similarly, with accounting. You could adopt your own rules but no one else would understand the accounting information prepared on that basis and it would not be very useful.

Unlike a card or a board game, however, no one sat down and devised a set of rules for preparing accounting information. What happened over a long period of time was that a common procedure gradually evolved. So much so that it is now possible to identify a number of accounting practices that appear to be generally accepted.

In this book we will refer to such practices as *accounting rules*, although some accountants use a number of other terms, e.g. assumptions, axioms, concepts, conventions, postulates, principles and procedures.

This chapter outlines those conventional accounting rules that are widely accepted. The chapter is divided into seven main sections. In the first main section we explain why this chapter is particularly important and relevant for non-accountants. This is followed by a review of the background to the subject. The next three sections outline the main accounting rules. We have classified them under three main headings: *boundary rules, measurement rules* and *ethical rules*. These sections are followed by a section that considers the possibility of preparing accounting information on the basis of what is called a 'conceptual framework'. Before we conclude the chapter we pose some questions that non-accountants should ask about the accounting rules adopted by their own particular entity.

Learning objectives

By the end of this chapter you should be able to:

- **identify the main accounting rules used in preparing accounting information;**

- **classify them into three broad groupings;**

- **describe each accounting rule;**

- **explain why each one of them is important;**

- **outline the main features of a conceptual framework of accounting.**

! Why this chapter is important for non-accountants

As a non-accountant, do you need to question the information that accountants give you? Do you have to know what procedures they use in preparing accounting information? Does it matter if you do not? We think that the answer to all three questions is 'yes'. As a senior manager, you will be ultimately responsible for any decisions made by the entity and you cannot fall back on the excuse that '*it was the accountants that did it*'.

In order to satisfy yourself that the accountants have got it right, you need to be aware of what procedure or rules they have used in preparing any information given to you. In general, they will have used a number of conventional rules that have evolved over many centuries. However, the detailed application of them is subject to a considerable amount of individual interpretation. This means that if you interpret the circumstances differently you can quite easily change the results. For example, it is easy to change the profit or loss that an entity has made by altering the amount charged for the depreciation of fixed assets (such as machinery) or the provision set aside for bad debts (these topics are considered in Chapter 5). Similarly, the cost of making a particular product can be altered by changing the way that overheads are charged to products (see Chapter 16).

We are not suggesting that accountants deliberately act mischievously or even fraudulently in presenting information to management. The important point to grasp is that a considerable amount of individual judgement is required in preparing accounting information. Hence you, as a senior non-accounting manager, need to approve the assumptions and estimates adopted by your accountants. You cannot do that in a meaningful way if you have no idea how accountants go about preparing the information they present to you.

The first step in understanding what they have done is to know what rules they have adopted. The second step is to consider whether they are appropriate for that particular entity. And the third step (if need be) is to challenge the accountants' adoption or interpretation of the rules that they have adopted. It follows that this chapter is a vital one underpinning all that follows in the rest of the book.

We will turn to those rules shortly but first we want to give you more of the background to the subject. We do so in the next section.

Historical development

The practice of accounting has evolved slowly over many centuries. Accounts were prepared originally for stewardship purposes and it is only in more recent times that they have become more widely used. This has meant that some of the traditional practices have had to be adapted to suit more recent requirements. For example, the demand to produce accounts on an annual basis means that a number of arbitrary decisions have to be taken to deal with some events that last for more than one year, such as the building of a power plant.

Users of accounts are not always aware of such difficulties. They sometimes expect accounts to be prepared in a certain way and then they become upset when they find that this not the case. We referred to this phenomena in the last chapter as the 'expectations gap'. It follows that in order to bridge the expectations gap users should be aware of the basis upon which accounts have been prepared, i.e. they have to know the rules.

Until the middle of the nineteenth century accounting rules were largely conventions. They were the ones that had gradually become generally accepted by custom and practice. A number of laws were then introduced to regulate company accounting practices but it was not until 1948 that accounting become much more rule based. Nevertheless, accountants still had a great deal of discretion in how they prepared a set of financial accounts for companies. With other types of entities they had almost complete freedom to do as they wished.

A major change took place in 1971 when the various professional bodies began to issue a series of guides called *Statements of Standard Accounting Practice* (SSAPs). The responsibility for issuing accounting standards was taken over in 1991 by a body called the Accounting Standards Board (ASB). The ASB took responsibility for the existing SSAPs but it also began to issue its own guides called Financial Reporting Standards (FRSs). It is mandatory for professionally qualified accountants to follow the requirements of both SSAPs and FRSs.

SSAPs and FRSs lay down in much greater detail than any legal requirement the way that financial statements must be prepared and presented. They are not absolutely prescriptive but a professionally qualified accountant would have to have some good reasons for ignoring their requirements. We shall be returning briefly to the work of the ASB later in the chapter and then in more detail in Chapter 9.

In this chapter we are going to deal with the conventional rules of accounting that have been developed over a period of time. There are a considerable number that may be identified (perhaps over 100) but we are going to deal with only 14 of them. For convenience we are going to classify them as follows:

1 boundary rules;
2 measurement rules;
3 ethical rules.

A diagrammatic representation of them is shown in Figure 2.1. The way that we have chosen to classify these rules is largely arbitrary. It has been done this way to make it easier for you to understand them. For convenience we also show these accounting rules in an Appendix at the end of the chapter.

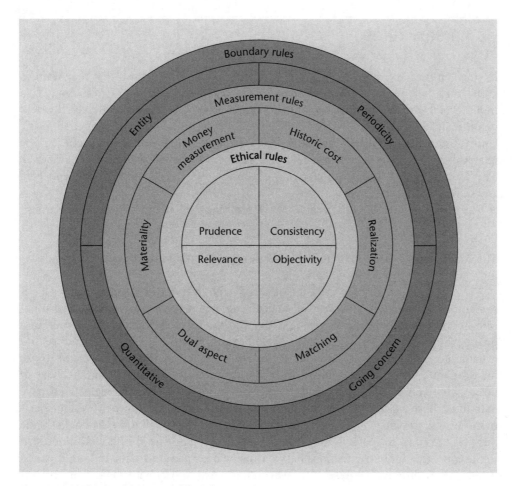

Figure 2.1 **The basic accounting rules**

Activity 2.1	Consult a reputable dictionary (such as the Oxford English) and write down the meaning of the following words. They may each have several meaning so extract the ones that relate more to fact or truths.

(a) assumptions
(b) axioms
(c) concepts
(d) conventions
(e) postulates
(f) principles
(g) procedures.

Consider the definitions that you have extracted carefully. Do they all have a similar meaning?

Boundary rules

In small entities, the owners can probably obtain all the information that they want to know by finding out for themselves. In larger entities this is often impracticable, and so a more formal way of reporting back to the owners has to be devised. However, it would be difficult to inform the owners about literally *everything* that had happened to the entity. A start has to be made, therefore, by determining what should and should not be reported. Hence, accountants have devised a number of what we will call *boundary rules*. The boundary rules attempt to place a limit on the amount and type of data collected and stored within the entity.

There are four main boundary rules, and we examine them in the following subsections.

Entity

There is so much information available about any entity that accountants start by drawing a boundary around it (see Figure 2.2).

The accountant tries to restrict the data collected to that of the entity itself. This is sometimes very difficult, especially in small entities where there is often no clear distinction between the public affairs of the entity and the private affairs of the owner. In a profit-making business, for example, the owners sometimes charge their household expenditure to the business, and they might also use their private bank account to pay for goods and services meant for the business. In such situations, accountants have to decide where the business ends and the private affairs of the owners begin. They have then to establish exactly what the business owes the owner and the owner owes the business. The accountants will, however, only be interested in recording in the books of the business the effect of these various transactions on the *business*; they are not interested in the effect that those transactions have on the owner's private affairs. Indeed, it would be an entirely different exercise if the accountants were to deal with the owner's private affairs. This would mean that they were accounting for different entities altogether, i.e. private entities instead of public ones, although there may be a great deal of overlap between the two types.

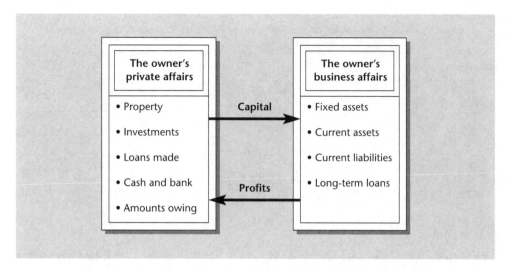

Figure 2.2 **The entity rule: the owner's business and private affairs are kept quite separate**

Periodicity

Most entities have an unlimited life. They are usually started in the expectation that they will operate for an indeterminate period of time, but it is clearly unhelpful for an owner to have to wait years before any report is prepared on how an entity is doing. The owner would almost certainly wish to receive regular reports at frequent short intervals.

If an entity has an unlimited life, any report must be prepared at the end of what must inevitably be an arbitrary period of time. In practice, financial accounting statements are usually prepared annually. Such a time period has developed largely as a matter of custom. It does, however, reflect the natural agricultural cycle in Western Europe, and there does seem to be a natural human tendency to compare what has happened this year with what happened last year. Nevertheless, where entities have an unlimited life (as is usually the case with manufacturing organizations), the preparation of annual accounts presents considerable problems in relating specific events to appropriate accounting periods. We shall be having a look at these problems in Chapter 5.

Apart from custom, there is no reason why an accounting period could not be shorter or longer than twelve months. Management accounts are usually prepared for very short periods, but sometimes this also applies to financial accounts. In the fashion industry, for example, where the product designs may change very quickly, managers may want (say) quarterly reports. By contrast, the construction industry, faced with very long-term contract work, may find it more appropriate to have (say) a five-year reporting period. In fact, irrespective of the length of the main accounting period (i.e. whether it is quarterly or five-yearly), managers usually need regular reports covering a very short period. Cash reports, for example, could be prepared on a weekly, or even on a daily basis.

It must also not be forgotten that some entities (e.g. limited liability companies) are required by law to produce annual accounts, and as tax demands are also based on a calendar year it would not be possible for most entities to ignore the conventional twelve-month period. In any case, given the unlimited life of most entities, you will appreciate that *any* period must be somewhat arbitrary, no matter how carefully a particular entity has tried to relate its accounting period to the nature of its business.

Activity 2.2	List three advantages and disadvantages of preparing financial accounts only once a year.

Advantages	Disadvantages
1	1
2	2
3	3

Going concern

The periodicity rule requires a regular period of account to be established, regardless either of the life of the entity or of the arbitrary nature of such a period. The going concern rule arises out of the periodicity rule. This rule requires an assumption that an entity will continue in existence for the foreseeable future unless some strong evidence exists to suggest that this is not going to be the case. It is important to make absolutely certain that this assumption is correct, because a different set of accounting rules need to be adopted if an entity's immediate future is altogether uncertain.

Quantitative

Accountants usually restrict the data that are collected to those that are easily quantifiable. For example, it is possible to count the number of people that an entity employs, but it is difficult to quantify the *skill* of the employees. Such a concept is almost impossible to put into numbers and it is, therefore, not included in a conventional accounting system.

Measurement rules

The boundary rules determine *what* data should be included in an accounting system, whereas the measurement rules explain *how* those data should be recorded. There are six main measurement rules, and we outline them briefly below.

Money measurement

It would be very cumbersome to record information simply in terms of quantifiable amounts. It would also be impossible to make any fair comparisons between various types of assets (such as livestock and farm machinery), or different types of transactions (such as the sale of eggs and the purchase of corn). In order to make meaningful comparison, we need to convert the data into a common recognizable measure.

As we suggested in Chapter 1, the monetary unit serves such a purpose. It is a useful way of converting accounting data into a common unit, and since most quantifiable information is capable of being translated into monetary terms, there is usually no difficulty in adopting the monetary measurement rule.

Historic cost

The historic cost rule is an extension of the money measurement rule. It requires transactions to be recorded at their *original* (i.e. their historic) cost. Subsequent changes in prices or values, therefore, are usually ignored. Increased costs may arise because of a combination of an improved product, or through changes in the purchasing power of the monetary unit, i.e. through inflation.

Inflation tends to overstate the level of accounting profit as it is traditionally calculated. Over the last 35 years, there have been several attempts in the United Kingdom to change the method of accounting in order to allow for the effects of inflation. There has been so much disagreement on what should replace what is called *historic cost accounting* (HCA) that no other method has been acceptable. Throughout most of this book, we shall be adopting the historic cost rule.

Realization

One of the problems of putting the periodicity rule into practice is that it is often difficult to relate a specific transaction to a particular period. For example, assume that a business arranges to sell some goods in 2004, it delivers them in 2005, and it is paid for them in 2006. In which year were the goods *sold*: 2004, 2005 or 2006? In conventional accounting it would be most unusual to include them in the sales for 2004, because the business has still got a legal title to them. They could be included in the accounts for 2006 when the goods have been paid for. Indeed, this method of accounting is not uncommon. It is known as *cash flow accounting* (CFA). In CFA, transactions are only entered in the books of account when a cash exchange has taken place. By contrast, in HCA it is customary to enter most transactions in the books of account when the legal title to the goods has been transferred from one party to another and when there is an *obligation* for the recipient to pay for them. This means that, in the above example, under HCA the goods would normally be considered to have been sold in 2005.

The realization rule covers this point. It requires transactions relating to the sale of goods to be entered in the accounts for that period in which the legal title for them has been transferred from one party to another. In the jargon of accounting, they are then said to be *realized*. It is important to appreciate that for goods and services to be treated as realized, they do not need to have been paid for: the cash for them may be received during a later period (or for that matter, may have been received in an earlier period).

The realization rule is normally regarded as applying to sales, but *purchases* (meaning goods that are intended for resale) may be treated similarly. Thus, they would not be included in an entity's accounts until it had a legal title to them (i.e. until in law it would be regarded as owning them).

The realization rule can produce some rather misleading results. For example, a company may treat goods as having been sold in 2004. In 2005 it finds that the purchaser cannot pay for them. What can it do? Its accounts for 2004 have already been approved and it is too late to change them, but obviously the sales for that year were overstated (and so too, almost certainly, was the profit). The customer defaults in 2005, and so how can the *bad debt* (as it is known) be dealt with in *that* year? We shall be explaining how in Chapter 5.

Activity 2.3

A contracting company divides each of its orders into five stages: (1) on order; (2) on despatch; (3) on installation; (4) on commissioning; and (5) on completion of a 12-month warranty period. Assume that an order for Contract A (worth £100,000) is signed on 1 January 2004 and the warranty period ends on 31 December 2006. In which accounting period or periods would you treat the £100,000 as revenue (i.e. sales)? Would it be appropriate to apportion it over the three years of the contract?

Matching

The realization rule relates mainly to the purchase and sale of goods, in other words to what are known as *trading items*. However, a similar rule known as the *matching rule* applies to other incomes (such as dividends and rents received) and expenditure (such as electricity and wages). The matching rule is illustrated in Figure 2.3.

A misleading impression would be given if the cash received during a particular period was simply compared with the cash paid out during the same period. The exact period in which the cash is either received or paid may bear no relationship to the period in which the business was transacted. Thus, accountants normally adjust cash received and cash paid on what is known as an *accruals and prepayments* basis. An accrual is an amount that is *owed* by the entity at the end of an accounting period in respect of services received during that period. A prepayment is an amount that is *owing* to the entity at the end of the accounting period as a result of it paying in advance for services to be rendered in respect of a future period.

The conversion of cash received and cash paid to an accruals and prepayments basis at the end of an accounting period often involves a considerable amount of arithmetical adjustment. Account has to be taken for accruals and prepayments at the end of the previous period (i.e *opening* accruals and prepayments), as well as for accruals and prepayments at the end of the current period (i.e. *closing* accruals and prepayments). Accruals and prepayments are covered in more detail in Chapter 5.

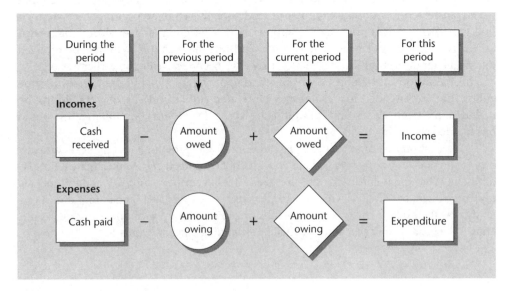

Figure 2.3 **Illustration of the matching rule**

An accruals and prepayments system of accounting enables the incomes of one period to be matched much more fairly against the costs of the same period. The comparison is not distorted by the accidental timing of cash receipts and cash payments. However, as the matching rule requires the accountant to estimate the level of both accruals and prepayments at the end of each accounting period, a degree of subjectivity is automatically built into the estimate.

Dual aspect

The dual aspect rule is a useful practical rule, although it really only reflects what is obvious. It is built round the fact that every time something is given, someone (or something) else receives it. In other words, every time a transaction take place, there is always a twofold effect. For example, if the amount of cash in a business goes up, someone must have given it; or if the business buys some goods, then someone else must be selling them.

We explained in Chapter 1 that this twofold effect was recognized many centuries ago. It gave rise to the system of recording information known as *double-entry book-keeping*. This system of book-keeping is still widely used. Although the concept is somewhat obvious, it has proved extremely useful, so much so that even modern computerized recording systems are based on it. From long experience, it has been found that the system is a most convenient way of recording all sorts of useful information about the entity, and of ensuring some form of control over its affairs.

There is no real need to adopt the dual aspect rule in recording information: it is entirely a practical rule that has proved itself over many centuries. Voluntary organizations (such as a drama club or a stamp collecting society) may not think that it is worthwhile to adopt the dual aspect rule, but you are strongly recommended to incorporate it into your book-keeping system in any entity with which you are concerned. If you do, you will find that it gives you more control over the entity's affairs besides providing you with a great deal more information.

Double-entry book-keeping will be examined in more detail in the next chapter.

Materiality

Strict application of the various accounting rules may not always be practical. It could involve a considerable amount of work that may be out of all proportion to the information that is eventually obtained. The materiality rule permits other rules to be ignored if the effects are not considered to be *material*, that is, if they are not significant.

Hence, the materiality rule avoids the necessity to follow other accounting rules to the point of absurdity. For example, it would normally be considered unnecessary to value the closing stock of small amounts of stationery, or to maintain detailed records of inexpensive items of office equipment. However, it should be borne in mind that what is immaterial for a large organization may not be so for a small one.

If you decide that a certain item is immaterial, then it does not matter how you deal with it in the accounts, because it cannot possibly have any significant effect on the results. When dealing with insignificant items, therefore, the materiality rule permits the other accounting rules to be ignored.

Ethical rules

There is an old story in accounting about the company chairman who asked his chief accountant how much profit the company had made. The chief accountant replied by asking how much profit the chairman would like to make. Accountants recognize that there is some truth in this story, since it is quite possible for different accountants to use the same basic data in preparing accounting statements yet still arrive at different levels of profit!

You might think that by faithfully following all of the accounting rules, *all* accountants should be able to calculate exactly the same amount of profit. Unfortunately this is not the case since, as we have seen, most of the main accounting rules are capable of wide interpretation. The matching rule, for example, requires an estimate to be made of amounts owing and owed at the end of an accounting period, while the materiality rule allows the accountant to decide just what is material. Both rules involve an element of subjective judgement, and so no two accountants are likely to agree precisely on how they should be applied.

In order to limit the room for individual manoeuvre, a number of other rules have evolved. These rules are somewhat ethical in nature and, indeed, some authors refer to them as accounting *principles* (thereby suggesting that there is a moral dimension to them). Other authors, however, refer to *all* of the basic accounting rules as principles, but it really does not matter what you call them as long as you are aware of them. Basically, the ethical rules require accountants to follow not just the letter but the spirit of the other rules.

There are four main ethical accounting rules. They are reviewed below.

Prudence

The prudence rule (which is sometimes known as *conservatism*) arises out of the need to make a number of estimates in preparing periodic accounts. Managers and owners are often naturally over-optimistic about future events. As a result, there is a tendency to be too confident about the future, and not to be altogether realistic about the entity's prospects. There may, for example, be undue optimism over the creditworthiness of a particular customer. Insufficient allowance may therefore be made for the possibility of a bad debt. This might have the effect of overstating profit in one period and understating it in a future period. We shall come across this problem again in Chapter 5.

The prudence rule is sometimes expressed in the form of a simple maxim:

> *If in doubt, overstate losses and understate profits.*

Activity 2.4	Supermarket companies sometimes receive a discount in advance from suppliers for meeting a specified sales target. Such discounts may be paid in advance. The accounting treatment of the discount could be dealt with in several ways: (1) it could be included in the profit and loss account for the period in which it was received; or (2) it could be amortized (apportioned) over the span of the contract; or (3) it could be included in the profit and loss account for the period in which the sales target is met.
	To what extent is the accounting treatment of such discounts an ethical decision? Prepare some notes indicating how you think this problem should be dealt with.

Consistency

As we have seen, the preparation of traditional accounting statements requires a considerable amount of individual judgement to be made in the application of the basic accounting rules. To compensate for this flexibility, the consistency rule states that, once specific accounting policies have been adopted, they should be followed in all subsequent accounting periods.

It would be considered quite unethical to change rules just because they were unfashionable, or because alternative ones gave better results. Of course, if the circumstances of the entity change radically it may be necessary to adopt different policies, but this should only be done in exceptional circumstances. If different policies are adopted, then the effect of any change should be clearly highlighted and any comparative figure adjusted accordingly.

The application of this rule gives confidence to the users of accounting statements, because if the accounts have been prepared on a consistent basis they can be assured that they are comparable with previous sets of accounts.

Objectivity

Accounts should be prepared with the minimum amount of bias. This is not an easy task, since individual judgement is required in interpreting the rules and adapting them to suit particular circumstances. Owners may want, for example, to adopt policies which would result in higher profit figures, or in disguising poor results.

If optional policy decisions are possible within the existing rules, it is advisable to fall back on the prudence rule. Indeed, it tends to be an overriding one. If there is any doubt about which rule to adopt (or how it should be interpreted), the prudence rule tends to take precedence.

It must be recognized, however, that if the prudence rules is always adopted as the easy way out of a difficult problem, someone preparing a set of accounts could be accused of lacking objectivity. In other words, you must not use this rule to avoid making difficult decisions. Indeed, it is just as unfair to be as excessively cautious as it is to be wildly optimistic. Extremism of any kind suggests a lack of objectivity, so you should avoid being either over-cautious or over-optimistic.

Relevance

The amount of information that could be supplied to any interested party is practically unlimited. If too much information is disclosed, it becomes very difficult to absorb, and so it should only be included if it is it going to help the user.

The selection of relevant information requires much experience and judgement, as well as a great understanding of the user's requirements. The information needs to be designed in such a way that it meets the *objectives* of the specific user group. If too much information is given, the users might think that it is an attempt to mislead them and, as a result, all of the information may be totally rejected.

A conceptual framework

This chapter discusses the basic accounting rules, which have evolved over a period of time; nobody worked them out on paper before they were applied in practice. This means that when some new accounting problem arises, we do not always know how to deal with it. Some accountants (especially university lecturers) argue that what is needed is a *conceptual framework*. In other words, we ought to devise a theoretical model of accounting, and then any new accounting problem could be solved merely by running it through the model.

It sounds very sensible, but it is not easy to devise such a model. Several attempts have been made, and none of them has been particularly successful. Basically, there are two approaches that can be adopted:

1 We can list all the accounting rules that have ever been used, and then extract the ones that are the most widely used. There are two main problems in adopting this approach:
   (a) To be meaningful, we would have to conduct an extremely wide survey of existing practice. As yet, the sheer scale required by this exercise has defeated most researchers.
   (b) Such an exercise would simply freeze existing practice: it would not improve it.
2 Alternatively, we could determine:
   (a) who uses accounting statements;
   (b) what they want them for (i.e. we would need to establish *user objectives*); and
   (c) what rules we need to adopt to meet those objectives.

The Accounting Standards Board (ASB) referred to at the beginning of the chapter has attempted to construct a conceptual framework using the second approach. The details are contained in a document published in 1999 called *Statement of Principles for Financial Reporting*.

The Statement is not an accounting standard and it is not mandatory for professionally qualified accountants to adopt it. Nevertheless, it is highly influential. It sets out the basic principles that the ASB believes should underpin what it calls 'general purpose financial statements' such as annual financial statements, financial statements in interim reports, preliminary announcements and summary financial statements.

The Statement is 30 pages long and it is divided into eight chapters. A brief summary of its contents is outlined below.

Chapter 1 lays down the objectives of financial statements, i.e. 'to provide information that is useful to those for whom they are prepared'. However, consideration needs to be given to those parties who use the information, what information they need and what role financial statements play in that process.

Chapter 2 identifies those entities that ought to publish financial statements. These include those entities that are cohesive economic units and where there is a legitimate demand for the information contained within such statements.

Chapter 3 describes the qualitative characteristics of financial information. As it complements much of the material in *this* chapter, it would be useful if we outline its main contents in a little more detail. The Statement argues that in order to make financial information useful it should consist of the following qualities:

1 *Materiality*. Information should be provided to users if their economic decisions would be affected either by its omission or by misstating it.

2 *Relevance.* Information should be capable of (a) influencing the economic decisions of users; and (b) being provided in time to influence the decisions. You will recall that earlier we regarded 'relevance' as being an 'ethical' rule.

3 *Reliability.* Information should (a) reflect the substance of events and transactions; (b) be free from deliberate bias and material error; and (c) incorporate a degree of caution when containing uncertain circumstances.

4 *Comparability.* Information should be presented in such a way that it is possible to ascertain similarities and spot differences over time and between entities.

5 *Comprehensibility.* The ASB does not object to information being provided even if some users would not understand it. Generally, it expects users to have a 'reasonable knowledge of business and economic activities and accounting and a willingness to study with reasonable diligence the information provided'. Now you know why you are studying accounting.

Chapter 4 identifies the main elements that should go to make up the financial statements such as assets (what the entity owns) and liabilities (what the entity owes). It refers to these elements as 'building blocks'. In subsequent chapters of this book, we will be dealing with the 'building blocks' of accounting.

Chapter 5 considers when events and transactions should be recognized in financial statements. We dealt with this particular aspect in the earlier part of this chapter when outlining the 'measurement' rules. *Chapter 6* complements Chapter 5 and considers how assets and liabilities should be measured. Again, we have covered much of this topic in our 'measurement rule' section earlier in this chapter. *Chapter 7* considers the characteristics of 'good' presentation so that financial statements are communicated clearly and effectively.

Chapter 8 is a highly specialized chapter involving the inclusion of information in financial statements that reflects an entity's interest in other entities. We shall only be dealing briefly with this topic in Chapters 10 and 11 of this book.

You will appreciate from the above summary that the Statement is couched in very general terms. It does not provide a precise set of rules for the preparation of financial statements and it certainly is not prescriptive. Thus it is not like the instructions that you get if you purchase a board game such as *Cluedo* or *Monopoly*. Rather, the ASB has put forward some basic concepts underpinning the preparation of financial statements. You then need to know how to apply those concepts when you prepare a set of financial statements. Part 2 of this book aims to provide you with the guidance you need.

You may have found it disappointing (especially if you are an engineer or a scientist) that by the end of this section we have not been able to provide you with a precise conceptual framework equivalent to a laboratory or a physical model for the presentation of financial statements. Unfortunately, there are so many variable factors in the social sciences that this is almost an impossible task.

Thus to a non-accountant, the ASB's *Statement of Principles* may appear totally unsatisfactory. Nevertheless it is a considerable landmark in the history of accounting. There has been much opposition to the ideas being pursued by the ASB and the Board has not felt itself to be in a position to make its principles mandatory. It is likely to be very many years before that position is reached and it is even more doubtful whether a more detailed framework can ever be formulated.

Activity 2.5

As a non-accountant you probably approach the idea of a conceptual accounting framework with an open mind. What are your ideas about the users of financial statements and what they want from such statements? Suggest some rules that should be adopted in preparing financial statements for those users that you have identified. But don't just copy ones outlined in this chapter.

Possible users	What they want	Rules to be followed

❗ Questions non-accountants should ask

This is a most important chapter. Apart from preparing the foundation for what follows in the rest of the book, it provides you with a number of important accounting issues that are extremely relevant and important in the real world. While you may be advised by your accountants, ultimately you will be responsible for any action taken by the entity you work for. So it is important that you know what your accountants have done and why.

Some of the accounting rules outlined in this chapter are fairly non-controversial. The entity, periodicity, quantitative, money measurement, matching and dual aspect rules do not normally cause too much of a problem. The application of the remaining rules can cause a problem, so you must question the application of them. We suggest that you pose the following questions.

- What absolute assurances can you give me that the entity is a going concern?
- What justification is there for including all our transactions at their historic cost?
- Can we use a more up-to-date cost for some items, e.g. property?
- How would we then value and depreciate such items?
- Is the method used for the determination of income absolutely cast-iron?
- What method have you used for determining what is an immaterial item?
- To what extent has the need for prudence been overridden by the need to be objective?
- Are there any items in the accounts that could be justifiably left out or presented in a different way without any problems?

Conclusion

In this chapter we have identified 14 basic accounting rules that accountants usually adopt in the preparation of accounting statements. We have described four of these rules as boundary rules, six as measurement rules and four as ethical rules. We have argued that the boundary rules limit the amount and type of information that is traditionally collected and stored in an accounting system. The measurement rules provide some guidance on how that information should be recorded, and the ethical rules lay down a code of conduct on how all the other rules should be interpreted.

The exact number, classification and description of these various accounting rules is subject to much debate among accountants. Most entities can adopt what rules they like, although it would be most unusual if they did not accept the going concern, matching, prudence and consistency rules.

In the next chapter, we shall examine the dual aspect rule in a little more detail. This rule is at the heart of double-entry book-keeping and most modern accounting systems are based upon it.

Key points

1 In preparing accounting statements, accountants adopt a number of rules that have evolved over a number of centuries.

2 There are four main boundary rules: entity, periodicity, going concern, and quantitative.

3 Measurement rules include: money measurement, historic cost, realization, matching, dual aspect, and materiality.

4 Ethical rules include: prudence, consistency, objectivity, and relevance.

5 No satisfactory conceptual framework of accounting has yet been developed by the accountancy profession. The ASB has issued a *Statement of Principles for Financial Reporting*, but this Statement is neither highly prescriptive nor mandatory.

Check your learning

The answers to these questions may be found within the text.

1 Name three other terms that mean the same as accounting rules.

2 What do the following initials stand for: (a) SSAP; (b) FRS; and (c) ASB?

3 List three categories of accounting rules.

4 What is meant by an 'entity'?

5 What accounting rule is used to describe a defined period of time?

6 What is a 'going concern'?

7   What types of qualitative information is normally included in financial statements?

8   Name three non-monetary items included in most financial statements.

9   Name one type of asset that may not be included at its historic cost in financial statements?

10 What is another term for 'matching'?

11 What does 'dual aspect mean?

12 How do you decide whether or not a transaction is 'material'?

13 Are *prudence* and *objectivity* compatible?

14 Is the consistency rule ever disregarded?

15 What concept is used to determine whether any items included in financial statements is relevant?

16 What is a conceptual framework?

17 What two approaches may be adopted in framing a conceptual framework?

18 What is the ASB's approach to the adoption of a conceptual framework?

19 Name the five qualities that the ASB regard as being desirable in order to make financial statements useful.

News story quiz

Remember the news story at the beginning of this chapter? Go back to that story and reread it before answering the following questions.

This news story deals with two companies (Capita and W S Atkins) both of whom are involved in the construction industry. If a contract takes longer than one year to complete, at what point should the company take any expected profit? A prudent approach would be to wait until the contract has finished. A highly imprudent one would be to take all the expected profit when the contract was signed. The accountancy profession's answer is to take some profit on account provided certain conditions are met.

Questions

1 What do you think the directors of Capita mean when they state that they have exceeded the requirements of various accounting standards?

2 Do you think that W S Atkins is adopting a conservative (i.e. prudent) accounting approach when it capitalizes building costs 'from the point at which its consortium is appointed sole preferred bidder and when such costs may be seen with virtual certainty as recoverable at financial close'? Is there such a thing as 'virtual certainty'?

3 In which accounting period should a construction company take the profit on a contract: (a) when the contract is signed; (b) apportioned over the life of the contract; (c) when the contract is completed; (d) when the warranty period is over; (e) when it is clear a profit will be made?

4 What are the repercussions of taking profit before the contracting company's obligations have completely ended?

5 What can such a company do if it takes a profit and then the contract ultimately results in a loss?

Tutorial questions

The answers to questions marked with an asterisk may be found in Appendix 4.

2.1 Do you think that when a set of financial accounts is being prepared, the prudence rule should override the objectivity rule?

2.2 'The law should lay down precise formats, contents, and methods for the preparation of limited liability company accounts.' Discuss.

2.3 The Accounting Standards Board now bases its Financial Reporting Standards on what might be regarded as a 'conceptual framework'. How far do you think that this approach is likely to be successful?

In questions 2.4, 2.5 and 2.6 you are required to state which accounting rule the accountant would most probably adopt in dealing with the various problems.

2.4* Electricity consumed in period 1 and paid for in period 2.
Equipment originally purchased for £20 000 which would now cost £30 000.
The company's good industrial relations record.
A five-year construction contract.
A customer who might go bankrupt owing the company £5000.
The company's vehicles, which would only have a small scrap value if the company goes into liquidation.

2.5* A demand by the company's chairman to include every detailed transaction in the presentation of the annual accounts.
A sole-trader business which has paid the proprietor's income tax based on the business profits for the year.
A proposed change in the methods of valuing stock.
The valuation of a litre of petrol in one vehicle at the end of accounting period 1.
A vehicle which could be sold for more than its purchase price.
Goods which were sold to a customer in period 1, but for which the cash was only received in period 2.

2.6* The proprietor who has supplied the business capital out of his own private bank account.
The sales manager who is always very optimistic about the creditworthiness of prospective customers.
The managing director who does not want annual accounts prepared as the company operates a continuous 24-hour-a-day, 365-days-a-year process.

At the end of period 1, it is difficult to be certain whether the company will have to pay legal fees of £1000 or £3000.

The proprietor who argues that the accountant has got a motor vehicle entered twice in the books of account.

Some goods were purchased and entered into stock at the end of period 1, but they were not paid for until period 2.

2.7   The following is a list of problems which an accountant may well meet in practice:

The transfer fee of a footballer.
Goods are sold in one period, but the cash for them is received in a later period.
The proprietor's personal dwelling house has been used as security for a loan which the bank has granted to the company.
What profit to take in the third year of a five-year construction contract.
Small stocks of stationery held at the accounting year end.
Expenditure incurred in working on the improvement of a new drug.

Required:
State:
(1) which accounting rule the accountant would most probably adopt in dealing with each of the above problems; and
(2) the reasons for your choice.

2.8   FRS 18 (Accounting Policies) states that profits shall be treated as realized and included in the profit and loss account only when the cash due 'can be assessed with reasonable certainty' (para. 28).
How far do you think that this requirement removes any difficulty in determining in which accounting period a sale has taken place?

2.9   The adoption of the realization and matching rules in preparing financial accounts requires a great deal of subjective judgement.

Required:
Write an essay examining whether it would be fairer, easier, and more meaningful to prepare financial accounts on a cash received/cash paid basis.

Further practice questions, study material and links to relevant sites on the World Wide Web can be found on the website that accompanies this book. The site can be found at www.booksites.net/dyson

Appendix Summary of the accounting rules

It would be convenient at this stage if we summarized the basic accounting rules outlined in the chapter so that it will be easy for you to refer back when studying later chapters. In summary they are as follows.

Boundary rules

1 **Entity**. Accounting data must be restricted to the entity itself. The data should exclude the private affairs of those individuals who either own or manage the entity, except in so far as they impact directly on it.

2 **Periodicity**. Accounts should be prepared at the end of a defined period of time, and this period should be adopted as the regular period of account.

3 **Going concern**. The accounts should be prepared on the assumption that the entity will continue in existence for the foreseeable future.

4 **Quantitative**. Only data that are capable of being easily quantified should be included in an accounting system.

Measurement rules

1 **Money measurement**. Data must be translated into monetary terms before they are included in an accounting system.

2 **Historic cost**. Financial data should be recorded in the books of account at their historic cost, that is, at their original purchase cost or at their original selling price.

3 **Realization**. Transactions that reflect financial data should be entered in the books of account when the legal title to them has been transferred from one party to another party, irrespective of when a cash settlement takes place.

4 **Matching**. Cash received and cash paid during a particular accounting period should be adjusted in order to reflect the economic activity that has actually taken place during that period.

5 **Dual aspect**. All transactions should be recorded in such a way that they capture the giving and the receiving effect of each transaction.

6 **Materiality**. The basic accounting rules must not be rigidly applied to insignificant items.

Ethical rules

1 **Prudence**. If there is some doubt over the treatment of a particular transaction, income should be underestimated and expenditure overestimated, so that profits are more likely to be understated and losses overstated.

2 **Consistency**. Accounting rules and policies should not be amended unless there is a fundamental change in circumstances that necessitates a reconsideration of the original rules and policies.

3 **Objectivity**. Personal prejudice must be avoided in the interpretation of the basic accounting rules.

4 **Relevance**. Accounting statements should not include information that prevents users from obtaining a true and fair view of the information being communicated to them.

Unit 3:   Organisations and Behaviour

Learning hours: **60**

NQF level 4:   **BTEC Higher National — H1**

Content Selected: **Mullins, Management and Organisational Behaviour, Chapter 2**

Introduction from the Qualifications Leader

This unit looks at the nature of organisations, their structure and culture. Chapter 2 has been selected as it provides a good introduction and background reading to the nature of organisational behaviour.

Description of unit

This unit provides an introduction to the nature of organisations in relation to management practices. The unit examines the internal nature of organisations from both a theoretical and practical viewpoint. The unit is intended to develop an understanding of the behaviour of people within organisations and the significance of organisational design and characteristics. It also aims to provide the basis for, and to underpin further study in, specialist areas of business.

Summary of learning outcomes

To achieve this unit a learner must:

1   Explore **organisational structure and culture**

2   Examine different **approaches to management and leadership** and theories of organisation

3   Examine the relationship between **motivational theories**

4   Demonstrate an understanding of **working with others, teamwork, groups and group dynamics**.

Content

1   **Organisational structure and culture**

Types of organisation and associated structures: functional, product-based, geographically based, multifunctional and multidivisional structures, matrix, centralisation and de-centralisation

Organisational networks and linkages: internal and external network structures, flexible working

Organisational culture: classification of organisational culture – power culture, role culture, task culture, person culture, cultural norms and symbols, values and beliefs, development of organisational culture

Authority and power: organisational charts, spans of control

The human resource function: a stakeholder perspective, personnel management roles, personnel policies, strategies and operating plans, strategic goals for personnel

Diagnosing behavioural problems: concepts, principles, perspectives, methodology

Perception: definition, perceptual selection, perception and work behaviour, attitude, ability and aptitude, intelligence

Significance and nature of individual differences: self and self-image, personality and work behaviour, conflict

Individual behaviour at work: personality, traits and types, its relevance in understanding self and others

2   **Approaches to management and leadership**

Development of management thought: scientific management, classical administration, bureaucracy, human relations approach, systems approach, contingency approach

Functions of management: planning, organising, commanding, co-ordinating, controlling

Managerial roles: interpersonal, informational, decisional

Nature of managerial authority: power, authority, responsibility, delegation, conflict

Frames of reference for leadership activities: opportunist, diplomat, technician, achiever, strategist, magician, pluralistic, transformational, change

3   **Motivational theories**

Motivation theories: Maslow's Hierarchy of Needs, Herzberg's Motivation – Hygiene theory, Vroom and Expectancy theories, Maccoby, McCrae and Costa – personality dimensions

Motivation and performance: rewards and incentives, motivation and managers, rewards monetary and non-monetary

Leadership: leadership in organisations, managers and leaders, leadership traits, management style, contingency approach, leadership and organisational culture

Leadership and successful change in organisations: pluralistic, transformational, communications, conflict

4   **Working with others, teamwork, groups and group dynamics**

The nature of groups: groups and teams, informal and formal groups, purpose of teams

Teams and team building: selecting team members, team roles, Belbin's theory, stages in team development, team building, team identity, team loyalty, commitment to shared beliefs, multi-disciplinary teams

Team dynamics: group norms, decision-making behaviour, dysfunctional teams, cohesiveness

Impact of technology on team functioning: technology, communication, change, networks and virtual teams, global and cross-cultural teams

Outcomes and assessment criteria

Outcomes	Assessment criteria for pass
	To achieve each outcome a learner must demonstrate the ability to:
1 Explore **organisational structure and culture**	• compare and contrast different organisational structures and culture • analyse the relationship between an organisation's structure and culture and the effects on business performance • analyse the factors which influence individual behaviour at work
2 Examine different **approaches to management and leadership** and theories of organisation	• describe different leadership styles and the effectiveness of these leadership approaches • analyse how organisational theory underpins principles and practices of organising and of management • compare the different approaches to management and theories of organisation used by two organisations
3 Examine the relationship between **motivational theories**	• discuss different leadership styles and the effectiveness of these leadership approaches • explain the different motivational theories and their application within the workplace • assess the relationship between motivation theory and the practice of management
4 Demonstrate an understanding of **working with others, teamwork, groups and group dynamics**	• describe the nature of groups and group behaviour within organisations • investigate the factors that lead to effective teamwork and the influences that threaten success • evaluate the impact of technology on team functioning within a given organisation

2 THE NATURE OF ORGANISATIONAL BEHAVIOUR

The scope for the examination of behaviour in organisations is very wide. There is a multiplicity of interrelated factors which influence the behaviour and performance of people as members of a work organisation. It is important to recognise the role of management as an integrating activity and as the cornerstone of organisationa effectiveness. People and organisations need each other. The manager needs to understand the main influences on behaviour in work organisations and the nature of the people–organisation relationship.

Photo: Mark Renders/Getty Images

LEARNING OUTCOMES

After completing this chapter you should be able to:

► explain the meaning and nature of organisational behaviour and provide an introduction to a behavioural approach to management;

► detail main interrelated influences on behaviour in work organisations and explain the nature of behavioural science;

► outline contrasting perspectives of organisations and different orientations to work;

► recognise the importance of management as an inte-grating activity;

► assess the nature and importance of the new psychological contract;

► review the need for a cross-cultural approach and the importance of culture to the study of organisational behaviour;

► summarise the complex nature of the behaviour of people in work organisations.

Organizations are extremely complex systems. As one observes them they seem to be composed of human activities on many different levels of analysis. Personalities, small groups, intergroups, norms, values, attitudes all seem to exist in an extremely complex multidimensional pattern. The complexity seems at times almost beyond comprehension.

Chris Argyris
Integrating the Individual and the Organization, John Wiley & Sons (1964)

THE MEANING OF ORGANISATIONAL BEHAVIOUR

We live in an organisational world. Organisations of one form or another are a necessary part of our society and serve many important needs. The decisions and actions of management in organisations have an increasing impact on individuals, other organisations and the community. It is important, therefore, to understand how organisations function and the pervasive influences which they exercise over the behaviour of people.[1]

> Organizational Behaviour is one of the most complex and perhaps least understood academic elements of modern general management, but since it concerns the behaviour of people within organizations it is also one of the most central ... its concern with individual and group patterns of behaviour makes it an essential element in dealing with the complex behavioural issues thrown up in the modern business world.
>
> **Financial Times Mastering Management Series**[2]

The behaviour of people

Organisational behaviour is concerned with the study of the behaviour of people within an organisational setting. It involves the understanding, prediction and control of human behaviour.[3] Common definitions of organisational behaviour (OB) are generally along the lines of: **the study and understanding of individual and group behaviour, and patterns of structure in order to help improve organisational performance and effectiveness.**[4] There is a close relationship between organisational behaviour and management theory and practice. Some writers seem to suggest that organisational behaviour and management are synonymous, but this is something of an over-simplification because there are many broader facets to management. Organisational behaviour does not encompass the whole of management; it is more accurately described in the narrower interpretation of providing a behavioural approach to management.

> *It is important to emphasise that in most cases the term 'organisational behaviour' is, strictly, a misnomer: rarely do all members of an organisation, except perhaps very small organisations, behave collectively in such a way as to represent the behaviour of the organisation as a whole. In practice, we are referring to the behaviour of individuals, or sections or groups of people, within the organisation. For example, when we talk about a 'caring organisation', we are really talking about the philosophy, attitudes and actions of top managers and/or departmental managers, or possibly an individual manager. Nevertheless, the wording 'organisational behaviour' has become widely accepted and is found increasingly in textbooks and literature on the subject. The term 'organisational behaviour' is a convenient form of shorthand to refer to the large number of interrelated influences on, and patterns of, behaviour of people within organisations.*[5]

A framework of study

The behaviour of people, however, cannot be studied in isolation. It is necessary to understand interrelationships with other variables which together comprise the total organisation. To do this involves consideration of interactions among the formal structure, the tasks to be undertaken, the technology employed and methods of carrying out work, the process of management and the external environment.

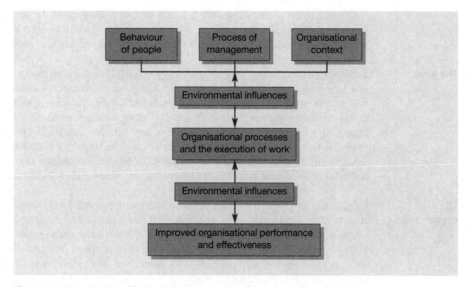

Figure 2.1 Organisational behaviour: a convenient framework of analysis

The study of organisational behaviour embraces therefore an understanding of:

■ the behaviour of people;
■ the process of management;
■ the organisational context in which the process of management takes place;
■ organisational processes and the execution of work; and
■ interactions with the external environment of which the organisation is part.

This provides us with a basic, but convenient, framework of analysis. (*See* Figure 2.1.)

Wilson, however suggests that the meaning of the term organisational behaviour is far from clear. She challenges what constitutes organisational behaviour and questions whether we should be interested only in behaviour that happens within organisations. There is a reciprocal relationship in what happens within and outside organisations. Wilson suggests that we also look outside of what are normally thought of as organisations and how we usually think of work. We can also gain insight into organisational life and organisational behaviour by looking at what happens in rest and play; by consideration of emotion and feeling; by the context in which work is defined as men's or women's work; and by looking at less organised work, for example work on the fiddle and the meaning of work for the unemployed.[6] These suggestions by Wilson arguably add an extra dimension to the meaning and understanding of organisational behaviour.

INFLUENCES ON BEHAVIOUR IN ORGANISATIONS

The variables outlined above provide parameters within which a number of inter-related dimensions can be identified – the individual, the group, the organisation and the environment – which collectively influence behaviour in work organisations.

The individual   Organisations are made up of their individual members. The individual is a central feature of organisational behaviour and a necessary part of any behavioural situation, whether acting in isolation or as part of a group, in response to expectations of the organisation, or as a result of the influences of the external environment. Where the needs of the individual and the demands of the organisation are incompatible, this can result in frustration and conflict. It is the task of management to integrate the individual and the organisation, and to provide a working environment which permits the satisfaction of individual needs as well as the attainment of organisational goals.

The group

Groups exist in all organisations and are essential to their working and performance. The organisation comprises groups of people and almost everyone in an organisation will be a member of one or more groups. Informal groups arise from the social needs of people within the organisation. People in groups influence each other in many ways, and groups may develop their own hierarchies and leaders. Group pressures can have a major influence over the behaviour and performance of individual members. An understanding of group structure and behaviour complements a knowledge of individual behaviour and adds a further dimension to organisational behaviour.

The organisation

Individuals and groups interact within the structure of the formal organisation. Structure is created by management to establish relationships between individuals and groups, to provide order and systems and to direct the efforts of the organisation into goal-seeking activities. It is through the formal structure that people carry out their organisational activities in order to achieve aims and objectives. Behaviour is affected by patterns of organisation structure, technology, styles of leadership and systems of management through which organisational processes are planned, directed and controlled. The focus of attention, therefore, is on the impact of organisation structure and design, and patterns of management, on the behaviour of people within the organisation. For example, *McPhee* refers to the growth in the nature and importance of organisational structures and their essence, and for greater emphasis on business-to-business (B2B) depth or group interviewing as part of an insight into business and organisational behaviour.[7]

The environment

The organisation functions as part of the broader external environment of which it is a part. The environment affects the organisation through, for example, technological and scientific development, economic activity, social and cultural influences and governmental actions. The effects of the operation of the organisation within its environment are reflected in terms of the management of opportunities and risks and the successful achievement of its aims and objectives. The increasing rate of change in environmental factors has highlighted the need to study the total organisation and the processes by which the organisation attempts to adapt to the external demands placed upon it. Increasing globalisation means that organisations must respond to different market demands and local requirements. 'In globalization, strategy and organization are inextricably twined.'[8] Globalisation impacts on organisational behaviour, and has placed greater emphasis on processes within organisations rather than functions of the organisation.

Contrasting but related approaches

These different dimensions provide contrasting but related approaches to the understanding of human behaviour in organisations. They present a number of alternative pathways for the study of the subject and level of analysis. It is possible, for example, to adopt a **psychological** approach with the main emphasis on the individuals of which the organisation is comprised. Psychological aspects are important but, by themselves, provide too narrow an approach for the understanding of management and organisational behaviour. Our main concern is not with the complex detail of individual differences and attributes *per se* but with the behaviour and management of people within an organisational setting.

It is also possible to adopt a **sociological** approach concerned with a broader emphasis on human behaviour in society. Sociological aspects can be important. A number of sociology writers seem set on the purpose of criticising traditional views of organisation and management. Many of the criticisms and limitations to which such writers refer are justified and help promote healthy academic debate. Unfortunately, however, much of the argument tends to be presented in the abstract and is lacking in constructive ideas on how, in practical terms, action can be taken to improve organisational performance.

BEHAVIOURAL SCIENCE – A MULTIDISCIPLINARY APPROACH

Whatever the approach, the study of organisational behaviour cannot be undertaken entirely in terms of a single discipline. It is necessary to provide a multidisciplinary, **behavioural science** approach (*see* Figure 2.2).

The wording 'behavioural science' has no strict scientific definition. It may be used as a collective term for the grouping of all the social sciences concerned with the study of people's behaviour. However, it is now more frequently used to refer to attempts to apply a selective, multidisciplinary approach to the study of human behaviour. In particular, the term is often taken as applying more narrowly and specifically to problems of organisation and management in the work environment.

Three main disciplines

There are areas of overlap among the various social sciences, their sub-divisions and related disciplines such as economics and political science. However, the study of behaviour can be viewed in terms of three main disciplines – **psychology**, **sociology** and **anthropology**. All three disciplines have made an important contribution to the field of organisational behaviour.

■ **Psychologists** are concerned, broadly speaking, with the study of human behaviour, with traits of the individual and membership of small social groups. The main focus of attention is on the individual as a whole person, or what can be termed the 'personality system', including, for example, perception, attitudes and motives.

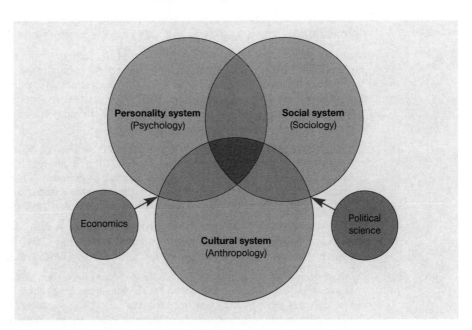

Figure 2.2 Behavioural science – a multidisciplinary approach

- **Sociologists** are more concerned with the study of social behaviour, relationships among social groups and societies, and the maintenance of order. The main focus of attention is on the analysis of social structures and positions in those structures – for example, the relationship between the behaviour of leaders and followers.
- **Anthropologists** are more concerned with the science of mankind and the study of human behaviour as a whole. As far as organisational behaviour is concerned the main focus of attention is on the cultural system, the beliefs, customs, ideas and values within a group or society, and the comparison of behaviour among different cultures – for example, the importance to Muslim women of wearing trousers to work. People learn to depend on their culture to give them security and stability, and they can suffer adverse reactions to unfamiliar environments.

The contribution of relevant aspects of psychology, sociology and anthropology aids our understanding of the behaviour of people in work organisations, and underpins the field of organisational behaviour. Behavioural science attempts to structure organisations in order to secure the optimum working environment. It is concerned with reconciling the needs of the organisation for the contribution of maximum productivity, with the needs of individuals and the realisation of their potential. Emphasis is on the application of relevant aspects of psychological and sociological theory and practice, and cultural influences, to problems of organisation and management in the work situation.

In terms of the applications of behavioural science to the management of people, we need also to consider the relevance and applications of philosophy, ethics and the law.

THE IMPORTANCE OF PEOPLE AND ORGANISATIONAL BEHAVIOUR

However one looks at the nature or disciplines of organisational behaviour it is important to remember, as *Morgan* reminds us, that: 'The reality of organizational life usually comprises numerous different realities!' [9]

Hellriegel, Slocum and Woodman suggest that:

... one way to recognise why people behave as they do at work is to view an organisation as an iceberg. What sinks ships isn't always what sailors can see, but what they can't see. [10]

The overt, formal aspects focus only on the tip of the iceberg (organisation). It is just as important to focus on what you can't see – the covert, behavioural aspects (*see* Figure 2.3).

As part of the *Financial Times Mastering Management* series, *Wood*, in his discussion of the nature of organisational behaviour (OB), suggests that in its concern for the way people behave in an organisational context, organisational behaviour can be regarded as the key to the whole area of management.

Is the study of behaviour in organisations important? I think it is vital. What the social sciences, humanities and the arts are to university education, OB is to business school education. The more technical a manager's training, the more important organisational behaviour becomes. It is arguably the one area that can carry the burden of bringing the collective wisdom of human history into the decision-making calculus of developing managers. And this is no trivial task. [11]

In the Foreword to Cloke and Goldsmith's thought-provoking book, *The End of Management, Bennis* claims that a distinct and dramatic change is taking place in the philosophy underlying organisational behaviour, calling forth a new concept of humanity.

This new concept is based on expanded knowledge of our complex and shifting needs, replacing an oversimplified, innocent, push-button idea of humanity. This philosophical shift calls for a new concept of organizational depersonalized, mechanistic value system of bureaucracy. With it comes a new concept of power, based on collaboration and reason, replacing a model based on coercion and threat ... The real push for these changes stems from the need not only to humanize organizations, but to use them as crucibles for personal growth and self-realization. [12]

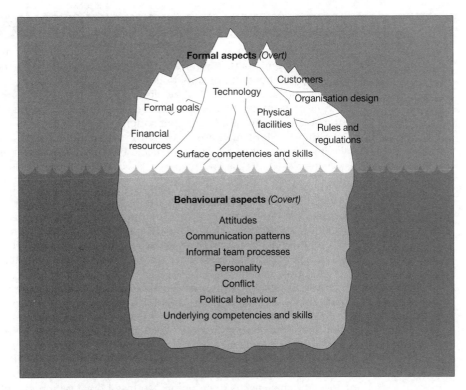

Figure 2.3 The organisational iceberg

Source: Don Hellriegel, John W. Slocum, Jr and Richard W. Woodman, *Organizational Behaviour*, Eighth edition, South-Western Publishing © (1998), p. 6. Reprinted with the permission of South-Western, a division of Thomson Learning: www.thomsonrights.com. Fax 800 730 2215.

People, capital and technology

In her discussion on 'putting people at the heart of corporate purpose', *Gratton* draws attention to the link between individual behaviour and organisational performance. People are uniquely different from capital and technology. As the challenge shifts from managing capital and technology to managing people, so this requires a fundamental shift in the way we consider resources and has profound implications for the organisations in which we work.

> *If we place people at the center of sustained competitive advantage then we have to take full account of the fundamental characteristics of human capital. What are these fundamental characteristics? What separates us from money or machines, and what are the implications of these differences? My view of this comes essentially from the perspective of an individual psychologist and from my experiences in organizations. For me the question of time is crucial, both because we humans operate in time with the past, the present and the future assuming importance; and because there are phases, sequences of time and rhythms, which are essentially human. Like many other psychologists, I have been influenced by the notion of meaning and of soul. Both are deeply philosophical terms, with roots as old as mankind. They are soft, perhaps even flaky, notions, but I believe to deny them is to create organizations fit for machines, not people. They may not be the terms with which you are most comfortable, perhaps other words suit you better, but somewhere within our views of organizations we need to acknowledge the differences between machines and man.*[13]

ORGANISATIONAL METAPHORS

Organisations are complex social systems which can be defined and studied in a number of different ways. A significant approach to this broad perspective on the nature of organisations and organisational behaviour is provided by *Morgan*. Through the use of metaphors, Morgan identifies eight different ways of viewing organisations – as machines, organisms, brains, cultures, political systems, psychic prisons, flux and transformation, and instruments of domination.

According to Morgan, these contrasting metaphors aid the understanding of the complex nature of organisational life and the critical evaluation of organisational phenomena.[14]

- **Machines**. This suggests that organisations can be designed as if they are machines with orderly relations between clearly defined parts. Viewing organisations as machines can provide the basis for efficient operation in a routine, reliable and predictable way. This form of bureaucratic structure provides form, continuity and security. However, it may have adverse consequences and limit the development of human capacities. Organisations viewed as machines function better in a stable and protected environment.
- **Organisms**. The organisation is seen as behaving like a living system. In the same way that biological mechanisms adapt to changes in their environment, so organisations, as open systems, adapt to the changing external environment. Organisations operating within a turbulent and dynamic environment require an adaptable type of structure.
- **Brains**. Viewing organisations as brains involves thinking about the organisation as inventive and rational, and in a manner that provides for flexibility and creative action. The challenge is to create new forms of organisation capable of intelligent change and that can disperse brainlike capacities.
- **Cultures**. This sees organisations as complex systems made up of their own characteristic sets of ideology, values, rituals, and systems of belief and practice. Attention to specific aspects of social development helps to account for variations among organisations.
- **Political systems**. In the sense that ways must be found to create order and direct people, organisations are intrinsically political. They are about authority, power, superior–subordinate relationships and conflicting interests. Viewing organisations as political systems helps in an understanding of day-to-day organisational life, the wheeling and dealing, and pursuit of special interests.
- **Psychic prisons**. This views organisations as psychic phenomena created and sustained by conscious and unconscious processes. Organisations and their members are constrained by their shadows or 'psychic prisons' and become trapped by constructions of reality. Their inherited or created mythical past places affects the representation of the organisation to the outside world. Viewing organisations as psychic prisons provides an understanding of the reality and illusions of organisational behaviour.
- **Flux and transformation**. The universe is in a constant state of flux, embodying characteristics of both permanence and change. Organisations can be seen as in a state of flux and transformation. In order to understand the nature and social life of organisations, it is necessary to understand the sources and logic of transformation and change.
- **Instruments of domination**. In this view organisations are associated with processes of social domination, and individuals and groups imposing their will on others. A feature of organisations is asymmetrical power relations that result in the pursuit of the goals of the few through the efforts of the many. Organisations are best understood in terms of variations in the mode of social domination and control of their members.

A broader view of organisational behaviour

Although the main concern of this book is with a managerial approach to organisational behaviour, these contrasting metaphors provide an interesting perspective on how to view organisations. They provide a broader view of the dynamics of organisational behaviour, and how to manage and design organisations. However, Morgan points out that these metaphors are not fixed categories and are not mutually exclusive. An organisation can be a mix of each, and predominantly a combination of two or three metaphors. Furthermore, these combinations may change over a period of time.

A number of writers involve the use of metaphors to help describe organisations. For example, in discussing the role and logic of viewing the organisation in terms of metaphors, *Drummond* raises questions such as what an organisation is like, and the power of metaphors in shaping our thinking; but also points out that all metaphors are partial and no metaphor can explain fully a particular phenomenon.[15]

ORIENTATIONS TO WORK AND THE WORK ETHIC

People differ in the manner and extent of their involvement with, and concern for, work. From information collected about the work situation, organisational participation and involvement with work colleagues, and life outside the organisation, *Goldthorpe et al.* identified three main types of orientation to work: instrumental, bureaucratic and solidaristic.[16]

- Individuals with an **instrumental orientation** defined work not as a central life issue but in terms of a means to an end. There is a calculative or economic involvement with work, and a clear distinction between work-related and non-work-related activities.
- Individuals with a **bureaucratic orientation** defined work as a central life issue. There is a sense of obligation to the work of the organisation and a positive involvement in terms of a career structure. There is a close link between work-related and non-work-related activities.
- Individuals with a **solidaristic orientation** defined the work situation in terms of group activities. There is an ego involvement with work groups rather than with the organisation itself. Work is more than just a means to an end. Non-work activities are linked to work relationships.

Different work situation

Some people may well have a set motivation to work, whatever the nature of the work environment. However, different work situations may also influence the individual's orientation to work. For example, the lack of opportunities for teamwork and the satisfaction of social expectations may result in an instrumental orientation to work, and a primary concern for economic interests such as pay and security. In other situations where there are greater opportunities to satisfy social needs, membership of work groups may be very important, and individuals may have a more solidaristic orientation to work.

According to *Herman*, the work ethic has been deeply challenged by two trends – the division of labour and the destruction of continuity in employment. Work has been fractured in task and sub-divided into specialised subtasks or branches into new kinds of work all together. The division of labour has now generated tens of thousands of discrete functions in the workplace. A more recent trend is the destruction of continuity in employment with many employees likely to re-enter the job market multiple times. This discourages the development of bonds of loyalty or employees investing themselves in their work with the hope of long-term employment.[17]

Knights and Willmott contend that most management textbooks do not make the connection between managing and everyday life. By drawing on a number of contemporary novels they attempt to 'bring to life' what they see as the reality of managing and organising, and dimensions of human experience at work and elsewhere. They explore, in an interesting way, the changing meaning of work and orientations to it, and how different kinds of work are meaningful to some people and not to others.[18]

Cultural influences

National culture is also a significant influence on orientations to work. For example, *Reeves* comments on the importance of conversation for effective organisational relationships but how this is resisted in the British work culture.

> *The Protestant version of the work ethic prevails, implying heads-down work, focused agendas, punctuality, efficiency. In French and Spanish offices, it takes the first hour to kiss everyone, the second to discuss local gossip and the third to pop out for a coffee and croissant. In Britain, these activities would count as sexual harassment, time-wasting and absenteeism. Many firms have built cafés or break out areas and then discovered people are too scared to use them for fear of looking work-shy.[19]*

As another example, the author experienced for himself how in parts of Australia work-related activities could often be undertaken comfortably in local coffee houses without concern about being seen as away from the place of work.

Cartwright comments on the psychological process of culture that has the power and authority not only to determine lifestyle but also to form individual personality traits, behaviours and attitudes.

> *It is the cultural environment that motivates people to do their best and to give of their best, often irrespective of or even in spite of their working or living environment. In this respect we make a clear distinction between social conditions and the cultural environment. In the same way that a first-class system does not guarantee first-class results, good living and working conditions do not, in themselves, guarantee high morale and motivation. People in the best working and living conditions can still have low morale and motivation without the benefit of a supportive culture.[20]*

Work/life balance

Popular newspaper articles often suggest that work is still a large component of what gives meaning to people's lives, and give examples of lottery or pools winners staying in work and often in their same old job. Other surveys and reports continue to suggest that the workplace is no longer a central feature of social activity. For a majority of people the main reason for work remains the need for money to fulfil the necessities of life. However, much still appears to depend on the extent of an individual's social contacts and activities outside of the work situation.

From a survey conducted among subscribers to *Management Today*, the majority of Britain's managers are engaged in a perpetual juggling act with the work/life balance, and in meeting both personal and work commitments. For many of those surveyed, however, work remains a huge source of satisfaction.[21] The work/life balance is discussed more fully in Chapter 18.

MANAGEMENT AS AN INTEGRATING ACTIVITY

Whatever the individual's orientations to work, it is through the process of **management** that the efforts of members of the organisation are co-ordinated, directed and guided towards the achievement of organisational goals. Management is an integral part of, and fundamental to, the successful operations of the organisation. Management is therefore the cornerstone of organisational effectiveness, and is concerned with arrangements for the carrying out of organisational processes and the execution of work (*see* Figure 2.4).

There are many aspects to management in work organisations, but the one essential ingredient of any successful manager is the ability to handle people effectively. The man-

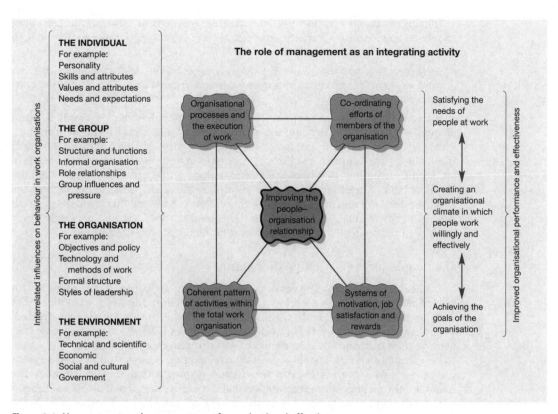

Figure 2.4 Management as the cornerstone of organisational effectiveness

ager needs to be conversant with social and human skills, and have the ability to work with and through other people. Without people there can be no organisation and no meaningful activity. **Behind every action or document in an organisation there are people**.

Patterns of human behaviour

It is the responsibility of management to manage. But organisations can only achieve their aims and objectives through the co-ordinated efforts of their members. This involves the effective management of human resources. However, it is important always to remember that it is people who are being managed and people should be considered in human terms. Unlike physical resources, people are not owned by the organisation. People bring their own perceptions, feelings and attitudes towards the organisation, systems and styles of management, their duties and responsibilities, and the conditions under which they are working. At the heart of successful management is the problem of integrating the individual and the organisation, and this requires an understanding of both human personality and formal organisations.[22]

> The fact is that management ultimately depends on an understanding of human nature. I suggest it goes much further than that. In the first place, good management depends on the acceptance of certain basic values. It cannot be achieved without honesty and integrity, or without consideration for the interests of others. Secondly, it is the understanding of human foibles that we all share, such as jealousy, envy, status, prejudice, perception, temperament, motivation and talent, which provides the greatest challenge to managers.
>
> HRH The Duke of Edinburgh, Institute of Management Patron[23]

Human behaviour is capricious, and scientific methods or principles of behaviour cannot be applied with reliability. For example, in his study of job satisfaction, *Bassett* comments that:

> There seem to be no universal generalizations about worker dissatisfaction that permit easy management policy solutions to absenteeism and turnover problems ... There are almost never any exact conditions of cause and effect in the realm of human behaviour.[24]

It is also widely observed that you cannot study the behaviour of people without changing it. Patterns of behaviour are influenced by a complex combination of individual, social and cultural factors. Tensions, conflicts and politics are almost inevitable, as are informal structures of organisation and unofficial working methods. We need to remind ourselves of the human aspects of the organisation and the idiosyncratic behaviour of individuals. For example, *Egan* refers to the importance of the shadow side of the organisation: that is, those things not found on organisation charts or in company manuals – the covert, and often undiscussed, activities of people which affect both the productivity and quality of working life of an organisation.[25]

The people–organisation relationship

In the belief of the author, the majority of people come to work with the **original** attitude of being eager to do a good job, and desirous of performing well and to the best of their abilities. **People generally respond in the manner in which they are treated**. Where actual performance fails to match the ideal this is largely a result of how staff perceive they are treated by management and the management function.

Many problems in the people–organisation relationship arise not so much from what management does, but **the manner in which it is done**. Often, it is **not so much the intent but the manner of implementation** that is the root cause of staff unrest and dissatisfaction. For example, staff may agree on the need to introduce new technology to retain the competitive efficiency of the organisation, but feel resentment about the lack of pre-planning, consultation, retraining programmes, participation in agreeing new working practices and wage rates, and similar considerations arising from the manner of its introduction.

Therefore, a heavy responsibility is placed on managers and the activity of management – on the processes, systems and styles of management. Accordingly, how managers exercise the responsibility for, and duties of, management is important. Attention must be given to the work environment, and appropriate systems of motivation, job satisfaction and rewards. It is important to remember that improvement in organisational performance will only come about through people.[26]

Providing the right balance   Management should, therefore, endeavour to create the right balance between the interrelated elements which make up the total organisation, and to weld these into coherent patterns of activity best suited to the external environment in which the organisation is operating. Consideration must be given to developing an organisational climate in which people work willingly and effectively.

People and organisations need each other. **Attention should be focused, therefore, on improving the people–organisation relationship**. Management is an integral part of this relationship. It should serve to reconcile the needs of people at work with the requirements of the organisation. Management is essentially an integrating activity which permeates every facet of the operations of the organisation. The style of management adopted can be seen as a function of the manager's attitudes towards people, and assumptions about human nature and behaviour (discussed in Chapter 7).

The general movement towards flatter organisation structures, flexible working and greater employee involvement has placed increasing emphasis on an integrating rather than a hierarchical/controlling style of management.

> Management processes in the new millennium will be much more behavioural in nature, focusing on the key human resource-driven issues: learning, team-based visions, driving human resource processes, incentives to enhance growth, holistic budgeting, and proactive controls.[27]

THE PSYCHOLOGICAL CONTRACT

One significant aspect of organisational behaviour and the relationship between the individual and the organisation is the concept of the **psychological contract**. This is not a written document, but implies a series of mutual expectations and satisfaction of needs arising from the people–organisation relationship. It involves a process of giving and receiving by the individual and by the organisation. The psychological contract covers a range of expectations of rights and privileges, duties and obligations, which do not form part of a formal agreement but still have an important influence on people's behaviour.[28]

The nature and extent of individuals' expectations vary widely as do the ability and willingness of the organisation to meet them. It is difficult to list the range of implicit expectations that individuals have and they change over time. These expectations are notwithstanding any statutory requirements placed upon the organisation; instead they relate more to the idea of a social responsibility of management, discussed in Chapter 5. The organisation will also have implicit expectations of its members. The organisational side of the psychological contract places emphasis on expectations, requirements and constraints that may differ from, and may conflict with, an individual's expectations. Some possible examples of the individual's and the organisation's expectations are given in Figure 2.5.

Process of balancing

It is unlikely that all expectations of the individual or of the organisation will be met fully. There is a continual process of balancing, and explicit and implicit bargaining. The nature of these expectations is not defined formally, and although the individual member and the organisation may not be aware consciously of them, they still affect relationships between them and have an influence on behaviour.

The psychological contract is a useful concept in examining the socialisation of new members of staff to the organisation. According to *Kotter*, for example, early experiences have a major effect on an individual's subsequent career in an organisation, and influence job satisfaction, attitude and level of productivity. The extent of the matches between individual and organisational expectations also influences the willingness of people to stay with the organisation and of the organisation to continue to employ them.[29]

Stalker suggests that successful companies are those that have the ability to balance the unwritten needs of their employees with the needs of the company. Such companies use a simple formula of Caring, Communicating, Listening, Knowing and Rewarding.

- **Caring** – demonstrating genuine concern for individuals working in the organisation.
- **Communicating** – really talking about what the company is hoping to achieve.
- **Listening** – hearing not only the words but also what lies behind the words.
- **Knowing** – the individuals who work for you, their families, personal wishes, desires and ambitions.
- **Rewarding** – money is not always necessary; a genuine thankyou or public recognition can raise morale.[30]

The significance of the psychological contract depends on the extent to which it is perceived as fair by both the individual and the organisation, and will be respected by both sides. *Cartwright*, for example, refers to mutuality as the basic principle of the psychological contract.

A psychological contract is not only measured in monetary value or in the exchange of goods or services, it is in essence the exchange or sharing of beliefs and values, expectations and satisfactions. Mutuality is the basic principle of the psychological contract and consensus or mutual understanding is the basis of mutuality. Ideally therefore self-interest should be balanced with common interest in a 'win–win' arrangement.[31]

Higher National in Business

INDIVIDUALS' EXPECTATIONS OF THE ORGANISATION

- provide safe and hygienic working conditions;
- make every reasonable effort to provide job security;
- attempt to provide challenging and satisfying jobs, and reduce alienating aspects of work;
- adopt equitable human resource management policies and procedures;
- respect the role of trade union officials and staff representives;
- consult fully with staff and allow genuine participation in decisions which affect them;
- implement best practice in equal opportunity policies and procedures;
- reward all staff fairly according to their contribution and performance;
- provide reasonable opportunities for personal development and career progression;
- treat members of staff with respect;
- demonstrate an understanding and considerate attitude towards personal problems of staff.

ORGANISATIONAL EXPECTATIONS OF THE INDIVIDUAL

- uphold the ideology of the organisation and the corporate image;
- work diligently in pursuit of organisational objectives;
- adhere to the rules, policies and procedures of the organisation;
- respect the reasonable authority of senior members of staff;
- not take advantage of goodwill shown by management;
- be responsive to leadership influence;
- demonstrate loyalty and not betray positions of trust;
- maintain harmonious relationships with work colleagues;
- not abuse organisational facilities such as email or Internet access;
- observe reasonable and acceptable standards of dress and appearance;
- show respect and consolidation to customers and suppliers.

Figure 2.5 The psychological contract: possible examples of individual and organisational expectations

The nature of the boss–subordinate relationship is clearly a central feature of the psychological contract. *Emmott*, for example, points out that good people-management practices are the basis for a positive psychological contract and this means managers having to deal with the 'soft stuff'. Properly managed the psychological contract delivers hard, bottom-line results and improved business performance.

Managers at all levels can have an influence on employees' perceptions of the psychological contract. It is, however, the relationship between individual employees and their line manager that is likely to have most influence in framing and managing employees' expectations.[32]

CHANGING NATURE OF THE PSYCHOLOGICAL CONTRACT

The changing nature of organisations has placed an increasing emphasis on the importance of effective human resource management, including the importance of the psychological contract within the employment relationship. For example, from a review of research, *McBain* maintains that human resource management plays a key role in ensuring the promotion of business success and managing change. This involves paying attention to the psychological contract and the establishment of expectations and obligations with all groups of employees within the organisation.[33] The Institute of Administrative Management has introduced a new module on 'The Individual and the Organisation in Context' which has come about because of the need to keep abreast of changes affecting the individual at work.

> There is a need for managers to be aware of the new psychological contracts the individual members of their teams are bringing to work. Managers will have to consider alternative management styles to meet this new need and to use new skills to motivate and train their staff. People no longer come to work to be 'told what to do', but are aspiring to be part of the whole, with a real role as stakeholders in the success of 'their' organisation. Wise managers will harness this commitment for the benefit of everyone concerned.[34]

Hiltrop suggests that the increasing pressure for organisations to change has prompted growing disillusionment with the traditional psychological contract based on lifetime employment and steady promotion from within. Companies must develop new ways to increase the loyalty and commitment of employees. This includes attention to reward strategies based on recognition of contribution rather than status or position; systematic training and development including the skills for working in cross-functional teams; and the training of managers in counselling, coaching and leadership skills.[35]

Performance management

Stiles et al. also draw attention to how new competitive conditions and dynamic environments have brought performance management to centre stage as a major element in the changing nature of the psychological contract. From an examination of three large UK organisations, the authors explore 'how performance management processes are being used to support moves from the traditional contract of job security and clear career paths, while attempting to maintain commitment and morale'. The authors conclude that there are two main areas of difficulty in changing the psychological contract so that it focuses on performance management. The presence of mixed messages from employers is undermining the employment relationship and changes are being driven in a top-down manner with a lack of consultation. There is also disenchantment and concern about the accuracy and fairness of performance management processes, with employees expressing scepticism towards managerial attempts to implement change.[36]

A new moral contract

The changing nature of organisations and individuals at work has placed increasing pressures on the awareness and importance of new psychological contracts. *Ghosal et al.* suggest that in a changing social context the law of masters and servants that underlies the old psychological contract is no longer acceptable to many people. Forces of global competition and turbulent change make employment guarantees unfeasible and also enhance the need for levels of trust and teamwork. The new management philosophy needs to be grounded in a very different moral contract with people. Rather than seeing people as a corporate asset from which value can be appropriated, people are seen as a responsibility and a resource to be added to. The new moral contract also demands much from employees who need to abandon the stability of lifetime employment and embrace the concept of continuous learning and personal development.[37]

ORGANISATIONAL PRACTICES

It is convenient, here, to consider two sets of observations on the nature of human behaviour and what may actually happen, in practice, in organisations: the Peter Principle, and Parkinson's Law. Although these observations are presented in a satirical manner, they nevertheless make a serious and significant point about the management and functioning of organisations, and the actual nature and practice of organisational behaviour.

THE PETER PRINCIPLE

This is concerned with the study of occupational incompetence and the study of hierarchies. The analysis of hundreds of cases of occupational incompetence led to the formulation of the '**Peter Principle**', which is:

In a hierarchy every employee tends to rise to their level of incompetence.[38]

Employees competent in their position are promoted and competence in each new position qualifies for promotion to the next highest position until a position of incompetence is reached. The principle is based on perceived incompetence at all levels of every hierarchy – political, legal, educational and industrial – and ways in which employees move upwards through a hierarchy, and what happens to them after promotion.

Among the many examples quoted by Peter are those from the teaching occupation. *A* is a competent and conforming college student who becomes a teacher following the textbook, curriculum guide and timetable schedule, and who works well except when there is no rule or precedent available. *A* never breaks a rule or disobeys an order but will not gain promotion because, although competent as a student, *A* has reached a level of incompetence as a classroom teacher.

B, a competent student and inspiring teacher, although not good with paperwork, is promoted to head of the science department because of success as a teacher. The head of science is responsible for ordering all science supplies and keeping extensive records and *B*'s incompetence becomes evident.

C, a competent student, teacher and head of department, is promoted to assistant principal, and being intellectually competent is further promoted to principal. *C* is now required to work directly with higher officials. By working so hard at running the school, however, *C* misses important meetings with superiors and has no energy to become involved with community organisations. *C* thus becomes regarded as an incompetent principal.

Means of promotion

Peter suggests two main means by which a person can affect promotion rate, 'Pull' and 'Push'.

- Pull is an employee's relationship – by blood, marriage or acquaintance – with a person above the employee in the hierarchy.
- Push is sometimes manifested by an abnormal interest in study, vocational training and self-improvement.

In small hierarchies, Push may have a marginal effect in accelerating promotion; in larger hierarchies the effect is minimal. Pull is, therefore, likely to be more effective than Push.

Never stand when you can sit; never walk when you can ride; never Push when you can Pull.[39]

Higher National in Business

PARKINSON'S LAW

A major feature of **Parkinson's Law** is that of the 'Rising Pyramid', that is, 'Work expands so as to fill the time available for its completion.'[40] General recognition of this is illustrated in the proverb, 'It is the busiest person who has time to spare.' There is little, if any, relationship between the quantity of work to be done and the number of the staff doing it. Underlying this general tendency are two almost axiomatic statements:

■ An official wants to multiply subordinates, not rivals.
■ Officials make work for each other.

Parkinson goes on to give the following example. If a civil servant, A, believes he is overworked there are three possible remedies: (i) resignation; (ii) ask to halve the work by having it shared with a colleague, B; or (iii) seek the assistance of two subordinates, C and D. The first two options are unlikely. Resignation would involve loss of pension rights, and sharing work with a colleague on the same level would only bring in a rival for promotion. So A would prefer the appointment of two junior members of staff, C and D. This would increase A's status. There must be at least two subordinates, so that by dividing work between C and D, A will be the only person to understand the work of them both. Furthermore, each subordinate is kept in order by fear of the other's promotion.

When, in turn, C complains of overwork, A, with the agreement of C, will advise the appointment of two assistants, E and F. However, as D's position is much the same and to avoid internal friction, two assistants, G and H, will also be recommended to help D. There are now seven people, A, C, D, E, F, G, H, doing what one person did before, and the promotion of A is almost certain.

People making work for each other

With the seven people now employed, the second stage comes into operation. The seven people make so much work for each other that they are all fully occupied and A is actually working harder than ever. For example, an incoming document comes before each of them in turn. E decides it is F's concern; F places a draft reply for C, who makes drastic amendments before consulting with D, who asks G to action it. But then G goes on leave and hands the file to H, who drafts a minute signed by D and returned to C, who revises the first draft and puts the new version before A. What does A do? A could find many excuses for signing C's draft unread. However, being a conscientious person, and although beset with problems created by subordinates both for A and for themselves, A reads through the draft carefully, deletes the fussy paragraphs added by C and H, and restores it to the format presented in the first instance by F.

Among other features of organisational practice that Parkinson discusses are: principles of personnel selection; the nature of committees; personality screen; high finance – and the 'Law of Triviality', which means in a committee that the time spent on any agenda item will be in inverse proportion to the sum involved; layout of the organisation's administration block; and 'injelitis' – the disease of induced inferiority.

Relevance of observations

Despite the light vein of Parkinson's writing, the relevance of his observations can be gauged from comments in the Introduction by HRH The Duke of Edinburgh.

The most important point about this book for serious students of management and administration is that it illustrates the gulf that exists between the rational/intellectual approach to human organization and the frequent irrational facts of human nature … The law should be compulsory reading at all business schools and for all management consultants. Management structures solve nothing if they do not take the facts of human nature into proper consideration, and one of the most important facts is that no one really likes having to make decisions. Consequently structures may generate a lot of activity but little or no useful work.[41]

I first read *Parkinson's Law* when studying for Economics A-level. Many of the laws are just as relevant today as they were then. They include: how to 'manage' a meeting, and how time spent in meetings is inversely proportional to the importance of each issue – his example is a short discussion on a £10 million power plant followed by a lengthy debate over a £350 bicycle shed. Ever been there? ... Parkinson's most famous law is that 'work expands to fill the time available – as we all make work for one another'. This is still true today.

Iain Herbertson, Managing Director of Manpower[42]

THE NEED FOR A CROSS-CULTURAL APPROACH

The international context of management and organisational behaviour

One major challenge facing managers in the early 21st century arises from what many commentators have identified as an increasingly international or **global** business environment. The following factors are frequently cited as potential explanatory factors underlying this trend:

- Improvements in international communication facilities leading to an increased consciousness of differences in workplace attitudes and behaviour in other societies.
- International competitive pressure – for example, the emergence of newly industrialised and/or free-market nations (the Far East region and ex-communist bloc countries are often viewed as examples of this phenomenon).
- The spread of production methods and other business processes *across* nations and regions.
- International business activity, for example: overseas franchising or licensing agreements; outsourcing of business units to other countries (call centres provide a topical example); direct foreign investment and the activities of multinational corporations which, by definition, operate outside national boundaries.

The European Parliament building in Strasbourg, France

Photo: European Parliament

It is not only businesses which choose to operate in more than one country or import foreign business and management techniques that are affected by cross-cultural concerns. *Tayeb* reported United States Department of Labor statistics indicating that in the period from 1985 to 2000, only 15 per cent of new entrants to the workforce in the USA were white males.[43] This highlights the importance of managing diversity in workforces *within* national boundaries.

Lessons from abroad?

One rationale for taking a cross-cultural approach to management lies in the potential benefits to be gained in performance terms. *Schneider and Barsoux*, in advocating cultural awareness of one's **own** society, note that:

> each country has its unique institutional and cultural characteristics, which can provide sources of competitive advantage at one point, only to become liabilities when the environment changes. Managers therefore need to evaluate the extent to which national culture can interfere with their company's efforts to respond to strategic requirements, now and in the future'.[44]

In addition to practically based benefits in considering our own 'home' culture, there has been a long tradition of looking to other cultures for examples of 'successful' practice which could be transplanted into work organisations in different societies. Different models may be dominant at different times. *Thompson and McHugh* note that: 'In the post-war period the giant US corporations transferred work organisation and managerial techniques across capitalist countries.'[45] However, in subsequent eras Scandinavian autonomous work group arrangements and Japanese management techniques were examined by and, to some extent, implemented in, organisations across the world. Such a search for good practice in other countries is, of course, ongoing and an awareness of how other cultures organise work and manage people is likely to be of continuing benefit in the future.

Managing people from different cultures

Another advantage of adopting a cross-cultural approach to the study of organisational behaviour, and to the management of people more generally, lies in the recognition of variations in workplace attitudes and behaviour between individuals and groups in different cultural contexts. *Brooks* notes that: 'Differences in national culture may have a bearing on how organisations deal with each other and also on behaviour within organisations which comprise a mix of nationalities.'[46] If we accept this fundamental point then it follows that key topics within the subject area of organisational behaviour may be influenced by national culture and that we should therefore re-evaluate models and concepts when applying them to other societies.

One leading writer in the field of cross-cultural studies, *Trompenaars*, commenting on his own work, suggests that: 'it helped managers to structure their experiences and provided new insights for them and their organisations into the real source of problems faced when managing across cultures or dealing with diversity'.[47] In examining the centrally important topic of motivation, *Francesco and Gold* inform their readers that: 'managers must develop organizational systems that are flexible enough to take into account the meaning of work and the relative value of rewards within the range of cultures where they operate.'[48]

A practical example of the impact of cultural diversity in the organisational behaviour area is provided in the recollections of an International Human Resource Manager cited in *Schneider and Barsoux*: 'Indonesians manage their culture by a group process, and everyone is linked together as a team. Distributing money differently among the team did not go over all that well; so we've come to the conclusion that pay for performance is not suitable for Indonesia.'[49] It may be extremely useful therefore to examine academic frameworks and research findings within the field of organisational behaviour to indicate the extent to which they are applicable worldwide or, alternatively, subject to meaningful variation in different cultural contexts.

IS ORGANISATIONAL BEHAVIOUR CULTURE-BOUND?

While it can be valuable to apply organisational behaviour concepts to diverse cultural settings it should also be borne in mind that some **universal** theories and models may, in reality, contain important culturally-derived assumptions. When examining classical frameworks for understanding organisation structure Schneider and Barsoux point out that: 'theories about how best to organise – Max Weber's (German) bureaucracy, Henri Fayol's (French) administrative model, and Frederick Taylor's (American) scientific management – all reflect societal concerns of the times as well as the cultural background of the individuals.'[50] That writers on work organisations may themselves be influenced by their own cultural backgrounds when compiling their work is unsurprising: however, it should equally not be ignored.

More significant still is the possibility that whole topics within organisational behaviour, *per se*, may be underpinned by a particular culturally-derived frame of reference. *Francesco and Gold*, addressing the issue of leadership, claim that: 'one difficulty is that not all cultures have the term leader'.[51] This raises the possibility that meanings we may assume to be taken for granted could be interpreted differently or **not even perceived at all** in different parts of the world.

Culture as understanding

'For our most basic common link is that we all inhabit this small planet, we all breathe the same air, we all cherish our children's future, and we are all mortal' (John. F. Kennedy, 10 June 1963). There are a number of very good reasons why we could usefully understand cultural difference (and similarity) at work, based on new awareness contributing to our own effectiveness and moreover to the accomplishment of organisational goals. It could also be true to say that an appreciation of culture and its effects may be of intrinsic value. There could therefore be advantages of cross-cultural awareness which include:

- increased self-awareness;
- sensitivity to difference;
- questioning our own assumptions and knowledge;
- lessening ignorance, prejudice and hatred.

However, it would be wrong to think that increased cross-cultural awareness or activity will automatically bring about any of these outcomes.

Adler listed the following inbuilt dangers when multi-cultural teams operate in a business setting.

- Mistrust – including stereotyping.
- Miscommunication with potential for reduced accuracy and resultant stress.
- Process difficulties, that is failure to agree when agreement is needed or even what constitutes agreement when arriving at decisions.

Adler goes on to examine research on the success of multi-cultural work teams and concludes that the evidence suggests that they either perform *much better or much worse* than teams composed of one cultural group.[52] There are clearly risks as well as benefits in working across cultures. It is hoped that an appreciation of cross-cultural aspects of organisational behaviour can help in this regard.

MODELS FOR UNDERSTANDING THE IMPACT OF CULTURE

The study of culture

Culture is a notoriously difficult concept to pin down. It is all too easy to assume that differences observed between societies may be attributed to culture *per se*, with little explanation of the reasons which may lie behind the differences, real or perceived. *Robbins* notes that: 'Most people are unaware of just how their culture will affect them. Culture is like fish to water. It is there all the time but the fish are oblivious to it.'[53] It is therefore necessary to be aware of one's own culture in order to appreciate fully differences between different groups. The Johari Window technique – see Chapter 14 – can be useful in identifying what may be known and not known regarding different cultures. Attempt to use this framework in respect of your own and one other culture to see its potential value. We should not assume that we are aware of all facets of our own culture or that others see us in a realistic and accurate way.

Matched pair comparisons

Some writers who have sought to conduct comparative research into workplace differences have frequently used a **matched pair** method of comparison. This involves selecting organisations for study which are similar in size, product or service, technologies employed and ownership pattern. It is claimed that any differences observed can be isolated and subjected to further detailed analysis to ascertain whether they are culturally-derived. An example of this methodological tradition is the work of *Maurice, Sorge and Warner* which is considered in Chapter 16.[54]

The danger of stereotyping

In Chapter 11 of this book we identify the concept of 'selective perception', that is the possibility of drawing inferences and conclusions from partial information. One example of this phenomenon is **stereotyping** which involves making judgements on an individual as a result of their membership of a group, which, we assume, itself contains shared characteristics. We clearly need to avoid stereotyping when approaching the subject of cultural differences at work. Writers such as *Hofstede* and *Trompenaars*, while identifying **clusters** of countries which they suggest may share particular features, nonetheless allow for divergence from the norm by referring to **central tendencies**. To take one example, Hong Kong is characterised by Hofstede as a **low uncertainty avoidance** culture which suggests a propensity for risk-taking and a tolerance of rapid change. However, it is eminently possible to conceive of an **individual** from Hong Kong who is 'risk averse' and conservative due to their own personality and upbringing.[55] It is, finally, necessary to take a non-judgemental approach when identifying cultural differences and academics in this area and crucially **successful international managers** tend to adopt an approach of 'not better nor worse – just different'!

Defining and conceptualising culture

Culture is a multifaceted concept. Models purporting to explain this topic typically distinguish between different **layers** or **strata** of culture. Trompenaars identifies three layers of culture; namely an outer, middle and core. Figure 2.6 depicts these layers as concentric circles. The outer circle identifies artifacts and products, the middle circle encompasses norms and values and the inner circle comprises basic assumptions held within the group.[56]

It may equally be useful to conceive of a three-layer model of culture comprising outer, middle and core layers. For our purposes an **outer layer** of culture refers to surface-level elements of culture which are quickly and easily understood on even a short visit to another country. Examples could include language, climate, dress and food and drink. The 1994 film *Pulp Fiction* provides an example in which a character in the film has recently returned to the USA after spending three years in Amsterdam. His description of the Netherlands is restricted to surface level anecdotes regarding fast

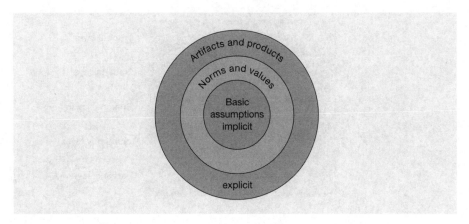

Figure 2.6   A model of culture

Source: Reproduced with permission from F. Trompenaars and C. Hampden-Turner, *Riding the Waves of Culture*, Second edition, Nicholas Brealey (1999), p. 22.

food and the comparative legality and availability of soft drugs. The viewer is invited to mock his failure to understand the greater subtleties of Dutch culture. Aspects of this outer layer can nonetheless be important to a successful cultural exchange in business. Giving a work colleague in the Czech Republic red flowers as a gift may be taken as expression of romantic interest while wearing a green hat in China may signify that one's partner is unfaithful!

A **middle layer** of culture is the one which will be of most relevance for us as it concerns expressed values, attitudes and behaviours. In terms of organisational behaviour, if we accept the evidence that indicates significant differences between cultures, we might anticipate that findings in the following topics should be re-examined to see whether they apply in different societies:

Leadership, Perception, Motivation, Work Groups, Organisation Structure, Human Resource Management and Management Control and Power.

The contribution of writers such as Hofstede, Trompenaars, and *Hall and Hall*[57] may also provide useful frameworks for understanding topics within organisational behaviour from a cross-cultural standpoint.

A **core layer** of culture relates to the deepest assumptions concerning people and nature held by a particular society. Such assumptions, which may be vestigial, often relate to the topography of a society or the level of threat posed by natural disasters. For example, it has been claimed that the Netherlands as a small country bounded by larger neighbours has developed a pragmatic flexible approach to business as a result of its location, bolstered by its historic struggle to keep the sea at bay. In the UK the relatively high degree of scepticism towards greater European integration may, in part, be explained by its island status. So-called group mentalities exhibited by some Asian countries could be traced back to patterns of agrarian production exhibited in previous times. Somewhat more arcane and, by definition, difficult to unravel, these core layer assumptions could conceivably manifest themselves in modern day cross-border business dealings.

In Figure 2.7 *Tayeb* shows with examples how culture can take effect at a number of levels; from the **global** through to the **personal**. Readers may wish to consider how significant cultural differences may occur at the **regional** and/or **community** levels in their own experience. Nonetheless studies of culture most usually take the country or nation state as the focus of attention.[58]

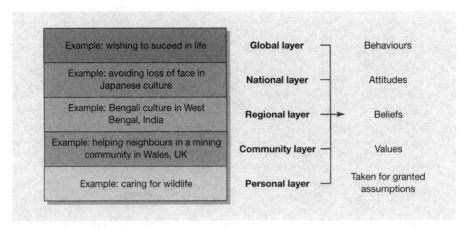

Figure 2.7 Major cultural layers

Source: Reproduced with permission from M. Tayeb, *International Management: Theories and Practice*, Financial Times Prentice Hall (2003), p. 14, with permission from Pearson Education Ltd.

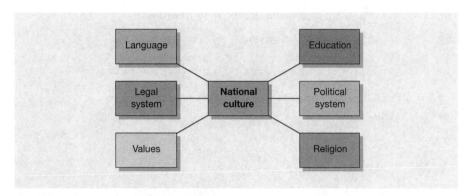

Figure 2.8 Factors affecting national culture

Source: Reproduced with permission from Ian Brooks, *Organisational Behaviour: Individuals, Groups and Organisation*, Second edition, Financial Times Prentice Hall (2003), p. 266, with permission from Pearson Education Ltd.

Brooks is one of several commentators who draw our attention to the interlinked nature of culture. Figure 2.8 illustrates the interplay between relevant factors affecting any one national culture.[59] You may wish to consider how these factors have combined to shape your own 'home' culture and that of one other country with which you are familiar.

FIVE DIMENSIONS OF CULTURE: THE CONTRIBUTION OF HOFSTEDE

Geert Hofstede is one of the most significant contributors to the body of knowledge on culture and workplace difference. His work has largely resulted from a large-scale research programme involving employees from the IBM corporation, initially in 40 countries. In focusing on one organisation Hofstede felt that the results could be more clearly linked to national cultural difference. Arguing that culture is, in a memorable phrase, **collective programming** or **software of the mind**, Hofstede initially identified four dimensions of culture; **power distance**, **uncertainty avoidance**, **individualism** and **masculinity**.[60] (*See* Table 2.1.)

■ **Power distance** is essentially used to categorise levels of inequality in organisations, which Hofstede claims will depend upon management style, willingness of subordinates to disagree with superiors, and the educational level and status accruing to particular roles. Countries which displayed a high level of power distance included France, Spain, Hong Kong and Iran. Countries as diverse as Germany, Italy, Australia and the USA were characterised as low power distance societies. Britain also emerged as a low power distance society according to Hofstede's work.

■ **Uncertainty avoidance** refers to the extent to which members of a society feel threatened by unusual situations. High uncertainty avoidance is said to be characteristic in France, Spain, Germany and many of the Latin American societies. Low-to-medium uncertainty avoidance was displayed in the Netherlands, the Scandinavian countries and Ireland. In this case Britain is said to be 'low-to-medium' together with the USA, Canada and Australia.

■ **Individualism** describes the relatively individualistic or collectivist ethic evident in that particular society. Thus, the USA, France and Spain display high individualism. This contrasts with Portugal, Hong Kong, India and Greece which are low individualism societies. Britain here is depicted as a high individualism society.

■ **Masculinity** is the final category suggested by Hofstede. This refers to a continuum between 'masculine' characteristics, such as assertiveness and competi-

Table 2.1 Classification of cultures by dimensions

I: More developed Latin	II: Less developed Latin	
high power distance	high power distance	
high uncertainty avoidance	high uncertainty avoidance	
high individualism	low individualism	
medium masculinity	whole range on masculinity	
Belgium	Colombia	
France	Mexico	
Argentina	Venezuela	
Brazil	Chile	
Spain	Peru	
	Portugal	
	Yugoslavia	

III: More developed Asian	IV: Less developed Asian	V: Near Eastern
medium power distance	high power distance	high power distance
high uncertainty avoidance	low uncertainty avoidance	high uncertainty avoidance
medium individualism	low individualism	low individualism
high masculinity	medium masculinity	medium masculinity
Japan	Pakistan	Greece
	Taiwan	Iran
	Thailand	Turkey
	Hong Kong	
	India	
	Philippines	
	Singapore	

VI: Germanic	VII: Anglo	VIII: Nordic
low power distance	low power distance	low power distance
high uncertainty avoidance	low-to-medium uncertainty avoidance	low-to-medium uncertainty avoidance
medium individualism	high individualism	medium individualism
high masculinity	low masculinity	low masculinity
Austria	Australia	Denmark
Israel	Canada	Finland
Germany	Britain	The Netherlands
Switzerland	Ireland	Norway
South Africa	New Zealand	Sweden
Italy	USA	

(Reproduced with permission from 'International Perspectives', Unit 16, Block V, Wider Perspectives, *Managing in Organizations*, ©The Open University (1985) p. 60.)

tiveness, and 'feminine' traits, such as caring, a stress upon the quality of life and concern with the environment. High masculinity societies included the USA, Italy, Germany and Japan. More feminine (low masculinity) societies included the Netherlands and the Scandinavian countries. In this case Britain was located within the high masculinity group.

A fifth dimension of culture, long-term/short-term orientation, was originally labelled **Confucian work dynamism**. This dimension developed from the work of *Bond* in an attempt to locate Chinese cultural values as they impacted on the workplace.[61]

Countries which scored highly on Confucian work dynamism or long-term orientation exhibited a strong concern with time along a continuum and were therefore both past- and future-oriented, with a preoccupation with tradition but also a concern with the effect of actions and policies on future generations. Table 2.2 indicates the score of ten countries along this fifth dimension. Unsurprisingly China scores highest on the LT column followed by Japan. Note the significantly lower scores of the USA and Western European countries surveyed.

Table 2.2 Cultural dimension scores for ten countries

	PD	ID	MA	UA	LT
USA	40L	91H	62H	46L	29L
Germany	35L	67H	66H	65M	31M
Japan	54M	46M	95H	92H	80H
France	68H	71H	43M	86H	30*L
Netherlands	38L	80H	14L	53M	44M
Hong Kong	68H	25L	57H	29L	96H
Indonesia	78H	14L	46M	48L	25*L
West Africa	77H	20L	46M	54M	16L
Russia	95*H	50*M	40*L	90*H	10*L
China	80*H	20*L	50*M	60*M	118H

PD=Power Distance; ID=Individualism; MA=Masculinity; UA=Uncertainty Avoidance; LT=Long-Term Orientation. H=top third, M=medium third, L=bottom third (among 53 countries and regions for the first four dimensions; among 23 countries for the fifth), *estimated

Reprinted with permission from Hofstede, G., 'Cultural Constraints in Management Theories', *Academy of Management Executive: The Thinking Manager's Source*, 7, 1993, p. 91.

Evaluation of Hofstede's work

Extremely influential; the seminal work of Hofstede has been criticised from certain quarters. In common with other writers in this area there is a focus on the national rather than regional level. The variations within certain countries, for example Spain, can be more or less significant. Again in common with other contributors Hofstede's classifications include medium categories which may be difficult to operationalise, accurate though they may be. Some may also find the masculinity/femininity dimension unconvincing and itself stereotypical. Other writers have questioned whether Hofstede's findings remain current. *Holden* summarises this view: 'How many people have ever thought that many of Hofstede's informants of three decades ago are now dead? Do their children and grandchildren really have the same values?'[62] Ultimately, readers can assess the value of his work in the light of their own experiences and interpretations of the business world. Hofstede in his extensive research has attempted to locate the essence of work-related differences across the world and to relate these to preferred management styles.

CULTURAL DIVERSITY: THE CONTRIBUTION OF TROMPENAARS

Another significant contributor to this area of study is provided by *Fons Trompenaars* whose later work is co-authored with *Charles Hampden-Turner*.[63] Trompenaars's original research spanned 15 years, resulting in a database of 50,000 participants from 50 countries. It was supported by cases and anecdotes from 900 cross-cultural training programmes. A questionnaire method comprised a significant part of the study which involved requiring participants to consider their underlying norms, values and attitudes. The resultant framework identifies seven areas in which cultural differences may affect aspects of organisational behaviour.

- Relationships and rules. Here societies may be more or less **universal**, in which case there is relative rigidity in respect of rule-based behaviour, or **particular**, in which case the importance of relationships may lead to flexibility in the interpretation of situations.
- Societies may be more oriented to the **individual** or **collective**. The collective may take different forms: the corporation in Japan, the family in Italy or the Catholic Church in the Republic of Ireland. There may be implications here for such matters as individual responsibility or payment systems.
- It may also be true that societies differ to the extent it is thought appropriate for members to show emotion in public. **Neutral** societies favour the 'stiff upper lip' while overt displays of feeling are more likely in **emotional** societies. Trompenaars cites a survey in which 80 employees in each of various societies were asked whether they would think it wrong to express upset openly at work. The numbers who thought it wrong were 80 in Japan, 75 in Germany, 71 in the UK, 55 in Hong Kong, 40 in the USA and 29 in Italy.
- In **diffuse** cultures, the whole person would be involved in a business relationship and it would take time to build such relationships. In a **specific** culture, such as the USA, the basic relationship would be limited to the contractual. This distinction clearly has implications for those seeking to develop new international links.
- **Achievement**-based societies value recent success or an overall record of accomplishment. In contrast, in societies relying more on **ascription**, status could be bestowed on you through such factors as age, gender or educational record.
- Trompenaars suggests that societies view **time** in different ways which may in turn influence business activities. The American dream is the French nightmare. Americans generally start from zero and what matters is their present performance and their plan to 'make it' in the future. This is 'nouveau riche' for the French, who prefer the 'ancien pauvre'; they have an enormous sense of the past.
- Finally it is suggested that there are differences with regard to attitudes to the **environment**. In western societies, individuals are typically masters of their fate. In other parts of the world, however, the world is more powerful than individuals.

Trompenaars' work is based on lengthy academic and field research. It is potentially useful in linking the dimensions of culture to aspects of organisational behaviour which are of direct relevance, particularly to people approaching a new culture for the first time.

The high- and low-context cultures framework

This framework for understanding cultural difference has been formulated by Ed Hall; his work is in part co-authored with Mildred Reed Hall.[64] *Hall* conceptualises culture as comprising a series of 'languages', in particular:

- Language of time
- Language of space
- Language of things
- Language of friendships
- Language of agreements

In this model of culture Hall suggests that these 'languages', which resemble shared attitudes to the issues in question, are communicated in very different ways according to whether a society is classified as 'high' or 'low' context.

The features of 'high' context societies, which incorporate Asian, African and Latin American countries, includes:

- a high proportion of information is 'uncoded' and internalised by the individual;
- indirect communication styles ... words are less important;
- shared group understandings;
- importance attached to the past and tradition;
- 'diffuse' culture stressing importance of trust and personal relationships in business.

'Low' context societies, which include the USA, Australia, Britain and the Scandinavian countries, exhibit contrasting features including:

- a high proportion of communication is 'coded' and expressed;
- direct communication styles ... words are paramount;
- past context less important;
- 'specific' culture stressing importance of rules and contracts.

Other countries, for example France, Spain, Greece and several Middle Eastern societies, are classified as 'medium' context.

To take one example as an illustration: American managers visiting China may find that a business transaction in that country will take more time than at home. They may find that it is difficult to interpret the true feelings of their Chinese host and may need to decode non-verbal communication and other signals. They may seek to negotiate a rules-based contract whereas their Chinese counterpart may lay greater stress upon building a mutually beneficial reciprocal relationship. There is scope for potential miscommunication between the two cultures and interesting differences in interpersonal perception. Inasmuch as much of the management literature canon originates from the Anglo-American context, there is again considerable merit in adopting a cross-cultural perspective.

SUMMARY: CONVERGENCE OR CULTURE-SPECIFIC ORGANISATIONAL BEHAVIOUR

There is evidence of a narrowing or even increasing elimination of cultural differences in business. *Grint* sees both positive and negative consequences of aspects of globalisation. While noting that: 'at last we are approaching an era when what is common between people transcends that which is different; where we can choose our identity rather than have it thrust upon us by accident of birth',[65] the same author goes on to suggest that: 'we are heading for global convergence where national, ethnic and local cultures and identities are swamped by the McDonaldization ... and/or Microsoftization of the world'.[66]

There is an undoubted narrowing of cultural differences in work organisations; and it may be the case that such narrowing may apply to individual and group behaviour at work. *Thompson and McHugh* note for example that: 'Russia is now experiencing rampant individualism and uncertainty following the collapse of the old solidaristic norms', thus implying convergence of work values.[67]

For the most part, however, it is argued here that growing similarity and harmonisation relate more often to production, IT and quality systems which are more likely to converge due to best-practice comparisons and universal computer standards. Human Resource Management is, contrastingly, less likely to converge due to national institutional frameworks and culturally derived preferences. Recent significantly different responses to the need for greater workplace 'flexibility' in Britain and France illustrate this point. Above all, those aspects of organisational behaviour which focus on individual differences, groups and managing people are the most clearly affected by culture and it is argued strongly here that it is and is likely to remain essential to take a cross-cultural approach to the subject.

CRITICAL REFLECTIONS

In your understanding of behaviour and managing people at work – as in life more generally – it is worth remembering the 'Bag of Gold' syndrome. However hard you try or whatever you do there will always be some people you just cannot seem to please. Give them a bag of gold and they will complain that the bag is the wrong colour, or it is too heavy to carry, or why could you not give them a cheque instead!

What are your own views?

What happens within organizations affects what happens outside and vice versa. Organizational behaviour is seen chiefly as being about the particular ways that individual's dispositions are expressed in an organizational setting and about the effects of this expression. While at work there is rest and play. What happens in rest and play, both inside and outside the organization, impacts on organizational life. We can also gain insight into organizational behaviour by looking at less organized work, like work 'on the fiddle', and what work means to the unemployed.

Wilson, F. M. *Organizational Behaviour: A Critical Introduction*, Oxford University Press (1999), pp. 1–2.

How would you explain the meaning and nature of organisational behaviour, and how it is influenced?

'The study of organisational behaviour is really an art which pretends that it is a science and produces some spurious research findings to try to prove the point.'

Debate.

SYNOPSIS

■ Organisations play a major and continuing role in the lives of us all, especially with the growth of large-scale business organisations. The decisions and actions of management in organisations have an increasing impact on individuals, other organisations and the community. It is important, therefore, to understand how organisations function and the pervasive influences they exercise over the behaviour of people. It is also necessary to understand interrelationships with other variables which together comprise the total organisation.

■ The behaviour of people in work organisations can be viewed in terms of multi-related dimensions relating to the individual, the group, the organisation and the environment. The study of organisational behaviour cannot be understood fully in terms of a single discipline. It is necessary to provide a behavioural science approach drawing on selected aspects of the three main disciplines of psychology, sociology and anthropology together with related disciplines and influences.

■ Organisations are complex social systems which can be defined and studied in a number of different ways. One approach is to view organisations in terms of contrasting metaphors. Gauging the effectiveness or success of an organisation is not an easy task, however, although one central element is the importance of achieving productivity through the effective management of people. People differ in the manner and extent of their involvement with, and concern for, work. Different situations influence the individual's orientation to work and work ethic. A major concern for people today is balancing work and personal commitments.

■ It is through the process of management that efforts of members of the organisation are co-ordinated, directed and guided towards the achievement of organisational objectives. Management is the cornerstone of organisational effectiveness. It is essentially an integrating activity and concerned with arrangements for the carrying out of organisational processes and the execution of work. How managers exercise the responsibility for, and duties of, management is important. Attention should be focused on improving the people–organisation relationship.

■ One particular aspect of the relationship between the individual and the organisation is the concept of the psychological contract. This is not a formal, written document but implies a series of mutual expectations and satisfaction of needs arising from the people–organisation relationship. There is a continual process of explicit and implicit bargaining. The nature of expectations has an important influence on the employment relationship and behaviour in work organisations. The changing nature of organisations and individuals at work has placed increasing pressures on the awareness and importance of a different moral contract with people.

■ A major challenge facing managers today arises from an increasingly international or global business environment. This highlights the need for a cross-cultural approach to the study of organisational behaviour and the management of people. In an increasingly global context, managers need to recognise and understand the impact of national culture. However, culture is a multifaceted concept and notoriously difficult to pin down. But it has important repercussions for the effective management of people, and the study and understanding of workplace behaviour.

REVIEW AND DISCUSSION QUESTIONS

1 Explain your understanding of (i) the nature of organisational behaviour and (ii) the meaning of behavioural science.

2 Suggest main headings under which interrelated factors can be identified which influence behaviour in work organisations. For each of your headings give examples from your own organisation.

3 Discuss how organisations may be viewed in terms of contrasting metaphors. Explain how you would apply these metaphors to an understanding of your own organisation.

4 Discuss the role of management as an integrating activity. Give your own views on the responsibility of management and the manner in which you believe this responsibility should be exercised.

5 Explain the nature of the people–organisation relationship. Why is it important to distinguish between the 'intent' and the 'implementation' of management decisions and actions?

6 Explain what is meant by the 'psychological contract'. List (i) the personal expectations you have of your own organisation and (ii) what you believe to be the expectations of the organisation. Discuss with supporting examples the changing nature of psychological contracts between the organisation and its members.

7 Why is it increasingly important for managers to adopt an international approach? Discuss critically the likely longer-term impact of Britain's membership of the European Union.

8 Debate fully the importance of national culture to the study of management and organisational behaviour. Where possible, give your own actual examples

ASSIGNMENT 1

A first step in understanding human behaviour and the successful management of other people is to know and understand yourself. For this simple exercise you are asked to select any one of the following shapes that you feel is 'YOU'.

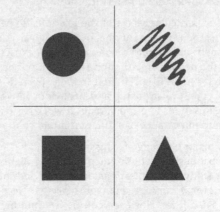

After you have made your selection discuss in small groups the reasons which prompted you to choose that particular shape. How much agreement is there among members of your group? You should then consider and discuss the further information provided by your tutor.

ASSIGNMENT 2

Provide for classroom discussion short descriptions (suitably disguised if necessary) to illustrate the practical application of:

1 The Peter Principle, and
2 Parkinson's Law.

Include in your descriptions what you believe to be the relevance of each of these sets of observations, and the effects on other members of staff.

PERSONAL AWARENESS AND SKILLS EXERCISE

OBJECTIVES

Completing this exercise should help you to enhance the following skills:

▶ Obtain a clearer picture of your own and other people's work ethic.

▶ Explore the importance of work to you and your fixed attitudes about work.

▶ Recognise the significance of individuals' orientations to work within an organisation.

EXERCISE

You are required to start by asking yourself this question: is it a good thing to be a worker? And then to think carefully about your responses to the following questions:

How do you feel ...

■ when you hear the word 'work'?

■ as you get ready for work?

■ when you know the day is over?

■ about the work you've accomplished?

■ about someone who chooses not to work?

■ about taking time off?

■ when you hear the word 'management'?

■ about taking control of your career?

Compare your responses with those of your colleagues. What conclusions do you draw about the work ethic?

DISCUSSION

■ What do you see as the character traits of a person with a healthy work ethic?

■ To what extent do you agree with the contention that: 'we are employed for our skills but valued for our attitude'?

■ What effect might different orientations to work have within an organisation and how might they all be accommodated?

Visit our website **www.booksites.net/mullins** for further questions, annotated weblinks, case material and Internet research material.

CASE STUDY 2.1

Eric and Kipsy: complexities of management and organisational behaviour

CONSIDER THE PLIGHT OF ERIC

Eric is a new manager of product information for a national firm which wholesales electrical components. He's proud because he was assigned a 'tough' office right out of management training. He's challenged because he can see as clearly as everyone else in the office that the work is not getting done on time – and that mistakes are far above the 2 per cent target. And he's scared because he finds himself utterly incapable of figuring out what he ought to do to make things better.

Eric's first day

The office is a new, one-storey building in a wooded suburban location – complete with carpeting on the floor and Muzak in the walls. There are 35 female employees, ranging from recent high school graduates in their first job to experienced middle-aged housewives. Their job is to provide salesmen in the field with current information about price, availability and delivery times of an exceptionally large inventory of electrical equipment and supplies.

Eric spent his first day on the job – some three months ago now – just watching and listening. While in management training, he had thought a lot about how he would handle that first day. He knew that everyone in the office would be as eager to find out what he was like as he was to learn about them and their jobs. And he wanted to make a good impression.

But Eric finally decided not to give a false impression. The fact was that he knew virtually nothing about the people he would be managing, or the kind of work they did. So why, he asked himself, act otherwise? Besides, if the people saw that he was genuinely interested in listening to them and learning from them, perhaps that would help establish good mutual rapport between him and his people. So he would just watch, and listen, and try to learn in his first few days on the job.

The first day was fun. Soon after arriving and being introduced to the four first-level supervisors, he asked to be 'plugged in' to one of the complicated-looking operating consoles at which the women received calls from the field. A green light would blink on the console, and the information clerk would be connected to the salesman in the field – all taken care of by an out-of-sight computer, which assigned calls sequentially to the waiting clerks. The salesman would ask for information about the availability of a certain piece of equipment. The clerk would then look up the stock number of that item in a large catalogue at her side and punch the number into a keyboard on the console. Immediately, the computer would present full information about stocks and delivery times of that item on an electronic display panel on the console, and the clerk would relay the appropriate information to the salesman. When the call ended, the green light would extinguish itself, and the clerk would then wait for the light to flash again, signalling the arrival of a new call.

Eric was fascinated by both the efficiency of the operation and the pleasantness of the surroundings. His biggest worry at that point was that everything was so efficiently designed that he, as manager, would not have anything to do with his time.

Beware first impressions

He soon learned how wrong he was. When, on his second day at the office, he began to attack a pile of paperwork on his desk, he found messages from nearly a dozen field salesmen, all wanting him to return their calls. Each of these salesmen, it turned out, had a significant complaint about the product information service – and some were obviously quite angry. Eric managed to maintain a calm, responsive stance in relation to the complaining salesmen, but he also felt his stomach tightening as he heard what they had to say. By the day's end, he had made a list of three general problems which seemed both frequent enough and serious enough to warrant his immediate attention and action:

1 Salesmen often were unable to get through quickly to information clerks. Since salesmen's calls usually were made from customer offices, this meant that they were left holding the telephone of a client for up to 10 or 15 minutes waiting for a clerk – while both the salesman and the customer became increasingly impatient.
2 Errors were excessive. Salesman after salesman reported that, on the basis of information provided by the clerks, they would promise delivery of materials on a specific date at a specific price – only to hear later from an irate customer that the materials had not been delivered, that the price was different from that quoted, or (all too often) both.

3 The clerks were often abrupt and unfriendly to the salesmen when they called. According to more than one salesman, the clerks acted as if they were being imposed upon, rather than providing the salesmen with help in carrying out the company's business.

The source of the problems

In the following week, as Eric attempted to track down the reasons for these difficulties, other problems came to light. First, absenteeism and turnover were extremely high. It appeared that the excessive delays were partly due to the fact that 15 to 20 per cent of the clerks were unlikely to show up for work on any given day – especially Monday and Friday – and that up to an hour's tardiness was not uncommon. This created call 'backups' on the computer. The computer, of course, calmly held the calls for as long as necessary, oblivious as only a machine can be to the rise in tempers in the customer's office.

When absenteeism was particularly high on any given day, part-time employees were called to fill in. Many of these individuals were not entirely familiar with the job and often did not remember some of the procedures to be used in looking up equipment numbers in the catalogue – resulting in wrong catalogue numbers and erroneous information being given to the customers. Worse, even experienced clerks had a high error rate. Eric's hope that the error problem was in the computerised information displayed on the clerks' consoles rather than a fault of the clerks themselves was clearly misplaced. Reports of errors arrived weeks after the information was provided (when orders failed to arrive on the customer's premises, or arrived with unexpected prices), and so it was usually impossible to determine who had made the mistake or why.

Finally, quite contrary to the impression he had received on his first day, Eric learned that loafing on the job not only was common practice among the clerks, but had indeed been developed into a rather elegant art form. It turned out that the clerks had devised ingenious ways to 'busy out' their consoles (i.e., to manipulate the console in order to provide the computer with a 'busy' indication when in fact the console was free). All a clerk needed to do, when she wanted a break from work, was to busy out her console and, if a supervisor happened to be nearby, act as if she were listening intently to a salesman on her headset.

Worse, there appeared to be a highly efficient system of informal communication among the clerks, which alerted everyone when a supervisor was about to appear on the scene (or was monitoring calls surreptitiously from the private listening room). This informal network was also popular for creative co-ordination of 'personals' (i.e., short breaks for visits to the toilet) and for making sure that none of the clerks was violating the generally accepted norms about how much work should be carried out on a given day.

Eric's challenge

Given his own observations and impressions, Eric was not surprised when, a few weeks after he had taken over management of the office, he was visited by the regional vice-president of the company. The vice-president informed him that sales were falling company-wide, and that at least part of the problem had to do with the quality of the information with which salesmen were being provided. Eric's operation was one of the most critical points of co-ordination in the entire company, he said, and it was important to everyone in the company that Eric reduce both the error rate and the number of delays salesmen currently were experiencing. The vice-president said he had enormous confidence in Eric's managerial ability, that he was sure the problems would be remedied quickly, and that he viewed Eric's future in the company with great optimism.

Eric panicked.

Eric's action plan

Within two days he had instituted a crash programme to increase efficiency, reduce call-in delays, and slash the error rate. He held a half-day meeting with his four first-level supervisors, impressing upon them the urgency of the situation and the need for them to work with their people, individually if necessary, to improve service. He held an evening meeting with all staff members (with everyone receiving both refreshments and overtime pay), at which he announced a set of office-wide performance goals, and encouraged each employee to do her best to help achieve the new goals. He even had one of the supervisors construct four large signs reading 'Increase Efficiency' (each with a line drawing of a smiling face under the words), which were placed on the four walls of the operating area.

Beginning the day after the kick-off meeting, all supervisory personnel (himself included) were to spend at least three hours a day on the floor, helping the employees improve their efficiency, making spot checks for errors, and generally doing anything possible to smooth the flow of work.

The first two days under the new programme seemed to go reasonably well: the average waiting time for incoming calls dropped slightly, spot checks of errors showed performance to be close to an acceptable level, and everyone seemed to be

Case study 2.1 continued

working hard and intently. No longer, for example, did the employees take time to look up from their work and smile or exchange a few words when Eric entered the room. That bothered him a bit because he always had enjoyed chatting with the clerks, but he accepted the loss of the smiles as a small price to pay for the increases in efficiency he hoped for.

On the third day, disaster struck. Eric did not notice until mid-morning that someone had carefully written 'IN' before 'Efficiency' on each of the four posters – and the smiles on the line drawings' faces had been extended into full-fledged, if subtly sarcastic, grins. Worse, everyone seemed to be studiously ignoring both the posters and him. Even the first-level supervisors said nothing to him about the posters, although Eric noticed that the supervisors, like the clerks, collected in pairs and threes for animated conversation when they were not aware of his presence. When he walked out into the operating area to start his three-hour stint, all eyes looked away and stayed there. He had never felt so completely alone.

That evening Eric stayed after everyone else had left; he removed the posters and pondered what to do next. With possibly one or two exceptions, he was sure that the people who worked for him were decent human beings. He knew that he himself was only trying to do his job, to get performance back up to standard. As he had told the employees at the kick-off meeting, this was in the best interest of everybody: the customers, the salesmen, the clerks, himself. So why the hostility towards him and his programme?

The root causes?

Gradually he began to suspect that the problems he had confronted – high errors and delays, excessive absenteeism and turnover – were merely outcroppings of some more basic difficulty. Perhaps, he thought, he had attacked the symptom rather than the disease.

But what was the disease? He considered each of the possibilities. He knew that there was a lot of complaining about the pay and the inflexibility of the hours. But the pay was actually very good, higher than for almost any other non-skilled job available to females in the suburban area – and every year there was a pay increase for everyone, which almost always was greater than the increase in the cost of living.

The hours were a problem, he knew, but even those employees who complained the most knew that he had tried mightily to convince the regional office to let him introduce a flexible scheduling plan that would allow the employees to better co-ordinate their personal and work lives. He had been told that company policy dictated an 8.30 to 5.00 workday and that hours (just like all other personnel policies) were centrally controlled in the interest of company-wide efficiency and regularity. Eric didn't like the decision (he felt he needed to be given much more personal authority to be able to run his own operation effectively). He did, however, understand that there was some need for central co-ordination of policy, and he thought that the employees should also be able to see the necessity for it. The hours, he decided, could not conceivably be the root of all the difficulties.

He considered briefly the possibility that the employees were simply not capable of doing the work at satisfactory levels of speed and accuracy. However, he knew that could not be the case: all had passed a company-administered ability test before they were hired and all had gone through a rigorous training programme which covered every contingency a person conceivably could face as an information clerk. Besides, the job was not all that difficult; he personally suspected that even the requirement of a high school diploma was superfluous, that anybody who could read and write could handle the job without significant difficulty. No, lack of ability was not the core of the problem.

Indeed, as Eric reflected further, it seemed that the reverse could be true: that perhaps the job was so simple and routine that the clerks were bored – and therefore chose to be absent a lot and to loaf whenever they could on the job. But surely the high pay and the pleasantness of the work setting should more than compensate for any such feelings of boredom? Furthermore, holding errors below 2 per cent could provide a real challenge, and loafing on the job would itself probably be more boring than working.

Supervision? It seemed most unlikely that this was the root of the difficulty. Each of the four supervisors had been information clerks themselves (although in the old days, when there was no computer and you had to look everything up in a set of reference manuals), and they knew the job inside out. Moreover, he knew from talking with the supervisors that they were genuinely committed to spending as much time as needed to help each clerk do as good a job as possible. Eric had observed each of them working on the floor many times, and there was no question in his mind about how much time and energy they spent in assisting and developing individual clerks.

Kipsy

Then what? Maybe, he finally concluded, the key was Kipsy. Kipsy had been a thorn in his side (the supervisors agreed) ever since Eric started the job. Although she herself had been working as a clerk for less than a year, she already had emerged as one of the informal leaders of the workforce. Eric found himself agreeing with one of his supervisors who had suggested over coffee one morning that Kipsy alone created as many problems as a dozen other clerks taken together. He was 99 per cent confident, for example, that it was she who had mutilated his signs. He had been recently hearing rumblings that Kipsy was informally talking up the possibility of the clerks unionising, probably even affiliating with some national outfit that had no understanding of the local situation.

He had tried to talk with her once. She had showed up unannounced at his office one day, with a long list of complaints about him and the work. His approach had been to listen and hear her out, to see what was troubling her, and then to do something about it – for her own sake, as well as for her supervisor and the company. Thinking back now, however, the main thing he remembered about the conversation (if you could call it a conversation) was her incredible anger. He was perplexed that he could not remember specifically what it was that she had been so mad about. Eric did recall telling her, as the conversation ended, that if she worked hard and effectively on her job for a year or two she would become eligible for enrolment in a company-run training course for a higher paying job. But again, he could not recall whether or not that had interested her.

In any case, it was clear that Kipsy was the link pin in the informal network among the clerks – and if they were turning against him and the company, you could be pretty sure that she was right in the middle of it. The question, though, was what to do about it. Fire her? In a very important sense, that would be admitting defeat – and publicly. Talk to her again? That probably would result in nothing more than his getting another load of hostility dumped in his lap, and that he didn't need.

Eric was in trouble, and he knew it. He realised it first when he could not think of a good way to repair the damage that his new motivational programme apparently had created. But he knew it for sure when he found that he was no longer thinking about work except when he was actually at his desk in the office and had to do so. When he started this job he had expected to become totally immersed in it; indeed, he had wanted to be. But now he was psychologically fleeing from his job as much as the clerks seemed to be fleeing from theirs.

CONSIDER THE PLIGHT OF KIPSY

Kipsy has been an information clerk in Eric's office for almost a year. In that year she has become increasingly frustrated and unhappy in her work – and she doesn't know quite what to do about it. Things certainly have not worked out as she had expected them to.

Early optimism ...

She had applied for the job because a friend told her that the company was a great place to work, that the pay was excellent, and that the people she would be working with were friendly and stimulating. Moreover, it was well known that the company was growing and expanding at a fast clip. That, Kipsy concluded, meant that there was a good chance for advancement for anyone who showed some initiative and performed well on the job.

Advancement was important. Throughout her high school years, Kipsy had always been seen as a leader by her classmates, and she had enjoyed that role much more than she had let on at the time. Her grades had been good – mostly As and Bs – and she knew if she had pushed a bit harder she could have obtained almost all As. However, she had decided that participation in school activities, doing after-school volunteer work, and (importantly) having friends and learning from them were just as important as grades; so she had deliberately let the grades slip a little.

The man who interviewed Kipsy for the job was extremely nice – and what he said about the job confirmed her high hopes for it. He even took her into the room filled with the complicated-looking consoles and let her watch some of the people at work. It seemed like it would be great fun – though perhaps a little scary – working with all that computerised equipment. She didn't know anything at all about computers.

When they returned to the hiring area from their visit to the console room, Kipsy's employment tests had been scored. The interviewer told her that she had scored in the top 10 per cent of all applicants for the job, that all signs pointed to a great future for her in the company, and that she could start training the next day if she wanted. Kipsy accepted the job on the spot.

Training for the job was just as exciting as she had expected it to be. The console seemed awfully complicated, and there was no end to the special requests and problems she had to learn how to deal with. The other people working on the job were also very nice, and Kipsy soon had made many new friends.

Case study 2.1 continued

... replaced by frustration and disappointment

After a few weeks, however, the fun wore off. The kinds of difficult problems she had been trained to solve on the console seemed never to occur. Instead, the calls began to fall into what Kipsy experienced as an endless routine: the green light flashes, the sales-man gives the name of a piece of equipment, you look it up in the book and punch the number on the key-board, you recite the information displayed by the computer back to the salesman, and the green light goes off. Then you wait – maybe only a second, maybe five minutes – for the light to go on again. You never know how long you are going to wait, so you can never think or read or even carry on an uninterrupted conversation with the girl next to you. It was, Kipsy decided, pretty awful.

Worse, many of her new friends were quitting. The rumour was that nearly 80 per cent of the people on the job quit every year, and Kipsy was beginning to understand why. Neither she nor any of her friends knew of anybody who had been pro-moted to management or to a better job from the ranks of the console operators, at least not in the last couple of years. Kipsy was also smart enough to realise that in time the whole operation would be automated – with salesmen punching in their requests for information directly from the field – at which time, she surmised, she and everyone else who had stuck out the job in hopes of something better would be laid off.

The only good thing about the job, she con-cluded, was that she was becoming the informal leader of the work group – and that had its moments. Like the time one of the girls had her planned vacation postponed at short notice, suppos-edly because absenteeism was so high that everyone had to be available for work merely to keep up with the flow of incoming calls. The girl (and two of her friends) had come to Kipsy and asked what she could do about it. Kipsy had marched straightaway into the manager's office with the girl, asked for an expla-nation, and got him to agree to let her take the vacation as planned. That felt awfully good.

But such moments were too infrequent to keep her interested and involved – so she found herself making up interesting things to do, just to keep from going crazy. She developed a humorous list, Rules for Handling Salesmen, which she surreptitiously passed around the office, partly in fun but also partly to help the new girls (there always were a lot of new girls) learn the tricks necessary to keep from getting put down by the always impatient, sometimes crude

salesmen. She also found that girls having difficulties on the job (again, usually the new workers) often came to her rather than to the supervisors for help – which she gladly gave, despite the obvious disap-proval of the supervisors. She even found herself assuming the role of monitor for the group, prodding girls who were not doing their share of the work, and showing new girls who were working too hard the various tricks that could be done to keep the pace of work at a reasonable level (such as 'busying out' the machine, when you just couldn't take any more and needed a break).

That was all fun, but as she reflected on it, it just didn't compensate for the basic monotony of the work or for the picky, almost schoolmarmish atti-tude of the supervisors. So she was buoyed up when she heard that a new manager was coming, fresh out of school. The rumour mill had it that he was one of the top young managers in the company, and she decided he surely would shake things up a bit as soon as he found out how miserable it was for people who worked in the office.

The new boss

Eric's first few days on the job confirmed her high hopes for him: he seemed genuinely interested in learning about the job and in hearing what changes people had to suggest. And he talked directly to the people doing the work, rather than keeping safely out of sight and listening only to what the school-marms said people thought and felt. All to the good.

Her opinion about Eric's managerial abilities dropped sharply a few weeks later, however, by what came to be known around the office as the 'flexible hours fiasco'. Kipsy and two other girls had come up with a proposal for pre-scheduling work hours so that there would be substantially more flexibility in the hours each person would work. The plan was designed so that management would know at least two days ahead of time who would be coming in when. The only cost to the company would be some additional clerical time spent on actually doing the scheduling, and Kipsy had obtained agreement from almost everyone in the office to share in the clerical tasks, in their own time.

Eric had seemed receptive to the plan when Kipsy first presented it to him, and said only that he would have to check it out with his superiors before instituting it. Nothing more was heard about the plan for about two weeks. Finally Eric called Kipsy into his office and (after a good deal of talking around the issue) reported that 'the people upstairs won't let us do it'.

Kipsy's respect for Eric plummeted. Rather than give a flat no, he had wriggled around for two weeks, and then lamely blamed the decision on 'the people upstairs'. She knew very well that the manager of an office could run his office however he pleased, so long as the work got done. And here was Eric, the bright new manager on the way up:

- He wouldn't go along with an employee-initiated proposal for making their life at work more bearable.
- He refused to take personal responsibility for that decision.
- He even had the gall to ask Kipsy to help 'explain to the girls' how hard he had tried to get the plan approved, and how sad he was that it had been turned down.

Kipsy's response was a forced smile, an elaborately sympathetic 'Of course I'll help', and a quick escape from his office.

Kipsy's demands

She took the Monday of the next week off, to think about whether or not she should quit and try to find a better job. At the end of the day, she made up a list of what she wanted from her work, what she was getting, and whether or not things would improve if she stuck with the job:

My wants	Am I getting them?	Hope for improvement
1 Good pay	OK, not great	Little, till my hair turns grey
2 Interesting people	Fine	No change, except friends keep leaving
3 Interesting work	Dismal	Zero
4 Chance to show initiative and personal responsibility	None	No hope
5 Chance to contribute to an organisation I believe in	Low	Ha!

The next day, Tuesday, she took her list and went to see Eric. After listening to a fatherly lecture on the importance of not missing work, especially on Mondays when the workload was heaviest, she began to tell him how upset she was. She told him that the only thing she got from working hard on the job was a backache every evening. She told him she had been misled about the chances for promotion on the job, and she asked him, as politely as she knew how, what he suggested she should do.

Eric's response blew her mind. There was a new programme, he said, in which people who did well on entry-level jobs for a few years could apply for advanced training in a technical specialty. This training would be done at company expense and in company time, and would qualify her for a promotional-type transfer, whenever openings in her chosen specialty developed. If she worked hard and was rated high on the quarterly supervisory assessments, Eric said, he would be prepared to nominate her for the advanced training. It was important, however, he emphasised, that she behave herself – no unnecessary absences, high work productivity, good ratings by her supervisors. Otherwise, she certainly would not be selected by 'the people upstairs' for the new programme.

Something snapped. What kind of a fool did he think she was? How long did he expect her to wait for a 'chance to be nominated' for some foggy 'technical training programme'? She started telling him, no holds barred now, no false politeness, exactly what she thought of the job, of the supervisors, even of the way he was running the office. The more she talked, the madder she got – until finally she got up, almost in tears, and ran out leaving behind only the reverberations of a well-slammed door.

Kipsy's dilemma

She was ashamed later, of course. She knew she would be, and she was, but she also was too embarrassed to go up to Eric and apologise. Which was too bad, because she suspected that behind it all Eric was probably a decent man, and maybe even somebody she could learn to like and respect – if only he would let himself be human once in a while. However, she knew there was nothing she could do to change the way Eric did his job; the first move clearly had to be his. It could be a long wait, Kipsy decided. In the meantime she would come to work, try to minimise her backaches and upsets, and continue to think about finding another job. Of one thing she was sure: no more 'bright ideas' for improving things at the office would come from her; they brought nothing but grief. Furthermore, she was no longer going to worry so much if she happened to misremember a catalogue number or accidentally disconnect a salesman. If all they wanted was a machine, that was all they were going to get.

Kipsy found herself much less able to be cavalier about her work than she had thought she could be.

Case study 2.1 continued

As hard as she tried not to care when she made errors, the distressing fact was that mistakes still *did* bother her. And she still felt like an unreconstituted sinner when she was a few minutes late for work.

It took the 'Increase Efficiency' programme to finally break her completely. It was not to be believed: an evening meeting, complete with supposedly inspirational messages from all the bosses about how we all had to pitch in and help the company make more money; grade school posters on all the walls imploring people to work harder; and, to top it all, all the bosses, even Eric, standing around for hours at a time, looking over everybody's shoulders, day after day.

Did Eric really believe that treating people like children would make them work harder? She could have told him straight out beforehand that the programme would make things worse rather than better. But of course he didn't ask.

Kipsy went on the offensive. She knew it was wrong, but she also knew she had to do *something* to preserve her sanity. Her first target was the signs; she and another girl stayed late in the rest room and, when everybody else had left, carefully changed the lettering of the signs to read 'Increase INEfficiency', and turned the smiling face on each sign into an obviously sarcastic grin. Kipsy also began discussing with the other girls the possibility of forming a club, which would be partly social but which could possibly develop into a vehicle for doing some hard-nosed bargaining with Eric.

It didn't work. Changing the signs, after the initial thrill, only made her feel more guilty. And even though virtually everyone in the office shared her dismay about the monotony of the work and was as upset as she about Eric and his 'Increase Efficiency' programme, nobody was very excited about forming a club. Some thought it wouldn't have any impact and would be a waste of time; others thought it sounded like the first step towards unionisation, which they didn't want. So the club idea died.

Kipsy was depressed. What should she do? Quit? Her preliminary explorations had not yet turned up any jobs which were much better – and most paid less than this one. Besides, to quit would be to admit publicly her inability to change anything in the office. She was supposed to be the leader of the girls in the office; she shouldn't become just one more tally towards the 80 per cent a year who left.

Talk to Eric again? She seriously doubted that he would listen to one word she said. And she doubted equally seriously that she could keep herself from blowing up again at him – which would accomplish nothing and help no one.

Shut up and stick it out? That was what she had been trying for the last three months. Without noticeable success.

What, then?

YOUR TASKS

(a) Analyse the issues of management and organisational behaviour which are raised in this case study.

(b) Suggest solutions to the problems faced by Eric and Kipsy.

NOTES AND REFERENCES

1. A summary of some merits in understanding organisational behaviour theory and the role of management is given in Mullins, L. J. 'The Organisation and the Individual', *Administrator*, vol. 7, no. 4, April 1987, pp. 11–14.
2. 'Introduction to Module 6, Organizational Behaviour', *Financial Times Mastering Management*, FT Pitman Publishing (1997), p. 216.
3. See, for example: Luthans, F. *Organisational Behaviour*, Seventh edition, McGraw-Hill (1995).
4. See, for example: Robbins, S. P. *Organizational Behavior: Concepts, Controversies, Applications*, Eighth edition, Prentice-Hall (1998).
5. For further details of recurring themes in organisational behaviour and premises about life in organisations see,
   for example: Porter, L. W., Lawler, E. E. and Hackman, J. R. *Behaviour in Organisations*, McGraw-Hill (1975).
6. Wilson, F. M. *Organzational Behaviour: A Critical Introduction*, Oxford University Press (1999).
7. McPhee, N. 'Gaining Insight on Business and Organisational Behaviour: the Qualitative Dimension', *International Journal of Market Research*, vol. 44, Winter 2002, pp. 53–72.
8. Yip, G. S. 'Global strategy in the Twenty-first Century', in Crainer, S. and Dearlove, D. (eds) *Financial Times Handbook of Management*, Second edition, Financial Times Prentice Hall (2001), p. 151.
9. Morgan, G. *Creative Organization Theory*, Sage Publications (1989), p. 26.

10. Hellriegel, D., Slocum, J. W. and Woodman, R. W. *Organizational Behavior*, Eighth edition, South-Western Publishing (1998), p. 5.

11. Wood, J. 'Deep Roots and Far From a "Soft" Option', *Financial Times Mastering Management*, FT Pitman Publishing (1997), p. 217.

12. Bennis, W. 'Foreword', in Cloke, K. and Goldsmith, J. *The End of Management and the Rise of Organizational Democracy*, Jossey-Bass (2002), p. ix.

13. Gratton, L. *Living Strategy: Putting People at the Heart of Corporate Purpose*, Financial Times Prentice Hall (2000), pp. 12–13.

14. Morgan, G. *Images of Organization*, Second edition, Sage Publications (1997).

15. Drummond, H. *Introduction to Organizational Behaviour*, Oxford University Press (2000).

16. Goldthorpe, J. H., Lockwood, D., Bechofer, F. and Platt, J. *The Affluent Worker*, Cambridge University Press (1968).

17. Herman, S.W. 'How Work Gains Meaning in Contractual Time: a narrative model for reconstructing the work ethic', *Journal of Business Ethics*, vol. 38, no. 1–2, June 2002, pp. 65–79.

18. Knights, D. and Willmott, H. *Management Lives: Power and Identity in Work Organizations*, Sage Publications (1999).

19. Reeves, R. 'Reality Bites', *Management Today*, March 2003, p. 35.

20. Cartwright, J. *Cultural Transformation*, Financial Times Prentice Hall (1999), p. 27.

21. Oliver, J. 'Losing Control', *Management Today*, June 1998, pp. 32–8.

22. See, for example, Argyris, C. *Integrating the Individual and the Organization*, John Wiley & Sons (1964).

23. 'In Celebration of the Feel-good Factor', *Professional Manager*, March 1998, p. 6.

24. Bassett, G. 'The Case against Job Satisfaction', *Business Horizons*, vol. 37, no. 3, May–June 1994, p. 62 and p. 63.

25. Egan, G. 'The Shadow Side', *Management Today*, September 1993, pp. 33–8.

26. See, for example, Robinson, G. 'Improving performance through people', *The British Journal of Administrative Management*, September/October 1999, pp. 4–5.

27. Chowdhury, S. *Management 21C*, Financial Times Prentice Hall (2000), p. 119.

28. See, for example: Schein, E. H. *Organizational Psychology*, Third edition, Prentice-Hall (1988).

29. Kotter, J. P. 'The Psychological Contract: Managing the Joining-Up Process', *California Management Review*, vol. 15, no. 3, 1973, pp. 91–9.

30. Stalker, K. 'The Individual, the Organisation and the Psychological Contract', *The Institute of Administrative Management*, July/August 2000, pp. 28, 34.

31. Cartwright, J. *Cultural Transformation*, Financial Times Prentice Hall (1999), p. 39.

32. Emmott, M. 'The Psychological Contract: Managers Do Make a Difference', *Manager*, The British Journal of Administrative Management, September/October 2001, p. 15.

33. McBain, R. 'The Role of Human Resource Management and the Psychological Contract', *Manager Update*, vol. 8, no. 4, Summer 1997, pp. 22–31.

34. Stalker, K. 'The Individual and the Organisation', *Student Adviser* Issue No. 51, The Institute of Administrative Management, Spring 2003.

35. Hiltrop, J. M. 'Managing the Changing Psychological Contract', *Employee Relations*, vol. 18, no. 1, 1996, pp. 36–49.

36. Stiles, P., Gratton, L., Truss, C., Hope-Hailey, V. and McGovern, P. 'Performance Management and the Psychological Contract', *Human Resource Management Journal*, vol. 7, no. 1, 1997, pp. 57–66.

37. Ghoshal, S., Bartlett, C. A. and Moran, P. 'Value Creation: The New Millennium Management Manifesto', in Chowdhury, S. *Management 21C*, Financial Times Prentice Hall (2000), pp. 121–40.

38. Peter, L. J. and Hull, R. *The Peter Principle*, Pan Books (1970), p. 22.

39. Ibid., p. 56.

40. Parkinson, C. N. *Parkinson's Law*, Penguin Modern Classics (2002), p. 14

41. HRH The Duke of Edinburgh, 'Introduction' to Parkinson, C. N. *Parkinson's Law*, Penguin Modern Classics (2002), pp. 9–10.

42. Herbertson, I. 'Books', *Management Today*, May 2000, p. 4.

43. Tayeb, M. *The Management of a Multicultural Workforce*, John Wiley & Sons (1996).

44. Schneider, S. C. and Barsoux, J. *Managing Across Cultures*, Second edition, Financial Times Prentice Hall (2003), p. 9.

45. Thompson, P. and McHugh, D. *Work Organisations: A Critical Introduction*, Third edition, Palgrave (2002), p. 81.

46. Brooks, I. *Organisational Behaviour: Individuals Groups and Organisation*, Second edition, Financial Times Prentice Hall (2003), p. 264.

47. Trompenaars, F. 'Trans-Cultural Competence', *People Management*, 22 April 1999, p. 31.

48. Francesco, A. M. and Gold, B. A. *International Organizational Behavior: Text, Readings, Cases and Skills*, Prentice Hall (1998), p. 103.

49. Schneider, S. C. and Barsoux, J. *Managing Across Cultures*, Second edition, Financial Times Prentice Hall (2003) p. 167.

50. Ibid., p. 86.

51. Francesco, A. M. and Gold, B A. *International Organizational Behavior: Text, Readings, Cases and Skills*, Prentice Hall (1998), p. 144.

52. Adler, N. J. *International Dimensions of Organisational Behaviour*, Third edition, South Western College Publishing (1997).

53. Robbins, S. *Essentials of Organizational Behaviour*, Third edition, Prentice Hall (1992), p. 14.

54. Maurice, M., Sorge, A. and Warner, M. 'Societal Differences in Organising Manufacturing Units', *Organisation Studies* (1980), vol. 1, no. 1, pp. 63–91.

55. Hofstede, G. *Culture's Consequences: International Differences in Work-related Values*, Sage Publications (1980).

56. Trompenaars, F. and Hampden-Turner, C. *Riding the Waves of Culture*, Second edition, Nicholas Brealey (1999)

57. Hall, E. T. and Hall, M. R. 'Key Concept: Underlying Structures of Culture', in Lane, H. W., Di Stefano, J. J., and Masnevski, M. L. *International Management Behavior*, Third edition, Cambridge, MA: Blackwell, (1997).

58. Tayeb, M. *International Management: Theories and Practices*, Financial Times Prentice Hall (2003).

59. Brooks, I. *Organisational Behaviour: Individuals, Groups and Organisation*, Second edition, Financial Times Prentice Hall (2003).

60. Hofstede, G. *Culture's Consequences: International Differences in Work-related Values*, Sage Publications (1980).

61. Hofstede, G. and Bond, M. H. 'The Confucius Connection: From Cultural Roots to Economic Growth' *Organisational Dynamics*, Spring 1988, pp. 4–21.

62. Holden, N. J. *Cross-Cultural Management: A Knowledge Management Perspective*, Financial Times Prentice Hall (2002), p. 51.

63. Trompenaars, F. and Hampden-Turner, C. *Riding the Waves of Culture*, Second edition, Nicholas Brealey (1999).

64. Hall, E. T. and Hall, M. R. *Understanding Cultural Differences*, Intercultural Press (1990).

65. Grint, K. *The Sociology of Work*, Second edition, Polity (1998), p. 298.

66. Ibid., p. 298.

67. Thompson, P. and McHugh, D. *Work Organisations: A Critical Introduction*, Third edition, Palgrave (2002), p. 74.

 Use the *Financial Times* to enhance your understanding of the context and practice of management and organisational behaviour. Refer to articles 1, 10, 12 and 19 in the BUSINESS PRESS section at the end of the book for relevant reports on the issues explored in this chapter.

Unit 4: Business Environment

Learning hours: 60

NQF level 4: BTEC Higher National — H1

Content Selected: Gammie, Hornby and Wall, Business Economics 2nd Edition, Chapter 1

Introduction from the Qualification Leader

This unit looks at the objectives of organisations, their operation in relation to the local, national and global environment and the influence of stakeholders. Chapter 1 has been chosen as background reading to the material needed for coverage of the outcomes of the unit.

Description of unit

The aim of the unit is to encourage learners to identify the objectives of organisations and the influence of stakeholders. Learners are also encouraged to investigate the operation of organisations in relation to the local, national and global environment. The unit also provides learners with a solid base of understanding of the parameters within which organisations act that can be built upon in further units.

Summary of learning outcomes

To achieve this unit a learner must:

1   Identify the mission, **objectives and responsibilities of an organisation** within its environment

2   Investigate the **economic, social and global environment** in which organisations operate

3   Investigate **the behaviour of organisations and the market environment**

4   Explore the significance of **international trade and the European dimension** for UK businesses.

Content

1 **Objectives and responsibilities of an organisation**

Categories of organisation: size, sector/type – private, public, voluntary, charitable; activity – primary, secondary tertiary

Mission, objectives and values of organisations: concept of corporate mission or vision, underlying values/philosophy, profit, market share, ROCE, sales, growth, level of service, customer/user perceptions and audits

Stakeholders: identification of stakeholders, stakeholder groups, conflict of expectations, attitude, power-influence matrix; satisfying stakeholder objectives, measuring performance

Responsibilities of organisations: to stakeholders, key legal responsibilities eg consumer, employment, disability discrimination and health and safety, diversity and equal opportunities, stakeholder pensions; wider responsibilities including ethical, environmental; ethical practice

2 **Economic, social and global environment**

Resource issues and types of economic system: basic economic problem, effective use of resources; type of economic systems – command, free enterprise, mixed, including transitional economies, public and private sector initiatives; private finance initiatives

Government policy: fiscal policy in the UK, monetary policy in the UK; MPC, industrial policy in the UK; social welfare policy in the UK; economic growth, economic performance/indicators influence of the CBI TUC stakeholder and interest groups, the influence of the global economy – trends, uncertainties, growth, impact on the economy, UK multinationals, World Bank

3 **Behaviour of organisations and the market environment**

Market types: perfect competition, monopoly, monopolistic competition, oligopoly, duopoly; competitive advantage, behaviour/strategies adopted by firms; role of Competition Commission, and regulatory bodies eg Oftel, Ofgas, Ofwat

Market forces and organisational responses: supply and demand, elasticity, customer perceptions and actions, issues relating to supply, cost and output decisions short run and long run, economies of scale, growth of organisations: reasons, methods, financing, MNCs/ TNCs joint ventures, outsourcing; core markets/skills, technology and innovation, labour market trends, cultural environment

4   **International trade and the European dimension**

The importance of international trade: to the UK economy, businesses, balance of payments, patterns and trends in international trade, UK trade with the EU, USA and other countries, trading blocs throughout the world, UK membership of the EU, enlargement of EU, direct/indirect exporting methods, trading opportunities, importance of global markets, implications for businesses of emerging markets, cultural diversity and clusters, TNCs, the economies of Europe EMU, EU budget import duties and levies, agricultural levies, VAT, competitor policy, European Single Market Act, social policy, The Social Chapter, tax harmonisation, CAP, regional policy

Outcomes and assessment criteria

Outcomes	Assessment criteria for pass **To achieve each outcome a learner must demonstrate the ability to:**
1 Identify the mission, **objectives and responsibilities of an organisation** within its environment	• identify the mission, values and key objectives of an organisation and assess the influence of stakeholders • evaluate the extent to which an organisation achieves the objectives of three stakeholders • explain the responsibilities of an organisation and strategies employed to meet them
2 Investigate the **economic, social and global environment** in which organisations operate	• explain how economic systems attempt to allocate and make effective use of resources • discuss the impact of social welfare and industrial policy initiatives on organisations and the wider community • evaluate the impact of macro economic policy measures and the influence of the global economy on UK-based organisations and stakeholders
3 Investigate **the behaviour of organisations and the market environment**	• explain how market structures in practice deviate from the model of perfect competition • use a range of examples to illustrate the relationship between market forces and organisational responses • explain the behaviour and competitive strategies employed by an organisation and discuss the role of the Competition Commission and regulatory bodies
4 Explore the significance of **international trade and the European dimension** for UK businesses	• discuss the importance of international trade, economic integration and global markets to UK business organisations • analyse the impact of two policies of the European Union on UK business organisations • explain the economic implications for the UK of entry into EMU

The domestic economic environment

Objectives

By the end of this chapter you will be able to:
➤ Understand the circular flow of income model of the economy.
➤ Identify the injections and withdrawals from the circular flow of income and assess their impact.
➤ Outline the key objectives of economic policy.
➤ Identify the causes of unemployment.
➤ Examine the factors causing inflation.
➤ Assess the causes of economic growth.
➤ Examine the domestic economic environment within which firms must operate.

Key concepts

Aggregate demand: the total level of demand for goods and services in the economy. It is made up of the expenditure of four sectors; namely, households (consumers' expenditure), business (investment expenditure), government sector (government expenditure) and the overseas sector (exports minus imports).

Cyclical unemployment: unemployment which is a direct result of the slump or depression in the economic cycle.

Deflationary gap: when the level of aggregate demand falls below the full employment level of national income.

Demand deficient unemployment: the level of unemployment created as a result of a deflationary gap.

Fiscal policy: the use of taxation as a means of controlling the economy.

Frictional unemployment: a type of short-term unemployment when people are 'between jobs'.

Full employment: a situation where all those who are seeking employment and who can be employed are employed. This has come to be regarded as being consistent with around 2–3 per cent unemployment.

Income effect: as taxes fall, people become better off. The income effect occurs when they no longer feel the need to work as hard or as long since they can achieve the same level of income with less effort.

Multiplier process: a process whereby increases in investment or government expenditure have a multiple effect on the level of aggregate demand.

Prices and incomes policy: a policy of direct control over wages and prices in which the government sets pay and price norms and creates bodies to 'police' increases above these norms.

1

Primary objectives of policy: these are the macroeconomic goals of government policy; namely, stable prices, full employment, economic growth and a balance of payments equilibrium.

Public sector borrowing requirement (PSBR): this is the deficit of the central and local government and the deficits of the nationalised industries.

Structural unemployment: this is the name given to unemployment that is the result of changes to the structure of the economy; for example, when there is a decline in the manufacturing sector which is not matched by an increase in employment in other sectors of the economy.

Substitution effect: this refers to the effect of, for example, a cut in taxes on work effort. As a result of the tax cut this results in an increase in the rewards for an extra hour's effort. In other words, there is an increase in the costs of taking additional leisure. The substitution effect says that if people are acting rationally they will substitute extra leisure for additional work.

Technological unemployment: this refers to unemployment created by changes to technology; for example, the decline of the employment of traditional printers in the newspaper industry as a result of changes in the technology of producing newspapers.

Transfer payments: those payments that represent a transfer of income from one group to another; for example, old age pensions, student grants and welfare benefits are paid for out of tax revenues. These payments are thus excluded from the calculation of national income as to include them would result in double counting.

Introduction
....

The business environment within which an organisation operates is influenced to a very great extent by the way in which the economy is managed. Before we examine the objectives of policy and how governments attempt to achieve these objectives we must first try to understand how the economy works. To do this we will examine what economists call the circular flow of income model.

The circular flow of income model
....

In order to understand how the economy works we need to construct a simplified model. One of the best-known models is the circular flow of income model. The key components of this model are set out in Figure 1.1.

We can view the economy as consisting of five important sectors. These are

➤ The domestic sector
➤ The business sector
➤ The financial sector
➤ The government sector
➤ The overseas sector

Figure 1.1
The circular flow of income model

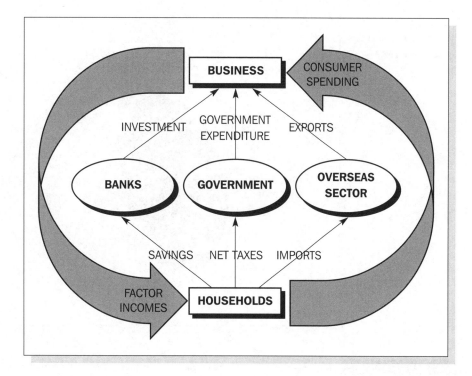

The domestic sector

This consists of households who can be viewed as supplying factors of production such as land, labour, capital and enterprise to the business sector. In return for these factors they receive what are called factor incomes such as wages, salaries, rent, interest, dividends, and profit. Figure 1.2 outlines the main sources of income in the UK in 1997.

As can be seen, about 60 per cent of all income is derived from wages and salaries with the remaining 40 per cent from all other sources of income. The household sector will spend its income either on domestically produced goods or on goods from abroad. If a household buys foreign goods then this is regarded as a leakage or a *withdrawal* from the circular flow of income model. In addition, government can also tax households by direct taxes on incomes or indirect taxes on our spending (VAT). This can also be viewed as a *withdrawal* from the circular flow of income.

PAUSE FOR THOUGHT 1 | *Taxpayers have an allowance that they can offset against income tax. In 1999–2000 the allowance for a single person under 65 was £4,335. These allowances are upgraded each year in line with inflation according to statutory provisions unless Parliament intervenes. What would be the effect on the circular flow of income if these allowances were frozen (i.e. not upgraded)?*

Figure 1.2
UK national income by category 1997

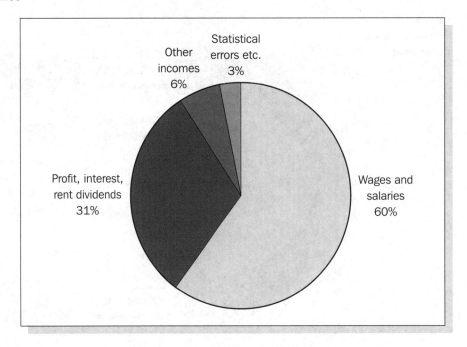

PAUSE FOR THOUGHT 2

Over half of all consumer spending is subject to VAT at the standard rate of 17.5 per cent, according to the Institute of Fiscal Studies (IFS 2000) with about 4 per cent taxable at a reduced rate. The reduced rate applies to domestic fuel, which had a VAT rate of 8 per cent but now has a rate of 5 per cent. From the summarised table (Table 1.1) work out what the effect on the circular flow of income would be if the government

(a) abolished the tax on domestic fuel and power but imposed VAT on books and newspapers
(b) imposed VAT on food
(c) imposed VAT on children's clothing and prescription drugs.

Table 1.1
Estimated costs of zero-rated, reduced-rated and exempt goods and services for VAT revenues, 1998–99

Goods	Estimated cost (£m)
Zero-rated	
Food	8,100
Construction of new dwellings*	2,150
Domestic passenger transport	1,700
International passenger transport	1,350
Books, newspapers and magazines	1,300
Children's clothing	1,000
Water and sewerage services	1,000
Drugs and medicines on prescription	750
Supplies to charities*	150
Ships and aircraft above a certain size	350
Vehicles and other supplies to people with disabilities	150

Table 1.1
Continued

Goods	Estimated cost (£m)
Reduced-rated	
Domestic fuel and power	1,900
VAT-exempt	
Rent on domestic dwellings*	2,750
Rent on commercial properties*	1,050
Private education	950
Health services*	500
Postal services	500
Burial and cremation	100
Finance and insurance*	100
Betting, gaming and lottery	950
Businesses with low turnover	100
Total	26,900

*Figures for these categories are particularly tentative and subject to a wide margin of error.

Source: HM Customs and Excise Annual Report 1997–98.

Households may also decide to save a proportion of their income and this can also be represented as a *withdrawal* of income from the circular flow of income.

PAUSE FOR THOUGHT 3 | *The savings ratio (i.e. the proportion of disposable income that is saved by households) is, in normal circumstances, quite stable at around 10–15 per cent. However, in the United States in recent years this ratio has fallen to almost zero across the economy as a whole. Can you explain the factors that may influence the savings ratio and what effect this will have on the circular flow of income in the USA and elsewhere?*

The business sector

Like domestic households, the business sector contributes to the circular flow of income. This sector demands factors of production such as land, labour, capital and enterprise and pays for this by different forms of income. The sector is also responsible for investing in plant and machinery which injects income into the circular flow of income. The amount of investment that is undertaken by the business sector depends on *the costs of borrowing* money and the likely *rate of return* that firms can earn (for details of how this is calculated, see Chapter 10). Future rates of return will be affected by such factors as the initial cost of the capital equipment and the income generated over the life of the asset, whether it is a machine or a factory. Of critical importance to this calculation is *the confidence that the business sector* has about the future. Thus, if businesses are apprehensive about future growth prospects, this can affect not only the amount the sector will invest but also the circular flow of income. Some of this investment is undertaken to replace capital, which has depreciated. Therefore, economists are more interested in the extent to which investment increases faster than the rate of depreciation since this adds to the flow of income in the economy. Equally, firms may decide to retain profits rather than pay them out as dividends. This form of corporate savings can be regarded as a *withdrawal* from the circular flow.

CASE STUDY **1.1**
....

UK manufacturing grows in confidence

In January 2000 there was an upsurge in optimism amongst the UK's leading manufacturers who claimed that demand was rising for the first time in almost two years despite the high value of sterling, according to the Confederation of British Industry's quarterly *Industrial Trends Survey*.

The survey showed business optimism continuing to rise with 23 per cent of firms being more optimistic and only 14 per cent less optimistic. The balance of +9 per cent compares with +13 in October and +5 in July. In addition, the survey claimed that optimism about export prospects had stabilised for the first time in more than three years, and that total orders had risen over the previous four months for the first time since April 1998 with 30 per cent of respondents indicating that orders were up and 21 per cent saying that they were down. The balance of +9 per cent compared with –5 in October 1999 and –19 in July. Export orders fell slightly but at the slowest rate since October 1996.

In addition, companies said total orders would grow steadily over the first four months of 2000, reflecting expectations that domestic demand would increase and export demand would level off. A balance of +9 per cent anticipate a rise. Firms also said that output rose for the first time since April 1998. Thirty-one per cent said output was up and 20 per cent said it was down. The balance of +11 per cent compares with –1 in October and –14 in July. Companies expect output to continue rising, with a balance of +11 per cent anticipating an increase over the next four months.

Nick Reilly, Chairman and Managing Director of Vauxhall Motors and head of the CBI's Economic Affairs Committee, said:

> '*Manufacturers have taken another step towards recovery. But we should not overstate the extent of the revival because domestic prices and employment continue to fall while investment plans remain weak. Companies are having to run much harder to stand still. Many firms are hanging on by their fingertips and the two-speed economy remains very much in evidence. Exports are stabilising but this is being driven by a rise in world demand. The strength of sterling is still holding back firms as they battle to compete. Another rise in interest rates would restrain economic growth unnecessarily when across the economy there is little evidence of inflation. Moreover, the impact of the millennium is still unclear. The Monetary Policy Committee [of the Bank of England] should keep rates on hold until the trends become more certain.*'

Source: Adapted from CBI Press release, 27 January 2000.

Questions

1 What are the main threats to the upsurge in confidence which the CBI survey indicates?

2 The Monetary Policy Committee did not take the CBI's advice and raised interest rates by 0.25 per cent. How would this affect the business sector and which components of the circular flow of income would be affected?

The financial sector

This sector contributes to the circular flow by the way in which money flows into and out of the sector. Savings are directed via such financial intermediaries as banks and building societies. The level of these savings can be affected by such things as interest rates, the amount of disposable income, and the rate of inflation and consumer confidence about the future.

Figure 1.3 outlines the savings ratio for the USA between 1987 and 1999.

PAUSE FOR THOUGHT 4   *From Figure 1.3 it can be seen that the standard savings ratio in the USA has fallen dramatically from about 10 per cent of disposable income in the 1970s to around 5 per cent by the late 1980s, finally falling to almost zero by the end of the 1990s. What factors could have caused this fall? What are the implications of the fall for the US economy and for the rest of the world? Is this a worry or a benefit for the UK economy according to the model of the circular flow of income?*

The government sector

The government can play an important part in injecting or withdrawing income from the circular flow of income. By raising taxes (*a withdrawal*) and lowering its own spending (*an injection*) it can create budget surpluses or deficits. When the economy is booming there is an automatic tendency for government taxes to increase as consumers spend more (and hence pay more expenditure taxes such as VAT). Companies will also pay more corporation tax, as profits will tend to rise in the boom phase. In addition this will tend to

Figure 1.3
United States personal savings ratio 1987–1998

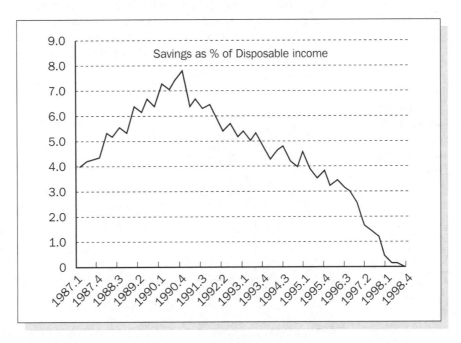

Adapted from P.D. Vujanovic (1999) *Habits and the savings–growth relationship: why US personal savings rates are at historic lows.*

reduce government spending on such things as unemployment or other welfare payments. The reverse, however, is also true when the economy is in a slump. Consumer and corporate taxes will tend to fall while government expenditure on social security will rise. This is known as the 'automatic fiscal stabilisers' and helps to iron out some of the worst of the economic cycles through which the economy runs from time to time. Of course the government can (and often does) try to anticipate this and adjust fiscal policy (i.e. taxes and spending) to take account of anticipated booms and slumps. This is particularly the case if the government is a believer in the Keynesian approach (see Chapter 3).

Figure 1.4 looks at the current budget surpluses and deficits over the last 40 years and clearly illustrates the cycles through which these surpluses and deficits have moved.

More recently the government has been forecasting a budget surplus (see Figure 1.5).

PAUSE FOR THOUGHT 5 | *What are the implications of Figure 1.5 for the circular flow of income in the period 1999–2002?*

The overseas sector

The final sector that has an influence on the circular flow of income is the overseas sector. Consumers from other parts of the world can add to the circular flow by demanding goods and services from UK firms. This clearly would represent an *injection* of income into the circular flow. The money that UK consumers spend on foreign imports represents a *withdrawal* of income from the circular flow. Equally, foreign companies investing in the UK would represent an injection into the circular flow whereas the setting up of a UK plant in South East Asia, for example, would represent a withdrawal of income from the UK. These aspects are reflected in the capital account. Table 1.2 shows the vari-

Figure 1.4
Current budget surpluses and deficits as a percentage of GDP, 1966–2000

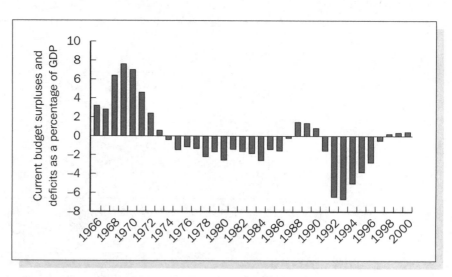

Source: HM Treasury Public Finances Database, December 1999 (Table A2).

Figure 1.5
Government receipts and spending as a percentage of GDP 1996–1997 to 2001–2002

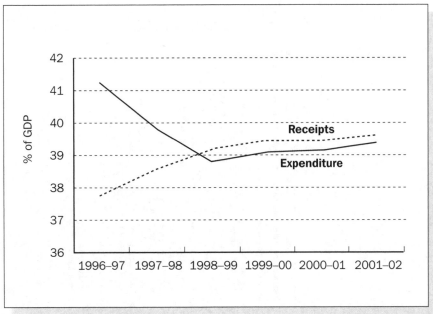

Source: IFS Green Budget 2000.

ous balances on goods and services (the visible account) as well as the balances on interest, dividends, profits and royalties (the invisible account). The capital account looks at the surpluses/deficits of this aspect.

Table 1.2
The balance of payment accounts, £ millions, 1979–1998

Period	Trade in goods	Total services	Current account		Capital account
			Visibles	Visibles+Invisibles	
1979	–3326	–	639	88	–
1980	1329	–	5046	3166	–
1981	3238	–	7072	6549	–
1982	1879	–	4948	4107	–
1983	–1618	–	2323	3299	–
1984	–5409	–	–1068	1209	–
1985	–3416	–	3203	2227	–
1986	–9617	6505	–3112	–2285	135
1987	–11698	6686	–5012	–5583	333
1988	–21553	4330	–17223	–17537	235
1989	–24724	3917	–20807	–23491	270
1990	–18707	4010	–14697	–19513	497
1991	–10223	4471	–5752	–8374	290
1992	–13050	5674	–7376	–10082	421
1993	–13319	6623	–6696	–10618	309
1994	–11091	6528	–4563	–1458	33
1995	–11724	8915	–2809	–3745	534
1996	–13086	8897	–4189	–600	736
1997	–11910	12414	504	6623	804
1998	–20537	12185	–8352	–482	473

Source: *Economic Trends* 1999.

Figure 1.6 **Some factors affecting the level of aggregate demand**

Consumer spending	plus	Investment	plus	Aggregate demand equals Government spending	plus	Exports	minus	Imports

Consumer spending

which depends upon

1. **Disposable income***
   which depends upon
   (a) TAXATION direct
       e.g. income tax and
   (b) TAXATION indirect
       e.g. VAT*

   AND

2. **Savings**
   which depends upon
   (a) THE RATE OF INTEREST*
       and
   (b) THE PROPENSITY TO SAVE

   AND

3. **Consumer confidence**
   which depends upon
   (a) THE 'FEEL GOOD' FACTOR
       and
   (b) DISPOSABLE INCOME*

Investment

which depends upon

1. **The cost of borrowing**
   which depends upon
   THE RATE OF INTEREST*

   AND

2. **The rate of return**
   which depends upon
   (a) THE INITIAL CAPITAL COST
       and
   (b) THE NET CASH FLOW OVER
       THE LIFE OF THE ASSET
       and
   (c) BUSINESS CONFIDENCE

Government spending

which depends upon

The state of the economy*

AND

**Government policies
and commitments***

AND

Demographic factors

Exports

which depends upon

1. **The state of
   the world economy**

   AND

2. **The competitiveness
   of the economy**
   which depends upon
   (a) INFLATION RATE*
       VIS-À-VIS OUR COMPETITORS
       and
   (b) WAGES IN RELATION
       TO PRODUCTIVITY †
       and
   (c) EXCHANGE RATES
       and
   (d) DESIGN, DELIVERY, QUALITY
       OF PRODUCTS/SERVICES
       AND

3. **Growth rate of
   UK economy***

Imports

which depends upon

1. **The competitiveness
   of the UK economy**
   which depends upon
   (a) INFLATION RATE*
       VIS-À-VIS OUR COMPETITORS
       and
   (b) EXCHANGE RATES†

       AND

2. **Growth rate of
   UK economy***

Key:
* Factors over which the government has some influence
† Assumes UK remains outside the single currency

PAUSE FOR THOUGHT 6 *How has the trade in goods affected the circular flow of income? How about services? What effects has the trade on invisibles had on the circular flow? Are we net exporters or importers of capital and what effect does this part of the balance of payments have on the circular flow of income model?*

PAUSE FOR THOUGHT 7 *1 From Figure 1.6, which of the main components of aggregate demand would be more easily influenced by the authorities and why do you think this is the case?*

2 If the government decides to (a) reduce the level of income tax, (b) reduce corporation tax, (c) reduce the rate of VAT and (d) reduce interest rates, identify the components of aggregate demand that will be affected.

Withdrawals and injections

Each of the five sectors mentioned above can create withdrawals and injections, as shown in Table 1.3.

Table 1.3
Injections and withdrawals

Sector	Injection	Symbol	Withdrawal	Symbol
Households			Savings	S
Business	Investment	I	Savings	S
Financial	Investment	I	Savings	S
Government	Government expenditure	G	Government taxes	T
Overseas	• Export of goods/services • Income from overseas investments • Import of capital	X	• Import of goods/services • Income paid out to overseas investors • Export of capital	M

Therefore, to summarise the data in Table 1.3:

Injections (J) $= I + X + G$

Withdrawals (W) $= S + M + T$

and from this it can be seen that for the circular flow of income model to be in equilibrium, then $J = W$. This is not the same thing as saying that savings must always equal investment or that the government must always balance its books; or even that the balance of payments must always be in balance. However, if there is to be an equilibrium in the circular flow, then $W = J$. If for any reason they were temporarily out of balance, then the national income (Y) would rise or fall to ensure that balance is achieved, as shown in Figure 1.7.

At national income level OY_2 households consume CY_2 level of income (i.e. there is no saving or any other form of withdrawal). However, national expenditure is DY_2. Thus $J = CD$ while $W = $ zero. In these circumstances, national income would rise from OY_2 to OY_e. As it does, the level of withdrawals from the circular flow of income will also rise. Conversely, if national income is at the level OY_1, then $BH = $ the level of withdrawals (i.e. the difference between income $OY_1 = BY_1$ and consumer spending, HY_1). Injections J, on the other

Figure 1.7
Equilibrium national income

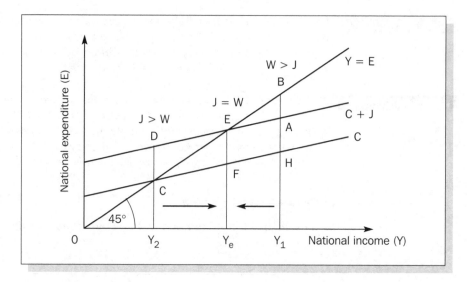

hand, is AH (the difference between C + J and C). Therefore, BH > AH (i.e. W > J). In these circumstances, national income would fall from OY_1 to OY_e. Only when J = W (i.e. at the point E where J = EF and W = EF) will national income reach a stable equilibrium.

Another way of looking at the same situation is to look at the graphs for both withdrawals (W) and injections (J), given in Figure 1.8.

From this diagram equilibrium national income occurs when W = J at income level OY_e where the first J graph (J_1) cuts the W graph at the point A. However, if the government wished to increase national income (let us imagine, for example, that at income level OY_e there was substantial unemployment) then it would be required to raise the J graph from J_1 to J_2.

Figure 1.8
Withdrawals and injections

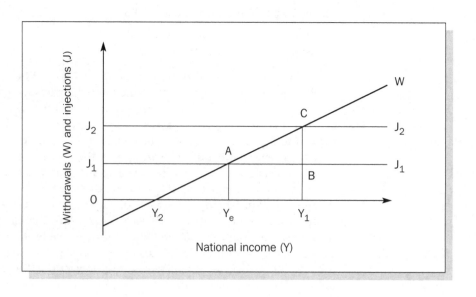

PAUSE FOR THOUGHT 8 *What factors could influence the J graph in Figure 1.8 to move from J_1 to J_2? What, if anything, could the government do to influence this?*

However, as can be seen from the figure, the change in J (BC) results in a bigger change in Y (Y_eY_1). This is known to economists as *the multiplier effect.*

The multiplier effect

The multiplier (k) can therefore be defined as follows:

> k = Change in national income/Change in injections
> = $\Delta Y / \Delta J$
> = Y_eY_1/BC
> = AB/BC
> = tangent of $\angle$CAB
> = slope of the W function

Therefore, as indicated in Figure 1.8, the size of the multiplier will be affected by the slope of the W function. The flatter the W function, the bigger will be the size of the multiplier. In other words, the more that people withdraw income from any increase in income, the greater will be the size of the multiplier. Economists use the concept of the marginal propensity to describe the extra income that is saved or taxed or spent on export. Thus a marginal 'propensity to save' of 0.2 indicates that consumers would save 20 per cent of any increase in their incomes. Therefore the more that people spend (and the less income is withdrawn from the circular flow of income) the bigger will be the multiplier.

The multiplier can then be rewritten to reflect this fact:

> k = 1/ (1 – mpw)

where mpw is defined as the marginal propensity to withdraw income from the circular flow, and

> mpw = mps + mpm + mpt

where mps is defined as the marginal propensity to save, mpm is the marginal propensity to import, and mpt is the marginal propensity to tax, from a given rise in income.

Thus, if mps = 0.2, mpm = 0.15 and mpt = 0.25, then mpw = 0.6 and k, the multiplier, is 1/ (1 – 0.6) = 1/0.4 = 2.5. Therefore, if these were the marginal propensities then an injection of £100 million into the economy would increase the national income by £250 million.

PAUSE FOR THOUGHT 9 *Complete Table 1.4 (the multiplier table) using the formulae:*
> ***k = 1/(1 – mpw)*** *and* ***mps + mpm + mpt = mpw***

Table 1.4

The multiplier

mps	mpm	mpt	mpw	k
0.05	0.05	0.10		
0.10	0.15		0.5	
	0.25	0.15	0.6	
0.30	0.15	0.25		
	0.25	0.35	0.8	
	0.30	0.36		25
	0.25	0.35		100

What do you notice about the results in this table?

CASE STUDY **1.2**

Japanese economy shows signs of recovery

By the beginning of 2000 it was clear that the Japanese economy had stopped deteriorating and begun to recover, with recovery most notable in exports and production, but there were still no signs of a self-sustained recovery in private-sector demand, although the environment surrounding such demand was gradually improving. The Central Bank of Japan (BOJ) therefore thought that it was appropriate for the Bank to maintain its zero-interest-rate policy, since the nation's economy had yet to reach a situation in which deflationary concerns have been eliminated. Under this 'ultra-easy policy' adopted in February 1999, the BOJ steered its target interest rate as close to zero as possible.

The central bank's Policy Board decided at its meeting on 17 January 2000 that the 'zero-interest-rate' policy should be kept intact, as Japan's economy still needed the support of low interest rates.

Although corporate earnings had improved, this had not yet spurred business activity. The income situation for households remained very poor and it was clear that the Central Bank would continue to keep a close watch on the possible effects of the yen's rise since the previous autumn on the economy and prices. There were some signs of recovery in the regions, as well as evidence of marginal improvements in the labour market. However, there were also signs of weakness, including sluggishness in consumer spending, the increasingly limited impact of public spending and the cautious attitude of firms about capital spending in some regions. As for consumer spending, it was argued that it was still falling short of recovery with the exception perhaps being the strong sales of home electronics centring on personal computers. On capital investment, many companies were still cautious about making investments because of excess capacity and concern over the business outlook. Investment was up by some firms, such as those in the information and telecommunications industries. On prices, it was predicted that they would remain stable for the time being, but the downward pressure on prices should also be watched carefully in view of declining income and the lack of clear signs of recovery in private demand.

Adapted from the Kyodo News Service, Tokyo, January 2000.

Questions

1   What does a policy of zero rates of interest mean and what are supposed to be its intended effects?

2   Using a 45-degree diagram, similar to Figure 1.7, explain the intended outcome of this policy.

3   Explain why the multiplier process has failed to take off in Japan.

CASE STUDY **1.3**
....

Tax revenue ready reckoner and the 2000 Budget

At the time of the Budget, the Treasury publishes what it calls the tax revenue ready reckoner which gives estimates of the effects of various tax changes. Table CS1.3.1 gives the data.

Table CS1.3.1
Direct effects of illustrative changes in taxation to take effect April 2000

	Cost/yield (Non-indexed base) 2000–01 (£m)
Income tax	
Rates	
Change starting rate by 1p	390
Change basic rate by 1p	2,650
Change higher rate by 1p	720
Change basic rate in Scotland by 1p	240
Allowances	
Change personal allowance by £100	560
Increase starting-rate limit by £100	290
Basic-rate limit	
Change basic-rate limit by 1%	140
Change basic-rate limit by 10%:	
increase (cost)	1,250
decrease (yield)	1,600
Allowances and limits	
Change all main allowances, starting- and basic-rate limits:	
increase/decrease by 1%	460
increase by 10% (cost)	4,400
decrease by 10% (yield)	5,000
Corporation tax	
Change main rate by 1 percentage point	1,100
Change smaller companies' rate by 1 percentage point	160
Capital gains tax	
Increase annual exempt amount by £500 for individuals and £250 for trustees	25
Inheritance tax	
Change rate by 1 percentage point	60
Increase threshold by £5,000	40
Excise duties*	
Beer up 0.3p a pint	30
Wine up 1.3p a bottle (75 cl)	10
Spirits up 6.4p a bottle (70 cl)	5
Cigarettes up 3p a packet (20 king-size)	60
Petrol up 0.5p a litre	115
Derv up 0.5p a litre	95
Change insurance premium tax (both standard and higher rates) by 1 percentage point	235
VAT	
Change both standard and reduced rates by 1 percentage point	3,175

Table CS1.3.1
Continued

	Cost/yield (Non-indexed base) 2000–01 (£m)
VAT coverage	**1999–2000**
Extend VAT to:	
food	7,800
domestic and international passenger transport	3,550
construction of new homes	2,750
books, newspapers, etc.	1,300
water and sewerage services	950
children's clothing	110
prescriptions	650

Source: HM Treasury Tax Ready Reckoner, November 1999.

Questions

1 In 2000 it was estimated that the Chancellor had about £7 billion extra to spend or to reduce taxes. Suppose that you were the Chancellor and you wanted to devote about half of this total to cutting taxes (i.e. £3.5 billion). Using Table CS1.3.1, work out a budget that would reduce taxes by this amount.

2 What would be the effects of your tax cuts?

3 What are the possible dangers if the Chancellor spends or reduces taxes by £7 billion?

The aims of macroeconomic policy

The remainder of this chapter looks at the main aims of government economic policy and at the current controversies that surround the conduct of macroeconomic policy.[1]

The macroeconomic environment is determined by the way in which the government attempts to achieve the four main aims of economic policy. Since the end of the Second World War every government has committed itself to these objectives, although the weight which successive governments have attached to each objective has varied over time. The four objectives are:

1 Full employment.
2 Stable prices.
3 Economic growth.
4 A balance of payments equilibrium.

Table 1.5 gives the data for the UK economy for the period 1979–2000.

Table 1.5

The UK economy: key economic Indicators

Year	Growth: % change in real GDP	Inflation: % change in RPI*	Unemployment (millions)	Current account as % of GDP
1979	2.8	13.4	1.1	−0.6
1980	−2.1	18.0	1.4	1.5
1981	−1.1	11.9	2.2	2.8
1982	1.7	8.6	2.5	1.7
1983	3.7	4.7	2.8	1.2
1984	2.0	5.0	2.9	0.5
1985	4.1	6.1	3.0	0.6
1986	3.8	3.4	3.0	−0.2
1987	4.6	4.1	2.8	−1.2
1988	4.5	4.9	2.3	−3.5
1989	2.1	7.8	1.8	−4.4
1990	0.6	9.5	1.6	−3.3
1991	−2.4	5.8	2.3	−1.3
1992	−0.5	3.7	2.8	−1.6
1993	2.0	1.6	2.9	−1.6
1994	3.6	3.8	2.6	−0.9
1995	3.7	4.2	2.3	−1.2
1996	2.3	2.5	2.1	−0.1
1997	3.5	3.1	1.6	0.8
1998	2.2	3.4	1.4	0.0
1999	1.5	1.6	1.3	−1.4
2000	2.4	2.2	1.3	−2.4
Averages	**2.0**	**5.9**	**2.2**	**−0.7**

*RPI inc. mortgages
Source: Goldman Sachs (1999) *The Economics Analyst*.

ACTIVITY **1.1**

The aims of macroeconomic policy

1   Using the data from Table 1.5 plot on a graph economic growth and unemployment against each year from 1979 to 1996. On a separate graph plot inflation against the current account balance. From the data in Table 1.5 and your graphs above can you detect any significant relationships between the key economic objectives as indicated?

2   How easy has it been for the government to achieve these objectives simultaneously?

Achievement of economic objectives

As can be seen from Activity 1.1, it has been difficult for governments to achieve these objectives simultaneously. Governments have often had to 'trade off' one objective in order to achieve others – a problem that is illustrated in Figure 1.9.

PAUSE FOR THOUGHT 10   *Before reading on, why do you think that it has been difficult to achieve these four objectives? What is the relationship between full employment and stable prices and between economic growth and the balance of payments? Why is it difficult to achieve a balance of payments and full employment? What do you think is the relationship between economic growth and stable prices?*

Figure 1.9
The trade off in economic objectives

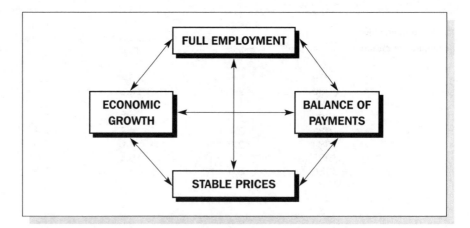

Full employment

Full employment has come to be defined as being consistent with around 2–3 per cent unemployment in advanced industrialised countries. Unemployment occurs where human resources are available for work, but are unable to find it. A number of types of unemployment are often identified.

➤ *Frictional unemployment* occurs because at any one time there will always be some people who are between jobs, or who are temporarily out of work for one reason or another.

➤ *Seasonal unemployment* occurs because demand for some goods and services varies with the times and seasons – for example, ski instructors or people employed as Santa Claus over the Christmas period.

➤ *Cyclical unemployment* occurs because of changes in the level of demand in times of recession or slump. Some workers will find that their jobs are among the first to feel the effects of such a downswing in the so-called business cycle. Some occupations seem to be more vulnerable than others in this respect; for example, construction workers are often the first to notice the effects of recession as firms postpone or delay capital projects and house building. This type of unemployment is a feature of the Boom–Bust cycle that dogged the UK economy over the past 30 or 40 years.

➤ *Structural unemployment* is caused by changes in the pattern of demand; for example, the decline of jobs in the manufacturing sector is often referred to as de-industrialisation (see Chapter 4).

➤ *Technological unemployment* refers to job losses resulting from changes in technology. For example, new technology completely revolutionised the way that newspapers were produced in the late 1980s, with the effect that a number of skilled print workers were made redundant. Car production has also been transformed by automated and robotic technologies and major changes in electronic/telecommunication technologies have had a dramatic effect on employment in areas such as television, banking and retailing.

PAUSE FOR THOUGHT 11 *Make a list of the different types of unemployment outlined above and give three examples of each type.*

The measurement of unemployment

The way in which unemployment is measured has aroused a considerable degree of controversy in recent years.[2] It has been calculated that the way in which unemployment is measured has been changed more than 30 times since 1979, although government ministers claimed at the time that only nine of these changes have had any significant impact on the unemployment total.

Unemployment is the measure of how many people are out of work in the economy. It is usually expressed as a percentage of the total workforce, on a monthly basis. There are several ways to measure unemployment, and they vary from country to country. In the United Kingdom, the government traditionally has counted the number of people who are claiming unemployment benefit – the so-called claimant count.

PAUSE FOR THOUGHT 12 *Before reading on, what are the problems in using the claimant count as the basis for measuring unemployment?*

But this leaves out those people who are not eligible for unemployment benefit but who may also be looking for jobs. It also leaves out the unemployed who are on special training schemes. In April 1998 the Labour government decided to publish *Labour Force Survey* (LFS) as a guide to unemployment figures. This measures the whole workforce, and then attempts to find all those who are seeking jobs, not just those who are receiving benefit. This method is recommended by the International Labour Organisation (ILO) and gives a more internationally comparable figure for unemployment. The government issues these ILO figures monthly instead of four times a year. The new number includes anyone who is actively available to start work within the next two weeks and has looked for work in the last four weeks or has already found a job but is waiting to start. The previous figures counted only those out of work and claiming unemployment benefit. By using this definition of 'unemployed', the figures should show that unemployment is much higher than the previous monthly figures indicated – as much as half a million higher.

PAUSE FOR THOUGHT 13 *Before reading on, identify the advantages and disadvantages of each of these measures.*

Advantages and disadvantages of different methods

It is argued that the claimant count gives the more precise figure for monthly unemployment as it is based on numbers collected by the government. This, however, has been widely criticised as being misleading. The old methods, as mentioned above, have had more than 30 changes in 20 years – and each time the change indicated a lower total. The Labour Party, when in opposition, complained about the method and promised to change the system once in power. For example, the previous methods excluded teenagers and anyone over 55 years old. The *Labour Force Survey* will be more consistent over time, but as it is based on a statistical survey it is therefore subject to sampling error. Because of this, the LFS is published on a rolling three-monthly basis and does not include all those who want jobs but are not actively seeking them (over 2 million in the winter of 1998).

PAUSE FOR THOUGHT 14

1 *What sectors of the economy or particular products or services are vulnerable to technological change in the next few years?*

2 *Can you speculate on what new products or services might begin to 'take off' in the early years of the new century?*

Stable prices and inflation

There are a number of different measures of inflation.[3] Firstly, there is the retail price index (RPI) which measures the average price level across a whole range of goods and services. These goods and services are weighted according to their importance in the average consumer's 'shopping basket'. If you can imagine that the shopping basket is worth £1,000, then Figure 1.10 gives the weighting factors, and it can be seen that about £100 out of the £1,000 in the shopping basket is spent on alcohol and tobacco.

PAUSE FOR THOUGHT 15

1 *Suppose that there was a 10 per cent increase in housing costs. What impact would this have on the overall RPI?*

2 *Apart from housing costs, which prices in which categories of expenditure have the biggest impact on the RPI?*

Figure 1.10
The Retail Price Index weighting factors 1999

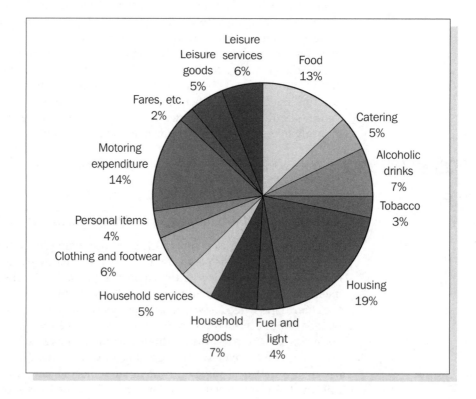

In addition to the RPI (sometimes referred to as the headline rate), two other measures are used. The second is called RPI-X, which takes out the distorting effects of changes in mortgage interest payments. Internationally, this is the most common method of calculating inflation. A rise in interest rates to curb inflation increases headline inflation in the short run as mortgage interest payments increase. Hence, RPI-X is sometimes called the underlying rate and is used as the government's target for inflation.

The third measure is called RPI-Y. This is inflation excluding mortgage interest payments and indirect taxes. Another key distorting effect results from indirect taxation. Value added tax rates rarely change, but new taxes on alcohol, tobacco and fuels may distort the inflation index figures. Measuring RPI-Y is most useful around December and January when budget duty increases come into effect.

The stability of prices can be affected by a number of factors which can be grouped under three main headings:

1 Demand factors
2 Cost factors
3 Monetary factors.

Demand inflation

Inflation can be defined as 'too much money chasing too few goods' and/or 'too many jobs chasing too few workers'. Figure 1.11 illustrates the situation.

The inflationary gap can be eliminated by bearing down on the components of aggregate demand. There are two principal weapons that governments can use to 'solve' the inflation problem, viz.:

➤ *fiscal policy*, involving changes in government spending and/or changes in taxation
➤ *monetary policy*, i.e. controlling the money supply or varying interest rates.

Figure 1.11
Inflationary gap

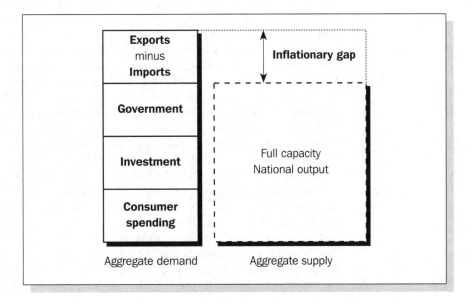

The aim of both of these policies is to bring aggregate demand more into line with aggregate supply or the productive potential of the economy.

PAUSE FOR THOUGHT 16 *Using Figure 1.11, outline the policy measures that could be used by the authorities to reduce an inflationary gap.*

Cost inflation

In the immediate post-war period, demand factors appeared to be the most significant cause of, and cure for, inflation. However, in the 1970s a number of other factors related to cost began to play a more significant role. For example, in 1972 the Organisation of Petroleum Exporting Countries (OPEC) raised the price of a barrel of oil by 400 per cent, and inflation became rampant. It was clear that demand management techniques were simply not capable of coping with this type of cost–push inflation. It is true that raising taxes and cutting government expenditure would eventually have worked, but this would only have been achieved by raising unemployment to extremely high levels. The Labour government at the time was unfortunately overwhelmed by the problem, and inflation hit 24 per cent by 1975. The effects on the government were devastating, as they were unable to control the inflationary forces that were unleashed. As the price of oil rose, so too did the cost of producing products which were derived from oil. Further, the costs of transport, energy and distribution also rose rapidly. Coupled with the decision to float the currency (for more details, see Chapter 3) the government experienced severe balance of payments difficulties, with the official gold and foreign exchange reserves in danger of running out. This prompted the government to introduce a prices and incomes policy to try to maintain price stability. This type of policy required the government to set up bodies to review all requests for increases in both wages and prices. It meant that these bodies were charged with the task of determining whether price increases were 'fair' and whether demands for pay increases were justified. In some cases the prices and incomes policies were 'voluntary' in that the recommendations of such bodies did not have the backing of the law. In other instances, the policy had statutory force, such as when the government imposed a pay and prices 'freeze'. However, with trade union militancy increasing in the face of rising prices, the government found that it was almost impossible to make such policies work and were forced to accept the intervention of the International Monetary Fund (IMF), who insisted on a massive dose of monetary medicine. Eventually, the Labour government found itself using all three conventional weapons in order to solve the inflation crisis; namely, deflationary fiscal policy, IMF-imposed monetary policy and a prices and incomes policy. Denis Healey, the then Chancellor of the Exchequer, was thus forced to introduce a series of measures which caused real wages to fall significantly but which also resulted in a rise in unemployment. Thus the UK had the worst of all worlds, with inflation still continuing to rise along with rises in unemployment. Stagflation (inflation coupled with a stagnant economy) was now rampant. Naturally enough, the trade unions did not take kindly to this, especially from a Labour government, and they exacted their revenge in the so-called Winter of Discontent of 1978/9. The Labour Party eventually lost the 1979 election and remained out of office for the next 18 years. This episode in our recent economic history demonstrates the various cost factors at work and the difficulties of controlling them.[4]

PAUSE FOR THOUGHT 17 *From the section above, identify as many cost–push factors as possible.*

Monetary theory

This episode heralded the introduction of a new Conservative government, which believed that the main cause of inflation was monetary. It is important to stress that these monetary theories pre-dated the 1979 Conservative government. Indeed, as we have seen, the first serious attempt to use monetary measures to solve inflation was introduced by a Labour government under Denis Healey. Even before that, Milton Friedman in the USA was writing about the importance for governments to control the money supply.[5]

The crux of this view stems from the classical theory of money. Simply stated this says that the following equation must hold:

$$MV = PQ$$

where M is the quantity of money circulating in the economy, V is the velocity of circulation of a given unit of money, P is the average price level and Q is the volume of goods and services an economy produces in a given time period.

PQ is Price × Quantity for the economy as a whole. In other words, it corresponds to the nominal value of national output or national income. It is therefore possible to derive V, the velocity of circulation of money, by dividing money national income by a suitable measure of the money supply, and there are several measures that can be used.

M0
> M0 equals notes and coins in circulation in the private sector
> *plus* private sector non-interest bearing sterling sight deposits
> *plus* Bankers' operational balances with the Bank of England.

M2
> M2 equals M0 *plus* private sector interest bearing retail sterling bank deposits with banks and building societies.

M4
> M4 equals private sector non-interest-bearing sterling sight bank deposits
> *plus* private sector interest-bearing sterling sight deposits
> *plus* private sector time bank deposits (including sterling certificates of deposit)
> *plus* private sector holdings of building society shares and deposits and sterling certificates of deposit.

This enables us to calculate various measures of the velocity of circulation (V). However, according to the monetarist view, the velocity of circulation is comparatively stable over a period, no matter which definition of the money supply one cares to take. Thus if we can regard V as stable, then this implies that there is a direct relationship between M, the money supply, and both P (the average price level) and Q (the volume of goods and services the economy is capable of producing). If we further assume that Q is capable of growing at a predictable rate, then we have a direct link between M (the money supply) and P (the average price level). Figure 1.12 gives the relationship between the money supply and price inflation for the period 1994–2000 using quarterly data.

Figure 1.12

**Money supply and
inflation 1994–1999**

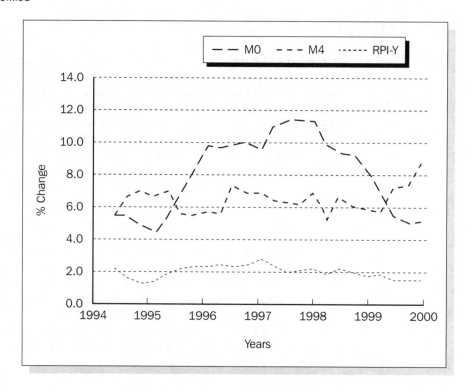

As can be seen, there is not much of a direct relationship between the two variables. Nevertheless, in spite of this apparent lack of support from the empirical evidence, the UK government still pursued the monetarist experiment from 1979 until about 1985. During that period the cornerstone of economic policy was the medium-term financial strategy (MTFS), which set monetary targets for the next three- or four-year period.

The results of pursuing monetarist policies were mixed and subsequently governments have abandoned attempts to control the money supply as the principal weapon in controlling inflation, preferring instead to pass responsibility for the control of inflation to the Bank of England and its monetary policy committee (MPC). In 1997 Gordon Brown set the MPC the inflation target of 2.5 per cent. The committee, which is independent, meets once a month to review a range of economic indicators and to set interest rates. While the announcement of an inflation target is no guarantee that the government will not be tempted to tinker with the economy for political reasons, it does at least ensure that there is some principle or objective by which to guide policy.

The government has therefore given much more independence to the Bank of England in the formulation of monetary policy. The Bank, it can be argued, is now totally independent.[6] Gordon Brown, the first Chancellor of the Exchequer in the Labour government of 1997, has gone much further than any of his predecessors in allowing the Bank of England a more independent voice. The Bank periodically publishes its own inflation report and offers the Chancellor independent advice on interest rates and exchange rate policy. The minutes of the monthly meeting between the Chancellor and the Governor of the Bank of England are now published and allow the public to see the kind of information and advice that the Chancellor is receiving. In those circumstances it is more difficult for the government to manipulate monetary policy for purely political purposes.[7]

| PAUSE FOR THOUGHT 18 | *Examine the case for giving the Bank of England independence in framing monetary policy. What are the dangers in this and how would you aim to overcome them?* |

Economic growth

The third key objective of economic policy is to achieve a fast rate of economic growth. Only by achieving economic growth can a society improve the economic well-being and living standards of its citizens. Before discussing the causes of economic growth it is important that we define the meaning of the term.

Economists usually define economic growth as the percentage change in real national income per head. Growth figures are therefore based on national income statistics and, as a result, suffer from all the imperfections of those statistics. For example, not all incomes are necessarily taken into account in these statistics. Some income is deliberately excluded because its inclusion would result in some 'double counting'. This is the case with so-called *transfer payments*. (This does not refer to the exorbitant prices paid by football clubs for the services of rather indifferent strikers!) Transfer payments refer to such things as students' grants, old age pensions and social security pensions, which are transferred from one section of the community to another via the tax and benefit system. It would be 'double counting' if transfer payments were included in the national income figures as the gross incomes used when calculating national income already include the tax element which funds these payments. However, some income is *not* declared, and this forms part of the 'black economy'. The black economy is almost impossible to quantify because of the very nature of the problem. Economists have attempted to put a figure on this with estimates ranging from 2 to 10 per cent of GNP. In addition, payments in kind, whereby goods and services are exchanged for other goods and services, also fail to be captured in the national income statistics. Taxation can distort the picture, especially expenditure taxes such as value added tax (VAT), which will tend to exaggerate the true size of the value of our national output. A similar argument applies to subsidies, which will have the opposite effect.

The way that national income is made up (i.e. its composition) can also have an effect on living standards. Imagine a situation in which two countries have identical national income per head figures but the first country spends 50 per cent of its income on defence while the second spends an equivalent amount on hospitals, schools and help for those below the poverty line. The national income per head figures will simply fail to detect any such differences although common sense tells us that there is bound to be a difference in the well-being and living standards of the two countries concerned. Similar arguments apply to the ways in which a country spends its income. In northern Europe central heating is much more prevalent and so national income statistics will be affected by such expenditure. In some parts of the world central heating is simply not needed to keep the population warm, yet the absence of such spending may result in those countries having an apparently lower national income per head.

It should also be remembered that the GNP per head figure is an average and takes no account of the way in which income is distributed. Thus an economy may experience significant rates of growth while at the same time inequalities in income may also grow. It can therefore be difficult to extrapolate from growth figures to living standards if these differences in income distribution exist.

Finally, if a large proportion of national income is exported it can be difficult to infer that increases in national income per head necessarily result in improved living standards.

Despite these difficulties, international league tables of economic growth involving national income are still published. Table 1.6 illustrates the pattern of economic growth around the world.

Table 1.6

International growth league table showing percentage change in GDP in 1994 and 1999

Country	1994	1999	Country	1994	1999
China	11.8	8.1	Italy	3.7	2.1
South Korea	9.3	13.0	France	3.6	3.2
Brazil	9.2	3.1	Germany	3.3	2.3
Malaysia	8.9	10.6	Holland	3.3	4.6
Singapore	8.7	7.1	Denmark	3.0	2.0
Thailand	8.4	6.5	Israel	2.9	3.0
Taiwan	7.0	6.8	Spain	2.8	4.0
Australia	6.4	4.3	Switzerland	2.6	3.0
Argentina	6.0	0.1	Austria	2.5	3.8
Canada	5.6	3.0	South Africa	2.1	2.1
Hong Kong	5.5	8.7	Hungary	2.0	5.9
Philippines	5.1	4.6	Belgium	1.7	4.5
Poland	5.0	6.2	Greece	1.1	3.7
India	4.7	5.5	Japan	0.9	0.0
Czech Republic	4.7	1.0	Sweden	0.4	3.4
Mexico	4.0	5.2	Portugal	−0.7	n.a.
USA	4.0	4.6	Venezuela	−3.3	−4.5
UK	3.9	3.0	Turkey	−8.9	−3.4
Chile	3.9	3.9	Russia	−14.0	7.3

Source: The Economist, 29 April 2000.

The table shows the figures for two years only and should therefore be treated with some caution. Nevertheless, it is interesting to note that the 'go–go' economies, where growth rates exceeded 6 per cent per annum, are mostly to be found in the Far East, with South Korea topping the table in 1999 with a phenomenal 13.0 per cent per annum. Some argue that the reason some countries can experience such fast rates of growth reflects the fact that these countries start from a relatively low economic base in terms of the GDP per head. However, in the case of the so-called 'tiger economies' of Hong Kong, Malaysia, Singapore and South Korea, the base level is not far behind that of the rest of the world's economies, with a GNP per head comparable with, and in some cases exceeding, the so called 'mature' economies. The middle-ranking economies (i.e. those whose growth rates were between 4 and 6 per cent) are a mixed set of economies, while most of the more mature economies of Western Europe fall into the next category of growers (i.e. those whose growth rates were between 2 and 4 per cent). Interestingly Japan, traditionally considered to be a model of economic rectitude, has had a disappointing period with a sluggish economy barely able to achieve any measurable increase in its economy in 1994 and with growth for 1999 negligible. Finally, those in the 'relegation zone' of our league table are undergoing very significant upheavals. It is perhaps not entirely coincidental that those economies that actually shrank in 1994 are also experiencing political upheavals of some kind (e.g. Turkey and Russia). By 1999, while the Russian economy had improved, Turkey and Venezuela were still experiencing severe economic dislocation.

PAUSE FOR THOUGHT 19 *Why do some economies grow faster than others? Before reading on, make a list of such factors.*

The growth rate of an economy can be affected by a number of factors, some of which have been identified as:

1 The quantity of the resources available.
2 The quality of the resources available.
3 The attitude of managers and workers.
4 Government policy.

Availability of resources

It is always possible for an economy to grow as a result of acquiring additional resources. West Germany's post-war economic miracle was helped by the influx of immigrant workers in the 1960s and, in Britain, the discovery of a new resource (North Sea oil) undoubtedly helped the economy to grow in the early 1980s when there was a very deep recession. (There is a view which links the two events, namely, the slump in manufacturing with the discovery of North Sea oil, but that will be considered later – see Chapter 4.)

PAUSE FOR THOUGHT 20 *Before you read the relevant section on this point, can you explain how the discovery of North Sea oil could have a damaging effect on the competitiveness of our manufacturing sector? (Hint: It links in with the effect of the discovery of oil on our exchange rate.)*

Quality of resources

As well as the quantity of resources available to an economy, one should also consider the quality of the resources available – in particular, the amount of investment that is undertaken in replacing outdated capital equipment and in developing new products that take advantage of technological developments. As well as the investment in plant and machinery, it is argued that investment in people is just as crucial to an economy's growth prospects. The appropriate kind of training is necessary to ensure that the economy has the requisite skills on which to call. The proportion of the workforce that is educated beyond school-leaving age can also have an influence, as can the type of education. The education system in the United Kingdom has been criticised for encouraging an 'anti-industry' and, in particular, an 'anti-manufacturing' attitude among school leavers. The UK's international competitors, it is claimed, are more sympathetic to the merits of vocational education. These criticisms are beginning to have less force than they had a decade ago, but they still persist.

Attitudes

The attitude to risk-taking can also be said to have an effect on the growth prospects of an economy. If entrepreneurs are encouraged to set up on their own and take risks, they may create business growth in areas that had not been considered previously. Martha Lane Fox and her partner set up the LastMinute.com web-based company selling last-minute deals on holidays, tickets for the theatre and sporting events. They saw an opportunity to develop a market that no-one at the time saw. They had the audacity to venture into an area of business that no-one else had spotted. Another example is Richard Branson who saw an opportunity to compete in the airline market in a way that few others would have believed possible. He also saw an opportunity to compete in the Cola drink market with the development of Virgin Cola. This sort of attitude creates added value for his business while at the same time adding to the country's economic growth.

Government policies

Governments can help or hinder economic growth by their own policies. In the past governments have been criticised for failing to provide the kind of stable economic climate in which firms can take long-term economic decisions (see also Chapter 12). The 'stop–go' cycle actually inhibited long-term growth because the economic environment was continually changing. A period of economic growth in which exports and investment are the main 'engines' of growth is likely to be more sustainable than a short consumer boom in which demand is artificially stoked up to levels that outstrip our ability to produce. The inevitable consequence of this type of growth is usually a balance of payments crisis and a run on the currency or an alarming reduction in our foreign exchange reserves (see section below on the balance of payments and exchange rates). Thus a well-managed economy can be a considerable advantage in securing sustainable economic growth. More recently, for example, the government has attempted to raise productivity by offering tax incentives for small firms to undertake Research and Development.[8]

However, while it is true that these factors play a significant role in the growth process it has been difficult to establish a direct 'cause-and-effect' relationship between each factor and economic growth. Does it follow, for example, that if an economy invests more then faster economic growth will automatically follow? Unfortunately, the answer is that it all depends! It depends, for example, on the quality of the investment decisions, rather than simply the volume. There is no simple relationship between the volume of investment and economic growth.

When an analysis of the main components of investment is conducted, one may discover for instance that a large proportion may be devoted to research and development of weapons systems for the defence industry or that investment in housing may form a significant proportion of a country's investment stock. The type of investment obviously has implications as to whether long-term economic growth is likely to be achieved. Thus a quantitative analysis that ignores these qualitative aspects is unlikely to give a definitive answer to the question of what causes economic growth. Similarly, simply increasing expenditure on education may not by itself necessarily increase economic growth. Again, qualitative aspects of the type of expenditure in education will play a part. There is, in fact, a strong scepticism about the economic benefits of educational expenditure. The 1960s and 1970s saw a significant expansion in expenditure on higher education in Britain, yet there was no noticeable improvement on our economic performance during that time. A closer examination of the ways in which this money was spent indicates that, unlike our international competitors, a large proportion of educational spending went on 'student maintenance' (i.e. students' living expenses) rather than directly on the educational process as such. While this expenditure is important, other countries found different ways of using their education budgets which laid greater emphasis on investing in the educational process itself. Again, simply looking at absolute numbers may mask a number of important qualitative issues.

Conclusions

In this chapter we have examined a simple model of how the domestic economy works and assessed the aims of economic policy. We will discuss in more detail the fourth objective (viz. achieving a balance of payments) in the next chapter. However, we have seen how difficult it has been for governments of all political persuasions to achieve these objectives simultaneously.

Notes

1 For a good website on this topic see www.bized.ac.uk/virtual/economy/
2 For details see the BBC's webpage at:
news2.thls.bbc.co.uk/hi/english/biz/the_economy/economy_reports/
3 For a good survey of the way to measure inflation and the RPI visit the Office of National Statistics webpage at: www.ons.gov.uk/data/cpgi/rpiguide.htm
4 For an insider's view of the difficulties of that period, see Healey, D. (1989) *The Time of My Life*, Michael Joseph, London, esp. ch. 19, Managing the Economy.
5 Friedman, M. (1968) The importance of monetary policy, *American Economic Review*, Vol. 58, March, pp. 1–17.
6 For an interesting analysis of how independent the Monetary Policy Committee is, see 'Bank at a crossroads as Whitehall rattles sabre: Independence would be better guaranteed if members were not eligible for reappointment', *The Independent*: London; May 30, 2000; Sarah Hogg.
7 For interesting evidence of the relationship between central bank independence and the control of inflation, see Posen, A. (1994) 'Why Central Bank Independence Does Not Cause Low Inflation' in *Finance and the International Economy*, No. 7, Amex Bank.
8 For details of this see The Institute of Fiscal Studies, *The Green Budget 1999*, London, or visit the IFS website at www.ifs.org.uk

References and additional reading

Curwin, P. ed. (1994) *Understanding the UK Economy*, Macmillan, London.
The Economist (1994) 'A bad case of arthritis', 26 February, pp. 92–3.
Ferguson, P.R., Ferguson, G.J. and Rothschild, R. (1993) *Business Economics: The Application of Economic Theory*, Macmillan, London, esp. ch. 13, pp. 249–67.

Friedman, M. (1968) 'The role of monetary policy', *American Economic Review*, March, Vol. 58, pp. 1–17.

Gough, J. (2000) *Introductory Economics for Business and Management*, McGraw-Hill, London, esp. ch. 12, pp. 307–44.

Griffiths, A. and Wall, S. (1997) *Applied Economics*, Longman, London, esp. ch. 19, pp. 468–90; ch. 20, pp. 492–519; ch. 24, pp. 602–28; and ch. 27, pp. 697–710.

Holden, K., Matthews, K. and Thompson, J. (1995) *The UK Economy Today*, Manchester University Press, Manchester.

Layard, R., Nickell, S. and Jackman, R. (1994) *Unemployment: Macroeconomic Performance and the Labour Market*, Oxford University Press, Oxford.

Perman, R. and Scouller, J. (1999) *Business Economics*, Oxford University Press, Oxford, esp. ch. 14.

Posen, A. (1994) 'Why Central Bank independence does not cause low inflation', *Finance and the International Economy*, No. 7, Amex Bank, New York.

Rifkind, J. (1995) *The End of Work?*, G.P. Putman & Sons, London.

Sloman, J. (2000) *Economics*, Financial Times, Prentice Hall, London, esp. chs. 13–22.

Unit 5: Common Law I

Learning hours: 60

NQF level 4: BTEC Higher National — H1

Content Selected: Elliott and Quinn, Contract Law 4th Edition, Chapter 1

Introduction from the Qualification Leader

This unit provides an introduction to the law of contract, with particular focus on the formation and operation of business contracts. It also introduces the law of Tort. Chapter 1 has been selected as it introduces material necessary for outcome 1 of the unit.

Description of unit

The aim of this unit is to provide an introduction to the law of contract, with a particular focus on the formation and operation of a business contract. Learners are encouraged to explore the contents of such an agreement and, in particular, to appreciate the practical application of standard-form business contracts. Additionally, the unit enables learners to understand how the Law of Tort differs from the law of contract and examines the Tort of Negligence and issues of liability pertinent to business.

Summary of learning outcomes

To achieve this unit a learner must:

1 Understand the **essential elements of a valid** and legally binding **contract** and its role in a business context

2 Explore the significance of **specific terms in a business contract**

3 Examine the role of the **Law of Tort in business activities** assessing **particular forms of tortious liability**

4 Understand and apply the **elements of the Tort of Negligence**.

Content

1 **Essential elements of a valid contract**

Essential elements: types of contractual agreements and their application in business; the making of a valid offer and its unconditional acceptance; the essential existence of a clear and unambiguous intention supported by sufficient consideration; the parties to the agreement possessing the necessary capacity and being privy to the agreement

2 **Specific terms in a business contract**

Specific terms: contents of a valid agreement and standard form business contracts; comparative analysis of express and implied terms; the effects of the breach of a condition, warranty or an innominate term; the legal effect on the agreement of the incorporation of an exemption clause

3 **The Law of Tort in business activities and particular forms of tortious liability**

The Law of Tort: fundamental aspects of tort; tortious liability and business operations; advantages of using tortious, as opposed to contractual, remedies

Types of tortious liability: the tortious liability of occupiers, employer's liability including vicarious liability for employees, health and safety issues, strict liability, difficulties of practical application

4 **Elements of the Tort of Negligence**

Negligence: the nature and scope of the duty of care and the standard of care; breach of duty, issues of causation and remoteness of damage

Outcomes and assessment criteria

Outcomes	Assessment criteria for pass To achieve each outcome a learner must demonstrate the ability to:
1 Understand the **essential elements of a valid** and legally binding **contract** and its role in a business context	• explain the different types of business agreement and the importance of the key elements required for the formation of a valid contract • apply the rules of offer and acceptance in a given scenario, also considering any impact of new technology • assess the importance of the rules of intention and consideration of the parties to the agreement • explain the importance of the contracting parties having the appropriate legal capacity to enter into a binding agreement
2 Explore the significance of **specific terms in a business contract**	• analyse specific contract terms with reference to their importance and impact if these terms are broken • apply and analyse the law on standard form contracts • discuss the effect of exemption clauses in attempting to exclude contractual liability
3 Examine the role of the **Law of Tort in business activities** assessing **particular forms of tortious liability**	• describe the nature of general tortious liability comparing and contrasting to contractual liability • explain the liability applicable to an occupier of premises • discuss the nature of employer's liability with reference to vicarious liability and health and safety implications • distinguish strict liability from general tortious liability
4 Understand and apply the **elements of the Tort of Negligence**	• explain and understand the application of the elements of the Tort of Negligence • analyse the practical applications of particular elements of the Tort of Negligence

1 Offer and acceptance

For a contract to exist, usually one party must have made an offer, and the other must have accepted it. Once acceptance takes effect, a contract will usually be binding on both parties, and the rules of offer and acceptance are typically used to pinpoint when a series of negotiations has passed that point, in order to decide whether the parties are obliged to fulfil their promises. There is generally no halfway house – negotiations have either crystallized into a binding contract, or they are not binding at all.

Unilateral and bilateral contracts

In order to understand the law on offer and acceptance, you need to understand the concepts of unilateral and bilateral contracts. Most contracts are bilateral. This means that each party takes on an obligation, usually by promising the other something – for example, Ann promises to sell something and Ben to buy it. (Although contracts where there are mutual obligations are always called bilateral, there may in fact be more than two parties to such a contract.)

By contrast, a unilateral contract arises where only one party assumes an obligation under the contract. Examples might be promising to give your mother £50 if she gives up smoking for a year, or to pay a £100 reward to anyone who finds your lost purse, or, as the court suggested in **Great Northern Railway Co** *v* **Witham** (1873), to pay someone £100 to walk from London to York. What makes these situations unilateral contracts is that only one party has assumed an obligation – you are obliged to pay your mother if she gives up smoking, but she has not promised in turn to give up smoking. Similarly, you are obliged to pay the reward to anyone who finds your purse, but nobody need actually have undertaken to do so.

A common example of a unilateral contract is that between estate agents and people trying to sell their houses – the seller promises to pay a specified percentage of the house price to the estate agent if the house is sold, but the estate agent is not required to promise in return to sell the house, or even to try to do so.

▶ Offer

The person making an offer is called the offeror, and the person to whom the offer is made is called the offeree. A communication will be treated as an offer if it indicates the terms on which the offeror is prepared to make a contract (such as the price of the goods for sale), and gives a clear indication that the offeror intends to be bound by those terms if they are accepted by the offeree.

An offer may be express, as when Ann tells Ben that she will sell her CD player for £200, but it can also be implied from conduct – a common example is taking goods to the cash desk in a supermarket, which is an implied offer to buy those goods.

Offers to the public at large

In most cases, an offer will be made to a specified person – as when Ann offers to sell her computer to Ben. However, offers can be addressed to a group of people, or even to the general public. For example, a student may offer to sell her old textbooks to anyone in the year below, or the owner of a lost dog may offer a reward to anyone who finds it.

In **Carlill** *v* **Carbolic Smoke Ball Co** (1893) the defendants were the manufacturers of 'smokeballs' which they claimed could prevent flu. They published advertisements stating that if anyone used their smokeball for a specified time and still caught flu, they would pay that person £100, and that to prove they were serious about the claim, they had deposited £1,000 with their bankers.

Mrs Carlill bought and used a smokeball, but nevertheless ended up with flu. She therefore claimed the £100, which the company refused to pay. They argued that their advertisement could not give rise to a contract, since it was impossible to make a contract with the whole world, and that therefore they were not legally bound to pay the money. This argument was rejected by the court, which held that the advertisement did constitute an offer to the world at large, which became a contract when it was accepted by Mrs Carlill using the smokeball and getting flu. She was therefore entitled to the £100.

A contract arising from an offer to the public at large, like that in **Carlill**, is usually a unilateral contract.

▶ Invitations to treat

Some kinds of transaction involve a preliminary stage in which one party invites the other to make an offer. This stage is called an invitation to treat. In **Gibson** *v* **Manchester City Council** (1979) a council tenant was interested in buying his house. He completed an application form and received a letter from the Council stating that it 'may be prepared to sell the house to you' for £2,180. Mr Gibson initially queried the purchase price, pointing out that the path to the house was in a bad condition. The Council refused to change the price, saying that the price had been fixed taking into account the condition of the property. Mr Gibson then wrote on 18 March 1971 asking the Council to 'carry on with the purchase as per my application'. Following a change in political control of the Council in May 1971, it decided to stop selling Council houses to tenants, and Mr Gibson was informed that the Council would not proceed with the sale of the house. Mr Gibson brought legal proceedings claiming that the letter he had received stating the purchase price was an offer which he had accepted on 18 March 1971. The House of Lords, however, ruled that the Council had not made an offer; the letter giving the purchase price was merely one step in the negotiations for a contract and amounted only to an invitation to treat. Its purpose was simply to invite the making of a 'formal application', amounting to an offer, from the tenant.

Confusion can sometimes arise when what would appear, in the everyday sense of the word, to be an offer, is held by the law to be only an invitation to treat. This issue arises particularly in the following areas.

Advertisements

A distinction is generally made between advertisements for a unilateral contract, and those for a bilateral contract.

Advertisements for unilateral contracts
These include advertisements such as the one in **Carlill** *v* **Carbolic Smoke Ball Co**, or those offering rewards for the return of lost property, or for information leading to the arrest or conviction of a criminal. They are usually treated as offers, on the basis that the contract can normally be accepted without any need for further negotiations between the parties, and the person making the advertisement intends to be bound by it. A recent illustration is provided by the Court of Appeal in **Bowerman** *v* **Association of British Travel Agents Ltd** (1996). A school had booked a skiing holiday with a tour operator which was a member of the Association of British Travel Agents (ABTA). All members of this association display a notice provided by ABTA which states:

> Where holidays or other travel arrangements have not yet commenced at the time of failure [of the tour operator], ABTA arranges for you to be reimbursed the money you have paid in respect of your holiday arrangements.

The tour operator became insolvent and cancelled the skiing holiday. The school was refunded the money they had paid for the holiday, but not the cost of the wasted travel insurance. The plaintiff brought an action against ABTA to seek reimbursement of the cost of this insurance.

He argued, and the Court of Appeal agreed, that the ABTA notice constituted an offer which the customer accepted by contracting with an ABTA member.

Advertisements for a bilateral contract

These are the type of advertisements which advertise specified goods at a certain price, such as those found at the back of newspapers and magazines. They are usually considered invitations to treat, on the grounds that they may lead to further bargaining – potential buyers might want to negotiate about the price, for example – and that since stocks could run out, it would be unreasonable to expect the advertisers to sell to everybody who applied.

In **Partridge** v **Crittenden** (1968), an advertisement in a magazine stated 'Bramblefinch cocks and hens, 25s each'. As the Bramblefinch was a protected species, the person who placed the advertisement was charged with unlawfully offering for sale a wild bird contrary to the Protection of Birds Act 1954, but his conviction was quashed on the grounds that the advertisement was not an offer but an invitation to treat.

It was held in **Grainger & Sons** v **Gough** (1896) that the circulation of a price-list by a wine merchant was not an offer to sell at those prices but merely an invitation to treat.

Shopping

Price-marked goods on display on the shelves or in the windows of shops are generally regarded as invitations to treat, rather than offers to sell goods at that price. In **Fisher** v **Bell** (1960) the defendant had displayed flick knives in his shop window, and was convicted of the criminal offence of offering such knives for sale. On appeal, Lord Parker CJ stated that the display of an article with a price on it in a shop window was only an invitation to treat and not an offer, and the conviction was overturned.

Where goods are sold on a self-service basis, the customer makes an offer to buy when presenting the goods at the cash desk, and the shopkeeper may accept or reject that offer. In **Pharmaceutical Society of Great Britain** v **Boots Cash Chemists (Southern) Ltd** (1953) Boots were charged with an offence concerning the sale of certain medicines which could only be sold by or under the supervision of a qualified pharmacist. Two customers in a self-service shop selected the medicines, which were price-marked, from the open shelves, and placed them in the shop's wire baskets. The shelves were not supervised by a pharmacist, but a pharmacist had been instructed to supervise the transaction at the cash desk. The issue was therefore whether the sale had taken place at the shelves or at the cash desk.

The Court of Appeal decided the shelf display was like an advertisement for a bilateral contract, and was therefore merely an invitation to treat.

The offer was made by the customer when medicines were placed in the basket, and was only accepted when the goods were presented at the cash desk. Since a pharmacist was supervising at that point no offence had been committed.

There are two main practical consequences of this principle. First, shops do not have to sell goods at the marked price – so if a shop assistant wrongly marks a CD at £2.99 rather than £12.99, for example, you cannot insist on buying it at that price (though the shop may be committing an offence under the Trade Descriptions Act 1968 – see Chapter 16 on consumer contracts). Secondly, a customer cannot insist on buying a particular item on display – so you cannot make a shopkeeper sell you the sweater in the window even if there are none left inside the shop. Displaying the goods is not an offer, so a customer cannot accept it and thereby make a binding contract.

Timetables and tickets for transport
The legal position here is rather unclear. Is a bus timetable an offer to run services at those times, or just an invitation to treat? Does the bus pulling up at a stop constitute an offer to carry you, which you accept by boarding the bus? Or, again, is even this stage just an invitation to treat, so that the offer is actually made by you getting on the bus or by handing over money for the ticket? These points may seem academic, but they become important when something goes wrong. If, for example, the bus crashes and you are injured, your ability to sue for breach of contract will depend on whether the contract had actually been completed when the accident occurred.

Although there have been many cases in this area, no single reliable rule has emerged, and it seems that the exact point at which a contract is made depends in each case on the particular facts. For example, in **Denton v GN Railway** (1856) it was said that railway company advertisements detailing the times at and conditions under which trains would run were offers. But in **Wilkie v London Passenger Transport Board** (1947) Lord Greene thought that a contract between bus company and passenger was made when a person intending to travel 'puts himself either on the platform or inside the bus'. The opinion was *obiter* but, if correct, it implies that the company makes an offer of carriage by running the bus or train and the passenger accepts when he or she gets properly on board, completing the contract. Therefore if the bus crashed, an injured passenger could have a claim against the bus company for breach of contract despite not having yet paid the fare or been given a ticket.

However, in **Thornton v Shoe Lane Parking Ltd** (1971) it was suggested that the contract may be formed rather later. If the legal principles laid down in **Thornton** are applied to this factual situation, it would appear that passengers asking for a ticket to their destination are making an invitation to treat. The bus company makes an offer by issuing the tickets, and the passengers accept the offer by keeping the tickets without objection. Fortunately, these questions are not governed solely by the law of contract as some legislation relevant to the field of public transport has since been passed.

There are other less common situations in which the courts will have to decide whether a communication is an offer or merely an invitation to treat. The test used is whether a person watching the proceedings would have thought the party concerned was making an offer or not (the objective approach discussed at p. 5).

▶ How long does an offer last?

An offer may cease to exist under any of the following circumstances.

Specified time

Where an offeror states that an offer will remain open for a specific length of time, it lapses when that time is up (though it can be revoked before that – see p. 16 below).

Reasonable length of time

Where the offeror has not specified how long the offer will remain open, it will lapse after a reasonable length of time has passed. Exactly how long this is will depend upon whether the means of communicating the offer were fast or slow and on its subject matter – for example, offers to buy perishable goods, or a commodity whose price fluctuates daily, will lapse quite quickly. Offers to buy shares on the stock market may last only seconds.

In **Ramsgate Victoria Hotel** *v* **Montefiore** (1866) the defendant applied for shares in the plaintiff company, paying a deposit into their bank. After hearing nothing from them for five months, he was then informed that the shares had been allotted to him, and asked to pay the balance due on them. He refused to do so, and the court upheld his argument that five months was not a reasonable length of time for acceptance of an offer to buy shares, which are a commodity with a rapidly fluctuating price. Therefore the offer had lapsed before the company tried to accept it, and there was no contract between them.

Failure of a precondition

Some offers are made subject to certain conditions, and if such conditions are not in place, the offer may lapse. For example, a person might offer to sell their bike for £50 if they manage to buy a car at the weekend. In **Financings Ltd** *v* **Stimson** (1962) the defendant saw a car for sale at £350 by a second-hand car dealer on 16 March. He decided to buy it on hire-purchase terms. The way that hire-purchase works in such cases is that the finance company buys the car outright from the dealer, and then sells it to the buyer, who pays in instalments. The defendant would therefore be buying the car from the finance company (the plaintiffs), rather than from the dealer. The defendant signed the plaintiff's form, which stated that the agreement would be binding on the finance company only when signed on its behalf. The car dealer did not have the authority to do this, so it had to be sent to the plaintiffs for signing. On 18 March the defendant paid the first instalment of £70. On 24 March the car was stolen from the dealer's premises. It was later found, badly damaged and the defendant no longer wanted to buy it. Not knowing this, on 25 March the plaintiffs signed the written 'agreement'. They subsequently sued the defendant for failure to pay the instalments. The Court of Appeal ruled in favour of the defendant, as the so-called 'agreement' was really an offer to make a contract with the plaintiffs, which was subject to the implied condition that the car remained in much the same state as it was in when the offer was made, until that offer was accepted. The plaintiffs were claiming that they had accepted the offer by signing the document on 24 March. As the implied condition had been broken by then, the offer was no longer open so no contract had been concluded.

Rejection

An offer lapses when the offeree rejects it. If Ann offers to sell Ben her car on Tuesday, and Ben says no, Ben cannot come back on Wednesday and insist on accepting the offer.

Counter offer

A counter offer terminates the original offer. In **Hyde** *v* **Wrench** (1840) the defendant offered to sell his farm for £1,000, and the plaintiff responded by offering to buy it at £950 – this is called making a counter offer. The farm owner refused to sell at that price, and when the plaintiff later tried to accept the offer to buy at £1,000, it was held that this offer was no longer available; it had been terminated by the counter offer. In this situation the offeror can make a new offer on exactly the same terms, but is not obliged to do so.

Requests for information

A request for information about an offer (such as whether delivery could be earlier than suggested) does not amount to a counter offer, so the original offer remains open. In **Stevenson** *v* **McLean** (1880) the defendant made an offer on a Saturday to sell iron to the plaintiffs at a cash on delivery price of 40 shillings, and stated that the offer would remain available until the following Monday. The plaintiffs replied by asking if they could buy the goods on credit. They received no answer. On Monday afternoon they contacted the defendant to accept the offer, but the iron had already been sold to someone else.

When the plaintiffs sued for breach of contract, it was held that their reply to the offer had been merely a request for information, not a counter offer, so the original offer still stood and there was a binding contract.

Death of the offeror

The position is not entirely clear, but it appears that if the offeree knows that the offeror has died, the offer will lapse; if the offeree is unaware of the offeror's death, it probably will not (**Bradbury** v **Morgan** (1862)). So if, for example, A promises to sell her video recorder to B, then dies soon after, and B writes to accept the offer not knowing that A is dead, it seems that the people responsible for A's affairs after death would be obliged to sell the video recorder to B and B would be obliged to pay the price to the executors.

However, where an offer requires personal performance by the offeror (such as painting a picture, or appearing in a film) it will usually lapse on the offeror's death.

Death of the offeree

There is no English case on this point, but it seems probable that the offer lapses and cannot be accepted after the offeree's death by the offeree's representatives.

Withdrawal of offer

The old case of **Payne** v **Cave** (1789) establishes the principle that an offer may be withdrawn at any time up until it is accepted. This is frequently described by lawyers as a 'revocation'. In **Routledge** v **Grant** (1828) the defendant made a provisional offer to buy the plaintiff's house at a specified price, 'a definite answer to be given within six weeks from date'. It was held that, regardless of this provision, the defendant still had the right to withdraw the offer at any moment before acceptance, even though the time limit had not expired.

There are a number of rules about revocation.

Revocation must be communicated

It is not enough for offerors simply to change their mind about an offer; they must notify the offeree that it is being revoked. In **Byrne** v **Van**

Tienhoven (1880) the defendants, a Cardiff company, had, on 1 October, posted a letter to New York offering to sell the plaintiffs 1,000 boxes of tinplates. On receiving the letter on 11 October, the plaintiffs immediately accepted by telegram. Acceptances sent by telegram take effect as soon as they are sent (see p. 25 below for details of the postal rule).

In the meantime, on 8 October, the defendants had written to revoke their offer, and this letter reached the defendants on 20 October. It was held that there was a binding contract, because revocation could only take effect on communication, but the acceptance by telegram took effect as soon as it was sent – in this case nine days before the revocation was received. By the time the second letter reached the plaintiffs, a contract had already been made.

Revocation of an offer does not have to be communicated by the offeror; the communication can be made by some other reliable source. In **Dickinson** *v* **Dodds** (1876) the defendant offered to sell a house to the plaintiff, the offer 'to be left open until Friday, June 12, 9 am'. On 11 June the defendant sold the house to a third party, Allan, and the plaintiff heard about the sale through a fourth man. Before 9 am on 12 June, the plaintiff handed the defendant a letter in which he said he was accepting the offer. It was held by the Court of Appeal that the offer had already been revoked by the communication from the fourth man, so there was no contract. By hearing the news from the fourth man, Dickinson 'knew that Dodds was no longer minded to sell the property to him as plainly and clearly as if Dodds had told him in so many words'.

An offeror who promises to keep an offer open for a specified period may still revoke that offer at any time before it is accepted, unless the promise to keep it open is supported by some consideration from the other party (by providing consideration the parties make a separate contract called an option).

In certain office situations, a great deal of mail may be received daily. Because of the volume, mail does not go directly to the person whose name is on the envelope, but is received, opened and sorted by clerical staff and then distributed to the relevant people. In these situations there may be some difficulty in pinpointing when the information in the letter can be said to be communicated: is it when the letter is received within the company, when it is opened, or when it is actually read by the relevant member of staff? There is no authority on the point but the approach would probably be that communication occurred when the letter was opened, even though there may in those circumstances be no true communication.

There are two main exceptions to the rule that the withdrawal must be communicated to the offeree. First, if an offeree moves to a new address without notifying the offeror, a withdrawal which was delivered to the offeree's last known address will be effective on delivery there. In the same way, where a withdrawal reaches the offeree, but the offeree simply

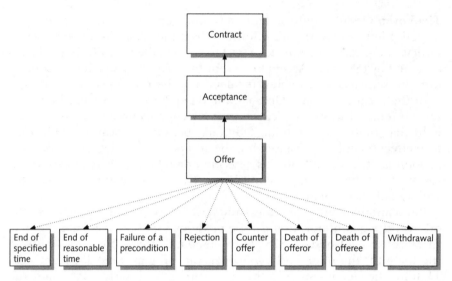

Figure 1.1 Termination of an offer

fails to read it, it probably still takes effect on reaching them (see *The Brimnes* (1975) p. 25 below). This would be the position where a withdrawal by telex or fax reached the offeror's office during normal business hours but was not actually seen or read by the offeree or by any of their staff until some time afterwards.

Second, where a unilateral offer is made to the world at large, to be accepted by conduct, it can probably be revoked without the need for communication if the revocation takes place before performance has begun. For example, if you place a newspaper advertisement offering a reward for the return of something you have lost, and then decide you might actually be better off spending that money on replacing the item, it would probably be impossible for you to make sure that everyone who knew about the offer knows you are withdrawing it – even if you place a notice of withdrawal in the newspaper, you cannot guarantee that everyone concerned will see it. It seems to be enough for an offeror to take reasonable steps to bring the withdrawal to the attention of such persons, even though it may not be possible to ensure that they all know about it. Thus, in the US case of **Shuey** (1875) it was held that an offer made by advertisements in a newspaper could be revoked by a similar advertisement, even though the second advertisement was not read by all the offerees.

Acceptance

Acceptance of an offer means unconditional agreement to all the terms of that offer. Acceptance will often be oral or in writing, but in some cases an offeree may accept an offer by doing something, such as delivering goods in response to an offer to buy. The courts will only interpret conduct as indicating acceptance if it seems reasonable to infer that the offeree acted with the intention of accepting the offer.

In **Brogden** v **Metropolitan Rail Co** (1877) Brogden had supplied the railway company with coal for several years without any formal agreement. The parties then decided to make things official, so the rail company sent Brogden a draft agreement, which left a blank space for Brogden to insert the name of an arbitrator. After doing so and signing the document, Brogden returned it, marked 'approved'.

The company's employee put the draft away in a desk drawer, where it stayed for the next two years, without any further steps being taken regarding it. Brogden continued to supply coal under the terms of the contract, and the railway company to pay for it. Eventually a dispute arose between them, and Brogden denied that any binding contract existed.

The courts held that by inserting the arbitrator's name, Brogden added a new term to the potential contract, and therefore, in returning it to the railway company, he was offering (in fact counter offering) to supply coal under the contract. But when was that offer accepted? The House of Lords decided that an acceptance by conduct could be inferred from the parties' behaviour, and a valid contract was completed either when the company first ordered coal after receiving the draft agreement from Brogden, or at the latest when he supplied the first lot of coal.

Merely remaining silent cannot amount to an acceptance, unless it is absolutely clear that acceptance was intended. In **Felthouse** v **Bindley** (1862) an uncle and his nephew had talked about the possible sale of the nephew's horse to the uncle, but there had been some confusion about the price. The uncle subsequently wrote to the nephew, offering to pay £30 and 15 shillings and saying, 'If I hear no more about him, I consider the horse mine at that price.' The nephew was on the point of selling off some of his property in an auction. He did not reply to the uncle's letter, but did tell the auctioneer to keep the horse out of the sale. The auctioneer forgot to do this, and the horse was sold. It was held that there was no contract between the uncle and the nephew. The court felt that the nephew's conduct in trying to keep the horse out of the sale did not necessarily imply that he intended to accept his uncle's offer – even though the nephew actually wrote afterwards to apologize for the mistake – and so it was not clear that his silence in response to the offer was intended to constitute acceptance. This can be criticized in that it is hard to see how there could have been clearer evidence that the nephew did actually intend to sell, but, on the other hand, there are many situations in which it would be undesirable and confusing for silence to amount to acceptance.

It has been pointed out by the Court of Appeal in **Re Selectmove Ltd** (1995) that an acceptance by silence could be sufficient if it was the offeree who suggested that their silence would be sufficient. Thus in **Felthouse**, if the nephew had been the one to say that if his uncle heard nothing more he could treat the offer as accepted, there would have been a contract.

Unilateral contracts are usually accepted by conduct. If I offer £100 to anyone who finds my lost dog, finding the dog will be acceptance of the offer, making my promise binding – it is not necessary for anyone to contact me and say that they intend to take up my offer and find the dog.

Acceptance must be unconditional

An acceptance must accept the precise terms of an offer. In **Tinn** *v* **Hoffman** (1873) one party offered to sell the other 1,200 tons of iron. It was held that the other party's order for 800 tons was not an acceptance.

Negotiation and the 'battle of the forms'

Where parties carry on a long process of negotiation, it may be difficult to pinpoint exactly when an offer has been made and accepted. In such cases the courts will look at the whole course of negotiations to decide whether the parties have in fact reached agreement at all and, if so, when.

This process can be particularly difficult where the so-called 'battle of the forms' arises. Rather than negotiating terms each time a contract is made, many businesses try to save time and money by contracting on standard terms, which will be printed on company stationery such as order forms and delivery notes. The 'battle of the forms' occurs where one party sends a form stating that the contract is on their standard terms of business, and the other party responds by returning their own form and stating that the contract is on **their** terms.

The general rule in such cases is that the 'last shot' wins the battle. Each new form issued is treated as a counter offer, so that when one party performs its obligation under the contract (by delivering goods for example), that action will be seen as acceptance by conduct of the offer in the last form. In **British Road Services** *v* **Crutchley (Arthur V) Ltd** (1968) the plaintiffs delivered some whisky to the defendants for storage. The BRS driver handed the defendants a delivery note, which listed his company's 'conditions of carriage'. Crutchley's employee stamped the note 'Received under [our] conditions' and handed it back to the driver. The court held that stamping the delivery note in this way amounted to a counter offer, which BRS accepted by handing over the goods. The contract therefore incorporated Crutchley's conditions, rather than those of BRS.

However, a more recent case shows that the 'last shot' will not always succeed. In **Butler Machine Tool Ltd** *v* **Ex-Cell-O Corp** (1979) the defendants wanted to buy a machine from the plaintiffs, to be delivered ten months after the order. The plaintiffs supplied a quotation (which was taken to be an offer), and on this document were printed their standard terms, including a clause allowing them to increase the price of the goods if the costs had risen by the date of delivery (known as a price-variation clause). The document also stated that their terms would prevail over any terms and conditions in the buyers' order. The buyers responded by placing an order, which was stated to be on their own terms and conditions, and these were listed on the order form. These terms did not contain a price-variation clause. The order form included a tear-off acknowledgement slip, which contained the words: 'we accept your order on the terms and conditions thereon' (referring to the order form). The sellers duly returned the acknowledgement slip to the buyers, with a letter stating that the order was being accepted in accordance with the earlier quotation. The acknowledgement slip and accompanying letter were the last forms issued before delivery.

When the ten months were up, the machine was delivered and the sellers claimed an extra £2,892, under the provisions of the price-variation clause. The buyers refused to pay the extra amount, so the sellers sued them for it. The Court of Appeal held that the buyers' reply to the quotation was not an unconditional acceptance, and therefore constituted a counter offer. The sellers had accepted that counter offer by returning the acknowledgement slip, which referred back to the buyers' conditions. The sellers pointed out that they had stated in their accompanying letter that the order was booked in accordance with the earlier quotation, but this was interpreted by the Court of Appeal as referring back to the type and price of the machine tool, rather than to the terms listed on the back of the sellers' document. It merely confirmed that the machine in question was the one originally quoted for, and did not modify the conditions of the contract. The contract was therefore made under the buyers' conditions.

The Court of Appeal also contemplated what the legal position would have been if the slip had not been returned by the sellers. The majority thought that the usual rules of offer and counter offer would have to be applied, which in many cases would mean that there was no contract until the goods were delivered and accepted by the buyer, with either party being free to withdraw before that. Lord Denning MR, on the other hand, suggested that the courts should take a much less rigid approach and decide whether the parties thought they had made a binding contract, and if it appeared that they did, the court should go on to examine the documents as a whole to find out what the content of their agreement might be. This approach has not been adopted by the courts.

Acceptance of unilateral offers

It has generally been assumed that there is no acceptance until the act has been completely performed – so if Ann says to Ben that she will give Ben £5 if Ben washes her car, Ben would not be entitled to the money until the job is finished, and could not wash half the car and ask for

£2.50. What then is the position if your teacher offers a prize for the best essay on contract, and then revokes the offer after the students have started work but before any essays are handed in? Unfortunately, the law gives no clear answer.

In **Luxor (Eastbourne) Ltd** *v* **Cooper** (1941) an owner of land had promised to pay an estate agent £10,000 in commission if the agent was able to find a buyer willing to pay £175,000 for the land. The arrangement was on the terms that are usual between estate agents and their clients, whereby the agent is paid commission if a buyer is found, and nothing if not. The House of Lords held that the owner in the case could revoke his promise at any time before the sale was completed, even after the estate agents had made extensive efforts to find a buyer, just as the estate agent could decide not to try to find a buyer, or to stop trying to do so. Although this decision might appear to support the view that offers of unilateral contracts are freely revocable until performance is complete, it may be more accurately seen as an approach specific to such estate agency arrangements.

In **Daulia Ltd** *v* **Four Millbank Nominees Ltd** (1978) the Court of Appeal stated decisively that once an offeree had started to perform on a unilateral contract, it was too late for the offeror to revoke the offer. It should be noted that this statement was *obiter*, since the court found that the offeree in the case had in fact completed his performance before the supposed revocation.

It now appears that there are some circumstances in which part-performance may amount to acceptance. In **Errington** *v* **Errington** (1952) a father bought a house in his own name for £750, borrowing £500 of the price by means of a mortgage from a building society. He bought the house for his son and daughter-in-law to live in, and told them that if they met the mortgage repayments, the house would be signed over to them once the mortgage was paid off. The couple moved in, and began to pay the mortgage instalments, but they never in fact made a promise to continue with the payments until the mortgage was paid off, which meant that the contract was unilateral.

When the father later died, the people in charge of his affairs sought to withdraw the offer. The Court of Appeal held that it was too late to do this. The part performance by the son and daughter-in-law constituted an acceptance of the contract and the father (or, after his death, his representatives) was bound by the resulting contract unless the son and daughter-in-law ceased to make the payments, in which case the offer was no longer binding.

Specified methods of acceptance

If an offeror states that his or her offer must be accepted in a particular way, then only acceptance by that method or an equally effective one will be binding. To be considered equally effective, a mode of acceptance should not be slower than the method specified in the offer, nor have any disadvantages for the offeror. It was stated in **Tinn** *v* **Hoffman** (1873) that where the offeree was asked to reply 'by return of post', any method which would arrive before return of post would be sufficient.

Where a specified method of acceptance has been included for the offeree's own benefit, however, the offeree is not obliged to accept in that way. In **Yates Building Co Ltd** *v* **J Pulleyn & Sons (York) Ltd** (1975) the sellers stated that the option they were offering should be accepted by 'notice in writing . . . to be sent registered or recorded delivery'. The purchaser sent his acceptance by ordinary letter post, but the court held that the acceptance was still effective. The requirement of registered or recorded delivery was for the benefit of the offeree rather than the offeror (as it ensured that their acceptance was received and that they had proof of their acceptance) and was not therefore mandatory.

The case of **Felthouse** *v* **Bindley** (see p. 19 above) shows that, although the offeror can stipulate how the acceptance is to be made, he or she cannot stipulate that silence shall amount to acceptance. In the same way, if the offeror states that the performance of certain acts by the offeree will amount to an acceptance, and the offeree performs those acts, there will only be an acceptance if the offeree was aware of the terms of the offer and objectively intended their acts to amount to an acceptance. In **Inland Revenue Commissioners** *v* **Fry** (2001) the Inland Revenue claimed over £100,000 of unpaid tax from Mrs Fry. Following negotiations, Mrs Fry wrote to the Inland Revenue enclosing a cheque for £10,000. In her letter she said that if the Inland Revenue accepted her offer of £10,000 in full and final settlement, it should present the cheque for payment. The Inland Revenue cashed the cheque but subsequently informed Mrs Fry that her offer was unacceptable. The High Court held that the Inland Revenue was entitled to the full amount of tax which it had claimed. The court explained that it was fundamental to the existence of a binding contract that there was a meeting of minds. An offer prescribing a mode of acceptance could be accepted by an offeree acting in accordance with that mode of acceptance. However, the Inland Revenue received thousands of cheques each day and there was no evidence that, when it cashed the cheque from Mrs Fry, it knew of the offer. The cashing of the cheque gave rise to no more than a rebuttable presumption of acceptance of the terms of the offer in the accompanying letter. On the evidence, that presumption had been rebutted, as a reasonable observer would not have assumed that the cheque was banked with the intention of accepting the offer in the letter.

An offeror who has requested the offeree to use a particular method of acceptance can always waive the right to insist on that method.

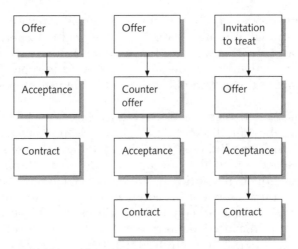

Figure 1.2 Three examples of how a contract can be made

Acceptance must be communicated

An acceptance does not usually take effect until it is communicated to the offeror. As Lord Denning explained in **Entores Ltd** *v* **Miles Far East Corporation** (1955), if A shouts an offer to B across a river, but just as B yells back an acceptance, a noisy aircraft flies over, preventing A from hearing B's reply, no contract has been made. A must be able to hear B's acceptance before it can take effect. The same would apply if the contract was made by telephone, and A failed to catch what B said because of interference on the line; there is no contract until A knows that B is accepting the offer. The principal reason for this rule is that, without it, people might be bound by a contract without knowing that their offers had been accepted, which could obviously create difficulties in all kinds of situations.

Where parties negotiate face to face, communication of the acceptance is unlikely to be a problem; any difficulties tend to arise where the parties are communicating at a distance, for example by post, telephone, telegram, telex, fax or messenger.

Exceptions to the communication rule

There are some circumstances in which an acceptance may take effect without being communicated to the offeror.

Terms of the offer

An offer may state or imply that acceptance need not be communicated to the offeror, although, as **Felthouse** *v* **Bindley** shows, it is not possible to state that the offeree will be bound unless he or she indicates that the offer is not accepted (in other words that silence will be taken as acceptance). This means that offerors are free to expose themselves to the risk of unknowingly incurring an obligation, but may not impose that risk on someone else. It seems to follow from this that if the horse in **Felthouse** *v* **Bindley** had been kept out of the sale for the uncle, and the uncle had then refused to buy it, the nephew could have sued his uncle, who would have been unable to rely on the fact that acceptance was not communicated to him.

Unilateral contracts do not usually require acceptance to be communicated to the offeror. In **Carlill** *v* **Carbolic Smoke Ball Co** (1893) the defendants argued that the plaintiff should have notified them that she was accepting their offer, but the court held that such a unilateral offer implied that performance of the terms of the offer would be enough to amount to acceptance.

Conduct of the offeror

An offeror who fails to receive an acceptance through their own fault may be prevented from claiming that the non-communication means they should not be bound by the contract. In the **Entores** case (1955) it was suggested that this principle could apply where an offer was accepted by telephone, and the offeror did not catch the words of acceptance, but failed to ask for them to be repeated; and in *The Brimnes* (1975), where the acceptance is sent by telex during business hours, but is simply not read by anyone in the offeror's office.

The postal rule

The general rule for acceptances by post is that they take effect when they are posted, rather than when they are communicated. The main reason for this rule is historical, since it dates from a time when communication through the post was even slower and less reliable than it is today. Even now, there is some practical purpose for the rule, in that it is easier to prove that a letter has been posted than to prove that it has been received or brought to the attention of the offeror.

The postal rule was laid down in **Adams** *v* **Lindsell** (1818). On 2 September 1817, the defendants wrote to the plaintiffs, who processed wool, offering to sell them a quantity of sheep fleeces, and stating that they required an answer 'in course of post'. Unfortunately, the defendants did not address the letter correctly, and as a result it did not reach the plaintiffs until the evening of 5 September. The plaintiffs posted their acceptance the same evening, and it reached the defendants on 9 September. It appeared that if the original letter had been correctly addressed, the plaintiffs could have expected a reply 'in course of post' by 7 September. That date came and went, and they had heard nothing from the plaintiffs, so on 8 September they sold the wool to a third party. The issue in the case was whether a contract had been made before the sale to the third party on 8 September. The court held that a contract was concluded as soon as the acceptance was posted, so that the defendants were bound from the evening of 5 September, and had therefore breached the contract by selling the wool to the third party. (Under current law there would have been a contract even without the postal rule, because the revocation of the offer could only take effect if it was communicated to the offeree – selling the wool to a third party without notifying the plaintiffs would not amount to revocation. However, in 1818 the rules on revocation were not fully developed, so the court may well have considered that the sale was sufficient to revoke the offer, which was why an effective acceptance would have to take place before 8 September.)

The postal rule was applied to acceptance by telegram in **Cowan** *v* **O'Connor** (1888), where it was held that an acceptance came into effect when the telegram was placed with the Post Office. These days the Post Office in England no longer offers a telegram service, but the same rule will apply to the telemessage service which replaced it. All the principles listed below concerning postal acceptances are also likely to apply to such telemessages.

Application of the postal rule

Use of the postal service must be reasonable. Only when it is reasonable to use the post to indicate acceptance can the postal rule apply. If the offer does not dictate a method of acceptance, appropriate methods can be inferred from the means used to make the offer. An offer made by post may generally be accepted by post, but it may be reasonable to accept by post even though the offer was delivered in some other way. In **Henthorn** *v* **Fraser** (1892) the defendant was based in Liverpool and the plaintiff lived in Birkenhead. The defendant gave the plaintiff in Liverpool a document containing an offer in Liverpool, and the plaintiff accepted it by posting a letter from Birkenhead. It was held that, despite the offer having been handed over in person, acceptance by post was reasonable because the parties were based in different towns.

Where an offer is made by an instant method of communication, such as telex, fax or telephone, an acceptance by post would not usually be reasonable.

Effect of the postal rule

The postal rule has two main practical consequences:

- A postal acceptance can take effect when it is posted, even if it gets lost in the post and never reaches the offeror. In **Household Fire Insurance** *v* **Grant** (1879) Grant had applied for (and therefore offered to buy) shares in the plaintiff company. The shares were allotted to him and his name was put on the register of shareholders. The company did write to say that the shares had been allotted to Grant, but the letter was lost in the post and he never received it. Some time later the company went into liquidation, and the liquidator claimed from Grant the balance owing on the price of his shares. It was held that Grant was bound to pay the balance, because the contract had been completed when the company's letter was posted.

It is likely that the same rule applies where the letter eventually arrives, but is delayed by postal problems.

- Where an acceptance is posted after the offeror posts a revocation of the offer, but before that revocation has been received, the acceptance will be binding (posted acceptances take effect on posting, posted revocations on communication). This point is illustrated by the cases of **Byrne** *v* **Van Tienhoven** (1880) and **Henthorn** *v* **Fraser** (1892).

Exceptions to the postal rule

Offers requiring communication of acceptance   An offeror may avoid the postal rule by making it a term of their offer that acceptance will only take effect when it is communicated to them. In **Holwell Securities** *v* **Hughes** (1974) the defendants offered to sell some freehold property to the plaintiffs but the offer stated that the acceptance had to be 'by notice in writing'. The plaintiffs posted their acceptance, but it never reached the defendants, despite being properly addressed. The court held that 'notice' meant communication, and therefore it would not be appropriate to apply the postal rule.

Instant methods of communication   When an acceptance is made by an instant mode of communication, such as telephone or telex, the postal rule does not apply. In such cases the acceptor will usually know at once that they have not managed to communicate with the offeror, and will need to try again.

In **Entores** *v* **Miles Far East Corporation** (1955) the plaintiffs were a London company and the defendants were an American corporation with agents in Amsterdam. Both the London company and the defendants' agents in Amsterdam had telex machines, which allow users to type in a message, and have it almost immediately received and printed out by the recipient's machine. The plaintiffs in London telexed the defendants' Amsterdam agents offering to buy goods from them, and the agents accepted, again by telex. The court case arose when the plaintiffs alleged that the defendant had broken their contract and wanted to bring an action against them. The rules of civil litigation stated that they could only bring this action in England if the contract had been made in England. The Court of Appeal held that because telex allows almost instant communication, the parties were in the same position as if they had negotiated in each other's presence or over the telephone, so the postal rule did not apply and an acceptance did not take effect until it had been received by the plaintiffs. Because the acceptance had been received in London, the contract was deemed to have been made there, and so the legal action could go ahead.

This approach was approved by the House of Lords in **Brinkibon** *v* **Stahag Stahl GmbH** (1983). The facts here were similar, except that the offer was made by telex from Vienna to London, and accepted by a telex from London to Vienna. The House of Lords held that the contract was therefore made in Vienna.

In both cases the telex machines were in the offices of the parties, and the messages were received inside normal working hours. In **Brinkibon** the House of Lords said that a telex message sent outside working hours would not be considered instantaneous, so the time and place in which the contract was completed would be determined by the intentions of the parties, standard business practice and, if possible, by analysing where the risk should most fairly lie.

There is no authority on when an acceptance by fax is binding, but as fax machines generally indicate whether or not a message has been successfully transmitted, the logical approach might be to treat an acceptance by fax as effective when sent, unless the sender is aware that the transmission was unsuccessful and was not received by the offeror. Even if the fax received is hard to read, the offeror will usually still know where it has come from, and has the opportunity to request clarification.

Misdirected acceptance Where a letter of acceptance is lost or delayed because the offeree has wrongly or incompletely addressed it through their own carelessness, it seems reasonable that the postal rule should not apply, although there is no precise authority to this effect. Treitel, a leading contract law academic, suggests that a better rule might be that if a badly addressed acceptance takes effect at all, it should do so at the time which is least advantageous to the party responsible for the misdirection.

Withdrawal of postal acceptance
Where the postal rule applies, it seems unlikely that an offeree could revoke a postal acceptance by phone (or some other instant means of communication) before it arrives, though there is no English case on the point. A Scottish case, **Dunmore** *v* **Alexander** (1830) does appear to allow such a revocation, but the court's views were only *obiter* on this point.

▶ Ignorance of the offer

It is generally thought that a person cannot accept an offer of which they are unaware, because in order to create a binding contract, the parties must reach agreement. If their wishes merely happen to coincide, that may be very convenient for both, but it does not constitute a contract and cannot legally bind them. Thus, if Ann advertises a reward for the return of a lost cat and Ben, not having seen or heard of the advertisement, comes across the cat, reads Ann's address on its collar and takes it back to Ann, is Ann bound to pay Ben the reward? No English case has clearly decided this point, and the cases abroad conflict with the main English case. On general principles Ben is probably unable to claim the reward.

In the American case of **Williams** *v* **Carwardine** (1833) the defendant offered a $20 reward for information leading to the discovery of the murderer of Walter Carwardine, and leaflets concerning the reward were distributed in the area where the plaintiff lived. The plaintiff apparently knew about the reward, but when she gave the information it was not in order to receive the money. She believed she had only a short time to live, and thought that giving the information might ease her conscience. The court held that she was entitled to the reward: she was aware of the offer and had complied with its terms, and her motive for doing so was irrelevant. A second US case, **Fitch** *v* **Snedaker** (1868), stated that a person who gives information without knowledge of the offer of a reward cannot claim the reward.

The main English case on this topic is **Gibbons** *v* **Proctor** (1891). A reward had been advertised for information leading to the arrest or conviction of the perpetrator of a particular crime and the plaintiff attempted to claim the reward, even though he had not originally known of the offer. He was allowed to receive the money, but the result does not shed much light on the problem because the plaintiff did know of the offer of reward by the time the information was given on his behalf to the person named in the advertisement.

Following the Australian case of **R** *v* **Clarke** (1927), it would appear that if the offeree knew of the offer in the past but has completely forgotten about it, they are treated as never having known about it. In that case a reward was offered by the Australian Government for information leading to the conviction of the murderers of two policemen. The Government also promised that an accomplice giving such information would receive a free pardon. Clarke was such an accomplice, who panicked and provided the information required in order to obtain the pardon, forgetting, at the time, about the reward. He remembered it later, but it was held that he was not entitled to the money.

Cross offers

These present a similar problem. If Ann writes to Ben offering to sell her television for £50, and by coincidence Ben happens to write offering to buy the television for £50, the two letters crossing in the post, do the letters create a contract between them? On the principles of offer and acceptance it appears not, since the offeree does not know about the offer at the time of the potential acceptance. The point has never been decided in a case but there are *obiter dicta* in **Tinn** *v* **Hoffman** (1873) which suggest there would be no contract.

Time of the formation of the contract

Normally a contract is formed when an effective acceptance has been communicated to the offeree. An exception to this is the postal rule, where the contract is formed at the time the acceptance is posted and there is no need for communication. A further exception to the general rule has been created by s. 11 of the Electronic Communications Act 2000. This establishes the precise time at which an electronic contract is made. Electronic contracts are concluded when the customer has both:

- received an acknowledgement that their acceptance has been received, and
- confirmed their receipt of that acknowledgement.

These communications are taken to be effective when the receiving party is able to access them. Section 11 applies unless the parties agree otherwise. Thus electronic contracts will normally be formed at a later stage than other contracts.

Offer and acceptance implied by the court

Sometimes the parties may be in dispute as to whether a contract existed between them. They may never have signed any written agreement but one party may argue that the offer and acceptance had been made orally or through their conduct. Thus, in **Baird Textile Holdings Ltd** *v* **Marks & Spencer plc (2001)** Marks & Spencer had been in a business relationship with Baird Textile Holdings (BTH) for 30 years. BTH were based in the United Kingdom and had been a major supplier of clothes to Marks & Spencer over the years. In October 1999, Marks & Spencer advised BTH that it was ending all supply arrangements between them with effect from the end of the current production season. BTH brought a legal action against Marks & Spencer alleging that they had a contract with the company, and that a term of this contract had been breached by Marks & Spencer's terminating their supply arrangements in this way. The Court of Appeal held that there was no contract governing the relationship between the two litigants and that therefore Marks & Spencer were not in breach of a contract. It held that a contract should only be implied if it was necessary to do so 'to give business reality to a transaction and to create enforceable obligations between parties who are dealing with one another in circumstances in which one would expect that business reality and those enforceable obligations to exist'. It would not be necessary to imply such a contract if the parties might have acted in just the same way as they did without a contract. Marks & Spencer had preferred not to be bound by a contract so that they had maximum flexibility. For business reasons BTH had accepted this state of affairs.

Auctions, tenders and the sale of land

The above rules of offer and acceptance apply to the sale of land and to sales by tender and auction, but it is useful to know how those rules apply in practice in these fairly common situations.

Auction sales

The parties to an auction sale are the bidder and the owner of the goods. The auctioneer simply provides a service, and is not a party to the contract between buyer and seller. Under the Sale of Goods Act 1979 (s. 57(2)), the general rule is that the auctioneer's request for bids is an invitation to treat, and each bid is an offer. Each bidder's offer lapses as soon as a higher bid is made, and an offer is accepted by the auctioneer (on behalf of the seller) on the fall of the hammer. Any bidder may therefore withdraw a bid before the hammer falls, and the auctioneer may also withdraw the goods on behalf of the seller before that point.

Advertisement of an auction

An advertisement that an auction is to take place at a certain time is a mere declaration of intention and is not an offer which those who attend at the specified time thereby accept. This was decided in **Harris** *v* **Nickerson** (1873), where the plaintiff failed to recover damages for travelling to an auction which was subsequently cancelled.

Auction 'without reserve'

In many cases, sellers at an auction specify reserve prices – the lowest prices they will accept for their goods. If nobody bids at least that amount, the goods are not sold. An auction 'without reserve', on the other hand, means that the goods will be sold to the highest bidder, however low their bid. We have seen that an advertisement announcing that an auction will be held is an invitation to treat and not an offer, but in **Warlow** *v* **Harrison** (1859) it was held that if such an advertisement includes the words 'without reserve', it becomes an offer, from the auctioneers to the public at large, that if the auction is held they will sell to the highest bidder (though it does not oblige the auctioneers to hold the sale in the first place). The offer is accepted when a person makes a bid and when doing so assumes that there is no reserve. That acceptance completes a contract, which is separate from any contract that might be made between the highest bidder and the owner of the property being sold. An auctioneer who then puts a reserve price on any of the lots breaches this separate contract.

In **Barry** v **Davies** (2000) the defendant auctioneers were instructed to sell two engine analysers, which were specialist machines used in the motor trade. The claimant had been told the sale would be 'without reserve'. New machines would cost £14,000 each. The auctioneer attempted to start the bidding at £5,000, then £3,000, but the claimant was the only person interested in the machines and placed a bid of just £200 for each machine. The auctioneer refused to accept that bid and withdrew the machines from the sale. The claimant sought damages for breach of contract and he was awarded £27,600. The defendants' appeal was dismissed and the case of **Warlow** v **Harrison** was followed. A contract existed between the auctioneer and the bidder that the auction would be without reserve, and that contract had been breached.

Tenders

When a large organization, such as a company, hospital, local council or government ministry, needs to find a supplier of goods or services, it will often advertise for tenders. Companies wishing to secure the business then reply to the advertisement, detailing the price at which they are willing to supply the goods or services, and the advertiser chooses whichever is the more favourable quotation. Tenders can also be invited for the sale of goods, in much the same way as bids are made at an auction.

As a general rule, a request for tenders is regarded as an invitation to treat (**Spencer** v **Harding** (1870)), so there is no obligation to accept any of the tenders put forward. The tenders themselves are offers, and a contract comes into existence when one of them is accepted.

In exceptional cases, however, an invitation for tenders may itself be an offer, and submission of a tender then becomes acceptance of that offer. The main example of this is where the invitation to tender makes it clear that the lowest tender (or the highest in the case of tenders to buy) will be accepted. In **Harvela Investments Ltd** v **Royal Trust Co of Canada (CI) Ltd** (1985) the defendants telexed two parties inviting them to submit tenders for the purchase of some shares, stating in the invitation 'we bind ourselves to accept the [highest] offer'. The House of Lords said that the telex was a unilateral offer to accept the highest bid, which would be followed by a bilateral contract with the highest bidder.

An invitation to tender may also be regarded as an offer to consider all tenders correctly submitted, even if it is not an undertaking actually to accept one. In **Blackpool and Fylde Aero Club Ltd** v **Blackpool Borough Council** (1990) the Council invited tenders from people wishing to operate leisure flights from the local airport. Those who wished to submit a tender were to reply to the Town Hall, in envelopes provided, by a certain deadline. The plaintiff returned his bid before the deadline was up, but the Council mistakenly thought it had arrived late. They therefore refused to consider it, and accepted one of the other tenders.

The plaintiff's claim for breach of contract was upheld by the Court of Appeal. Although the Council was not obliged to accept any of the tenders, the terms of their invitation to tender constituted an offer at least to consider any tender which was submitted in accordance with their rules. That offer was accepted by anyone who put forward a tender in the correct manner, and their acceptance would create a unilateral contract, obliging the Council to consider the tender. The Council was in breach of this unilateral contract.

In some cases a tenderer makes what is called a 'referential' tender, offering to top anyone else's bid by a specified amount. This occurred in **Harvela Investments Ltd** *v* **Royal Trust Co of Canada (CI) Ltd** (1985). Some shares were for sale, and the plaintiffs offered C$2,175,000 for them. Another party offered to pay C$2,100,000, or if this was not the highest bid, to pay C$101,000 'in excess of any other offer'. The House of Lords made it clear that the type of 'referential' tender made by the second party was not legally an offer, and was not permissible in such a transaction. Therefore the first defendants were bound to accept the plaintiffs' bid. Their Lordships explained their decision on the grounds that the purpose of a sale by fixed bidding is to provoke the best price from purchasers regardless of what others might be prepared to pay, and that referential bids worked against this. Such bids would also present practical problems if allowed: if everyone made referential bids it would be impossible to define exactly what offer was being made, and if only some parties made bids in that way, the others would not have a valid opportunity to have their offers accepted.

Acceptance of tenders
The implications of choosing to accept a tender depend on what sort of tender is involved.

Specific tenders Where an invitation to tender specifies that a particular quantity of goods is required on a particular date, or between certain dates, agreeing to one of the tenders submitted will constitute acceptance of an offer (the tender), creating a contract. This is the case even if delivery is to be in instalments as and when requested. If a company tenders to supply 100 wheelchairs to a hospital between 1 January and 1 June, their contract is completed when the hospital chooses the company's tender, and delivery must be made between those dates.

Non-specific tenders Some invitations to tender are not specific, and may simply state that certain goods may be required, up to a particular maximum quantity, with deliveries to be made 'if and when' requested. For example, an invitation to tender made by a hospital may ask for tenders to supply up to 1,000 test tubes, 'if and when' required. In such a case, taking up one of the tenders submitted does not amount to acceptance of an offer in the contractual sense, and there is no contract. Once the tender is approved, it becomes what is called a standing offer. The hospital may order no test tubes at all, may spread delivery over several instalments, or may take the whole 1,000 test tubes at once. If the hospital does buy the test tubes or some of them, whether in instalments or all at once, then each time it places an order it accepts the test tube manufacturer's offer, and a separate contract for the amount required is made on each occasion. The result is that when the hospital places an order, the company is bound to supply within the terms of the offer as required, but the company can revoke the offer to supply at any time, and will then only be bound by orders already placed.

This kind of situation would not oblige the hospital to order its test tubes only from the company whose tender it approved. In **Percival** *v* **LCC** (1918) Percival submitted a tender to the LCC for the supply of certain goods 'in such quantities and at such times and in such manner' as the Committee required. The tender was approved, but the LCC eventually placed its orders with other suppliers. Percival claimed damages for breach of contract, but the court held that acceptance of the non-specific tender did not constitute a contract, and the LCC were not obliged to order goods – although Percival was obliged to supply goods which were ordered under the terms of the standing offer, so long as the offer had not been revoked.

The nature of a standing offer was considered in **Great Northern Railway Co** *v* **Witham** (1873). The plaintiffs had invited tenders for the supply of stores, and the defendant made a tender in these words: 'I undertake to supply the Company for twelve months with such quantities of [the specified articles] as the Company may order from time to time.' The railway company accepted this tender, and later placed some orders, which were met by the defendant. The court case arose when the railway company placed an order for goods within the scope of the tender, and the defendant refused to supply them. The court found that the supplying company was in breach of contract because the tender was a standing offer, which the railway company could accept each time it placed an order, thereby creating a contract each time. The standing offer could be revoked at any time, but the tenderer was bound by orders already made, since these were acceptances of his offer and thereby completed a contract.

Sale of land

The standard rules of contract apply to the sale of land (which includes the sale of buildings such as houses), but the courts apply those rules fairly strictly, tending to require very clear evidence of an intention to be bound before they will state that an offer has definitely been made. The main reason for this is simply that land is expensive, and specific areas of land are unique and irreplaceable; damages are therefore often inadequate as a remedy for breach of contract in a sale of land, and it is better to avoid problems beforehand than put them right after a contract is made.

In **Harvey** v **Facey** (1893) the plaintiffs sent the defendants a telegram asking: 'Will you sell us Bumper Hall Pen? Telegraph lowest cash price.' The reply arrived, stating: 'Lowest price for Bumper Hall Pen, £900.' The plaintiffs then sent a telegram back saying: 'We agree to buy Bumper Hall Pen for £900 asked by you. Please send us your title deeds.' On these facts, the Privy Council held that there was no contract. They regarded the telegram from the defendants as merely a statement of what the minimum price would be if the defendants eventually decided to sell. It was therefore not an offer which could be accepted by the third telegram.

In practice the normal procedure for sales involving land is as follows:

Sale 'subject to contract'

First, parties agree on the sale, often through an estate agent. At this stage their agreement may be described as 'subject to contract', and although the effect of these words depends on the intention of the parties, there is a strong presumption against there being a contract at this stage (**Tiverton Estates Ltd** v **Wearwell Ltd** (1975)). If the parties sign a document at this point, it will usually be an agreement to make a more formal contract in the future, rather than a contract to go through with the sale. It was held in **Alpenstow Ltd** v **Regalian Properties plc** (1985) that there were some circumstances in which the courts may infer that the parties intended to be legally bound when signing the original document, even though it was said to be 'subject to contract', but such cases would arise only rarely.

The idea of making an agreement 'subject to contract' is to allow the buyers to check thoroughly all the details of the land (to make sure, for example, that there are no plans to build a new airport just behind the house they are thinking of buying, or that the house is not affected by subsidence).

Exchange of contracts

The next stage is that the buyer and seller agree on the terms of the formal contract (usually through their solicitors, though there is no legal reason why the parties cannot make all the arrangements themselves). Both parties then sign a copy of the contract, and agree on a date on which the contracts will be exchanged, at which point the buyer usually pays a deposit of around 10 per cent of the sale price. Once the contracts are exchanged, a binding contract exists (though it is difficult to see this transaction in terms of offer and acceptance). However, if the contract is breached at this point the buyer can only claim damages – the buyer has no rights in the property itself.

After exchanging contracts, the parties may make further inquiries (checking, for example, that the seller really does own the property), and then the ownership of the land and house is transferred to the buyer, usually by means of a document known as a transfer. At this stage the buyer pays the balance of the purchase price to the seller. The buyer then has rights in the property – in the event of the seller breaching the contract, the buyer can have her property rights enforced in court, rather than just claiming damages.

These principles are illustrated by **Eccles** *v* **Bryant** (1947). After signing an agreement 'subject to contract', the parties consulted their solicitors, who agreed a draft contract. Each party signed the contract, and the buyer forwarded his copy to the seller's solicitor so that contracts could be exchanged. However, the seller changed his mind about the sale, and his solicitor informed the buyer's solicitor that the property had been sold to another buyer. The buyer tried to sue for breach of contract, but the Court of Appeal held that the negotiations were subject to formal contract, and the parties had not intended to be bound until they exchanged contracts. No binding obligations could arise before this took place. The court did not say when the exchange would be deemed to have taken place – that is, whether it was effective on posting of the contracts, or on receipt. In many cases a contract will specify when an exchange will be considered complete, by stating, for example, that the contract will be binding when the contracts are actually delivered.

How important are offer and acceptance?

Although offer and acceptance can provide the courts with a useful technique for assessing at what point an agreement should be binding, what the courts are really looking to judge is whether the parties have come to an agreement, and there are some cases in which the rules on offer and acceptance give little help.

An example of this type of situation is **Clarke** *v* **Dunraven** (1897), which concerned two yacht owners who had entered for a yacht race. The paperwork they completed in order to enter included an undertaking to obey the club rules, and these rules contained an obligation to pay for 'all damages' caused by fouling. During the manoeuvring at the start of the race, one yacht, the *Satanita*, fouled another, the *Valkyrie*, which sank as a result. The owner of the *Valkyrie* sued the owner of the *Satanita* for the cost of the lost yacht, but the defendant claimed that he was under no obligation to pay the whole cost, and was only liable to pay the lesser damages laid down by a statute which limited liability to £8 for every ton of the yacht. The plaintiff claimed that entering the competition in accordance with the rules had created a contract between the competitors, and this contract obliged the defendant to pay 'all damages'.

Clearly it was difficult to see how there could be an offer by one competitor and acceptance by the other, since their relations had been with the yacht club and not with each other. There was obviously an offer and an acceptance between each competitor and the club, but was there a contract between the competitors? The House of Lords held that there was, on the basis that 'a contract is concluded when one party has communicated to another an offer and that other has accepted it or when the parties have united in a concurrent expression of intention to create a legal obligation'. Therefore responsibility for accidents was governed by the race rules, and the defendant had to pay the full cost of the yacht.

There are problems in analysing the contract between the entrants to the race in terms of offer and acceptance. It seems rather far-fetched to imagine that, on starting the race, each competitor was making an offer to all the other competitors and simultaneously accepting their offers – and in any case, since the offers and acceptances would all occur at the same moment, they would be cross offers and would technically not create a contract.

As we have seen, contracts for the sale of land are also examples of agreements that do not usually fall neatly into concepts of offer and acceptance. We will also see later that the problems arising from the offer and acceptance analysis are sometimes avoided by the courts using the device of collateral contracts (see p. 224 below).

Problems with offer and acceptance

Artificiality

Clearly there are situations in which the concepts of offer and acceptance have to be stretched, and interpreted rather artificially, even though it is obvious that the parties have reached an agreement. In **Gibson** *v* **Manchester City Council** (1979) Lord Denning made it clear that he was in favour of looking at negotiations as a whole, in order to determine whether there was a contract, rather than trying to impose offer and acceptance on the facts, but his method has largely been rejected by the courts as being too uncertain and allowing too wide a discretion.

Revocation of unilateral offers

The problem of whether a unilateral offer can be accepted by part-performance has caused difficulties for the courts. It can be argued that since the offeree has not promised to complete performance, they are free to stop at any time, so the offeror should be equally free to revoke the offer at any time. But this would mean, for example, that if A says to B, 'I'll pay you £100 if you paint my living room', A could withdraw the offer even though B had painted all but one square foot of the room, and pay nothing.

This is generally considered unjust, and various academics have expressed the view that in fact an offer cannot be withdrawn once there has been substantial performance. American academics have contended that the offeror can be seen as making two offers: the main offer that the price will be paid when the act is performed, and an implied accompanying offer that the main offer will not be revoked once performance has begun. On this assumption, the act of starting performance is both acceptance of the implied offer, and consideration for the secondary promise that the offer will not be withdrawn once performance begins. An offeror who does attempt to revoke the offer after performance has started may be sued for the breach of the secondary promise.

In England this approach has been considered rather artificial. Sir Frederick Pollock has reasoned that it might be more realistic to say that the main offer itself is accepted by beginning rather than completing performance, on the basis that acceptance simply means agreement to the terms of the offer, and there are many circumstances in which beginning performance will mean just that. Whether an act counts as beginning performance, and therefore accepting the offer, or whether it is just preparation for performing will depend on the facts of the case – so, for example, an offer of a reward for the return of lost property could still be revoked after someone had spent time looking for the property without success, but not after they had actually found it and taken steps towards returning it to the owner. This principle was adopted in 1937 by the Law Revision Committee.

Revocation of offers for specific periods

The rule that an offer can be revoked at any time before acceptance even if the offeror has said it will remain open for a specified time could be considered unfairly biased in favour of the offeror, and makes it difficult for the offeree to plan their affairs with certainty.

In a Working Paper published in 1975, the Law Commission recommended that where an offeror promises not to revoke the offer for a specified time, that promise should be binding, without the need for consideration, and if it is broken the offeree should be able to sue for damages.

An 'all or nothing' approach

The 'all or nothing' approach of offer and acceptance is not helpful in cases where there is clearly not a binding contract under that approach, and yet going back on agreements made would cause great hardship or inconvenience to one party. The problems associated with housebuying are well known – the buyer may go to all the expense of a survey and solicitor's fees, and may even have sold their own house, only to find that the seller withdraws the house from sale, sells it to someone else, or demands a higher price – generally known as 'gazumping'. So long as all this takes place before contracts are exchanged, the buyer has no remedy at all (though the Government is proposing to legislate to deal with some of these specific problems). Similarly, in a commercial situation, pressure of time may mean that a company starts work on a potential project before a contract is drawn up and signed. They will be at a disadvantage if in the end the other party decides not to contract.

Objectivity

The courts claim that they are concerned with following the intention of the parties in deciding whether there is a contract, yet they make it quite clear that they are not actually seeking to discover what **was** intended, but what, looking at the parties' behaviour, an 'officious bystander' might assume they intended. This can mean that even though the parties were actually in agreement, no contract results, as was the case in **Felthouse** *v* **Bindley** – the nephew had asked for the horse to be kept out of the sale because he was going to sell it to his uncle, but because he did not actually communicate his acceptance, there was no contract.

▶ ANSWERING QUESTIONS

1 At 9.00 am on Monday 13 August, Maurice, a car dealer, sends a telex to Austin offering to sell him a rare vintage car for £50,000. Austin receives the telex at 9.15 am and telexes his acceptance at 1.00 pm. Austin is aware that Maurice's office is closed for lunch between 1.00 and 2.00 pm. On his return to the office, Maurice does not bother to check whether he has received a telex from Austin and at 2.30 pm receives an offer for the car from Ford, which he accepts. At 4.00 pm Austin hears from another car dealer that Maurice has sold the car to Ford. He is advised that it will cost him an additional £2,000 to buy a similar car and he immediately sends Maurice another telex demanding that the original car be sold to him. Maurice receives this telex at 5.00 pm, at the same time as he reads the acceptance telex.

Advise Austin of his legal position and what remedies, if any, are open to him.
Oxford

Austin clearly wishes to establish that, at some point, he made a binding contract with Maurice; your task is to pinpoint when, if at all, that contract was made, using the rules of offer and acceptance. The clearest way to do this is to take each communication in turn, and consider its legal effect.

Maurice's first telex is clearly an offer; does Austin validly accept it? The general rule is that acceptance takes effect on communication; the application of this rule to telexed acceptances is contained in the cases of **Entores** and **Brinkibon**. Considering that the telex was sent outside working hours, when should it take effect, and considering the factors mentioned in **Brinkibon** – intentions of the parties, standard business practice – where should the risk lie? Obviously there is no clear answer, but in assessing where the risk should lie, you might take into account the fact that it seems reasonable for Austin to assume the telex would be read shortly after the lunch hour was finished, and to expect Maurice to check whether any reply had been received. This is relevant because in other cases on communication, the courts seem reluctant to bail out parties who fail to receive messages through their own fault (such as the requirement that telephone callers should ask for clarification if they cannot hear the other party – **Entores**). If Austin's telex acceptance is deemed to take effect when the telex is sent, a binding contract exists between them at that point, and this will take priority over the contract made with Ford. You should then consider the position if the rule that acceptance only takes effect on communication is strictly applied.

The next relevant communication is the other car dealer telling Austin that the car has been sold; **Dickinson v Dodds** makes it plain that information from a third party can amount to a revocation, and if this is the case, the offer ceases to be available and there is no contract between Austin and Maurice. However, in **Dickinson v Dodds** the message from the third party was such that the revocation was as clear as if the offeror had said it himself; if for any reason this was not the case here (if the dealer was known to be untrust-worthy, for example), there would be no revocation, and the offer would still be available for acceptance at 5 pm, at which point the contract would be made.

The issue of remedies is discussed fully in Chapter 15, but, assuming a contract was made, Austin is likely to be limited to claiming damages. Maurice could only be forced to sell the car if the courts granted specific performance, and this is only done when damages would be an inadequate way of putting the plaintiff in the position they should have enjoyed if the contract had been performed as agreed. Here this could be done by allowing Austin to claim the difference between the car's price and the cost of a replacement.

2 Peter's car has been stolen. He places an advertisement in the Morriston *Evening News* stating that a reward of £1,000 will be given to any person who provides information leading to the recovery of the car – provided the reward is claimed by 1 January. Andrew, a policeman, finds the car, which has suffered severe accident damage. His best friend Kelvin tells him about the reward and Andrew applies for it by a letter posted on 30 December. The letter arrives at Peter's house on 2 January.

Advise Andrew whether he has a contractual right to the reward. *WJEC*

This question concerns the issue of offer and acceptance and consideration in unilateral contracts. You first need to consider whether Peter's advertisement is an offer. It is worth pointing out that not all advertisements are seen as offers, although in this case the issue is fairly straightforward as there are several cases in which advertisements proposing unilateral contracts, and specifically involving rewards, have been recognized as offers.

The fact that Andrew did not see the advertisement but was told about it by a friend seems to raise the issue of whether an offer can be accepted by someone who does not know about it. The cases on this matter are inconclusive, but the fact that Andrew does know about the reward by the time he applies for it would seem to avoid the problem.

The next issue is whether Andrew applies for the reward in time. As you know, acceptance does not usually take effect until it is communicated, but acceptances sent by post may take effect on posting – the postal rule. The postal rule will apply so long as it is reasonable to submit the application by post, and here there seems no reason why it should not be. This means that the offer is accepted in time, even though the letter arrives after the specified closing date.

However, there is another important issue to examine: consideration (discussed in Chapter 6). Since Andrew is a policeman, it could be argued that finding the car and informing the owner of its whereabouts is no more than his public duty. In order to have provided consideration for the reward, he would need to have gone beyond this, as explained in cases such as **Glasbrook Brothers** v **Glamorgan County Council** and **Harris** v **Sheffield United** (see p. 73).

3 Critically evaluate what in law will amount to an 'offer'. *OCR*

Your introduction could start with a definition of an offer, which is stated at p. 10 to be a communication which indicates the terms on which the offeror is prepared to make a contract and gives a clear indication that the offeror intends to be bound by those terms if they are accepted by the offeree. Your introduction could also put the concept of an offer into the wider context of the principle of freedom of contract. Contract law's emphasis on the requirement of an offer is an example of the belief that the parties should be free to make contracts on any terms they choose.

You could then move on to distinguishing the concept of an offer from an invitation to treat. You might start by looking at bilateral contracts and examine the approach of the courts to the specific scenarios of advertisements, shopping, timetables and tickets for transport, tenders (p. 32), auctions (p. 31) and the sale of land (p. 34). Offers for unilateral contracts could then be considered, and in particular the case of **Carlill** v **Carbolic Smoke Ball Co**.

The next stage of your answer could contain an examination of how long an offer lasts (p. 14).

The question requires you to 'critically evaluate' and it will therefore not be enough to simply describe the law. One of the problem areas has been the 'battle of the forms' (p. 20), and you could look closely at cases such as **Butler Machine Tool Ltd** v **Ex-Cell-O Corp**. The case of **Clarke** v **Dunraven** (p. 36) provides an example of the type of scenario which does not fit comfortably within the concept of offer (and acceptance). Other criticisms of the law on offers can be found at p. 37 under the subheading 'Problems with offer and acceptance'.

Unit 6:   Business Decision Making

Learning hours: 60

NQF level 4:   BTEC Higher National — H2

Content Selected: Smailes and McGrane, Essential Business Statistics, Chapter 1

Introduction from the Qualification Leader

This unit looks at sources and techniques for collecting data as well as formats and appropriate software. Chapter 1 has been selected as background reading to outcome 1 as it introduces some elementary statistical concepts.

Description of unit

In business, good decision making requires the effective use of information. This unit gives learners the opportunity to examine a variety of sources and develop techniques for four aspects of information: data gathering, data storage, and the tools available to create useful information and present it.

Computers are used in business for much of this and thus the appreciation and use of appropriate IT software is central to the completion of this unit. Specifically, learners will use spreadsheets and other software for data analysis and the preparation of information. The use of spreadsheets for the manipulation of numbers, and understanding of how to apply the results, are seen as more important than the mathematical derivation of formulae used. They will also gain an appreciation of information systems currently used at all levels in an organisation as aids to decision making.

Summary of learning outcomes

To achieve this unit a learner must:

1   Use a variety of **sources for the collection of data**, both primary and secondary

2   Apply a range of **techniques to analyse data** effectively for business purposes

3   Produce **information in appropriate formats** for decision making in an organisational context

4   Use **software-generated information** to make decisions at operational, tactical and strategic levels in an organisation.

Content

1 **Sources for the collection of data**

   Primary sources: survey methodology, questionnaire design, sample frame, acceptance sampling methods, sample error

   Secondary sources: internet research, government and other published data, by-product data

2 **Techniques to analyse data**

   Representative values: mean, median, mode, calculation from raw data and frequency distributions and using the results to draw valid conclusions

   Measures of dispersion: maximum, minimum, standard deviation for small and large samples; typical uses – statistical process eg control, buffer stock levels

   Calculation: use of quartiles, percentiles, correlation coefficient

3 **Information in appropriate formats**

   Creation and interpretation of graphs using spreadsheets: line, pie, bar charts and histograms

   Scatter (XY) graphs and linear trend lines: extrapolation for forecasting – reliability

   Use of appropriate presentation software and techniques and report writing

4 **Software-generated information**

   Management information systems: computers and information processing tools for operational, tactical and strategic levels of the organisation

   Inventory control: economic order quantity, continuous and periodic review, Pareto analysis, material requirements, planning for manufacturing

   Project management: networking and critical path analysis, Gantt and Pert charts

   Financial tools: indices – discounted cash flow, internal rates of return (IRR function)

Outcomes and assessment criteria

Outcomes	Assessment criteria for pass To achieve each outcome a learner must demonstrate the ability to:
1 Use a variety of **sources for the collection of data**, both primary and secondary	• prepare and implement a plan for the collection of primary and secondary data for a given business problem • describe and justify the survey methodology and frame used • develop and use a questionnaire and justify its design for a particular purpose
2 Apply a range of **techniques to analyse data** effectively for business purposes	• create information for decision making by summarising data using representative values, and use the results to draw valid and useful conclusions in a business context • analyse data using measures of dispersion, and use to inform a given business scenario • calculate quartiles, percentiles, correlation coefficient, and use to draw useful conclusions in a business context
3 Produce **information in appropriate formats** for decision making in an organisational context	• using data from a given business scenario, prepare a range of graphs using spreadsheets – line, pie, bar charts and histograms, and draw valid conclusions based on the information derived • use trend lines in spreadsheet graphs to assist in forecasting for specified business information and thus inform decision making • prepare a business presentation using suitable software and techniques to disseminate information effectively and persuasively • prepare a formal business report
4 Use **software-generated information** to make decisions at operational, tactical and strategic levels in an organisation	• review management information systems and suggest appropriate information processing tools for operational, tactical and strategic levels of the organisation • review and evaluate inventory control systems in an organisation • prepare a spreadsheet to enable material requirements planning and calculate economic order quantities • prepare a project plan for an activity and determine the critical path • use financial tools – discounted cash flow and internal rates of return (IRR function) to evaluate the financial viability of proposed investments

CHAPTER 1

Collecting data

LEARNING OBJECTIVES

- To introduce some elementary statistical concepts and discuss available information sources;
- To discuss the different ways in which primary data is collected;
- To introduce and discuss the importance of sampling in the design of a survey;
- To consider some points in the formulation of questionnaires.

Introduction

Businesses need information to make decisions; part of this information will be 'statistical'.

A dictionary definition states that statistics are numerical facts collected systematically, arranged and studied.

For decision makers, the primary role of statistics is to provide them with the methods for obtaining and converting data (values, facts, observations, measurements) into useful information. Diagrammatically this can be seen in Figure 1.1.

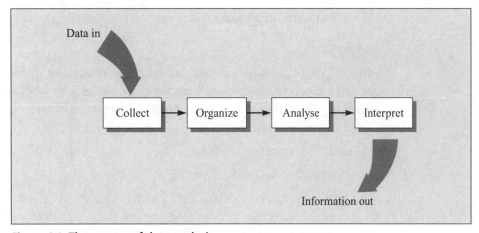

Figure 1.1 **The process of data analysis**

1

1.1   Types of data

Data comes in different forms, each of which is dealt with slightly differently on conversion to information. The main groups are shown in Figure 1.2 and further defined below.

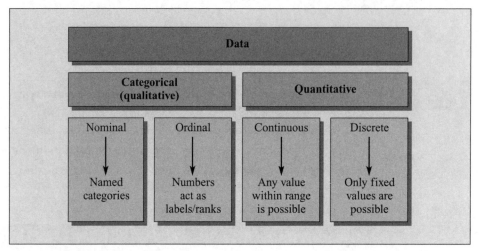

Figure 1.2 **Types of data**

Categorical (qualitative) data

Nominal data

These are data which can be divided into *non-measurable* named categories, for example colours of eyes, type of accommodation, makes of car and so on. Or the colours of shoes worn by 10 students in a lecture:

blue, brown, black, black, white, brown, red, black, black, white

Here, the results are shown in their raw form, a simple list.

Ordinal data

This is where numbers can act as labels or ranks. As the name suggests, it involves data representing some element of order. A year label would be a classic example. The classification of this type of data often causes confusion, as illustrated in the following example:

Levels of service are graded

1: Excellent   2: Good   3: Poor   4: Very poor

The words themselves (excellent, good etc.) are classified as nominal data. However, the accompanying codings are numbers specifically acting as ranks so these would be classified as ordinal data.

2

Note that there is a difference between ordering and coding. In the example opposite on shoe colours the colours could have been coded 1: black, 2: blue etc. but these numbers would *not* represent ordinal data because they do not give an order to the shoe colours.

Quantitative data

These are data which are measured, counted or quantified in some way. They can be divided into categories or classes according to their measurement. This type of data can be further subdivided into two types: continuous data and discrete data.

Continuous data

Continuous data are quantitative data for which any value within a continuous range of values is possible. It generally applies to data that are measured (e.g., heights, wages, times, weights). There is often debate about whether variables such as age and money should be classed as continuous data. In these cases common sense, with justification, prevails.

Table 1.1 **A table to show the heights of 80 people**

Height (cm)	Number* of people
150 to less than 160	12
160 to less than 170	24
170 to less than 180	28
180 to less than 190	16

Note: * The word 'frequency' is generally used to represent the number in each of the listed categories, and this term will be used from now on.

Consider Table 1.1. Here, height is the variable of interest.

Discrete data

These are quantitative data for which only certain fixed values (usually integers) are possible, for example counts, number of messages on an answerphone, number of visits to London and so on. Another example, with results shown in their raw form, follows:

Number of jewellery items worn by 15 students:

4, 5, 1, 0, 2, 3, 6, 2, 3, 0, 2, 4, 2, 0, 2

Table 1.2 shows the number of letters received each morning over a 30 day period. Here, the variable of interest is the number of letters.

Table 1.2 **Number of letters received over a 30 day period**

Number of letters each morning	Frequency
1	12
2	9
3	5
4	4

REVIEW ACTIVITY 1

State whether the following data are discrete, continuous, nominal or ordinal.

(a)   Daily temperatures in central Newcastle.

(b)   Days of the week.

(c)   Number of products sold by each shop in a chain of supermarkets.

(d)   Position in the music charts of UK singles.

Working:

Answers on page 215.

1.2   Sources of information

There are two basic sources of information, primary and secondary.

Primary data

These are data which have been collected specifically for a particular purpose.

Everyone at some time or other will have taken part in a data collection process. Every form filled in provides primary data to someone somewhere.

Often the information provided (say from questionnaires, interviews and feedback forms) is only collected from a relatively small number of people. This is called a **sample**. In much rarer circumstances (for example the 10 yearly UK census) data may be collected from the population, or as many people in the country as it is possible to reach. A **population** need not be made up of every person living in the UK or even people themselves. Populations may be, for example, every chocolate bar produced by a factory using a batch of raw materials, salmon at a fish farm or all employees at a large firm.

4

The word **census** is used to describe the collection of data from the complete population.

The word **survey** describes the collection of data from a sample selected from a population. Samples are generally used as they are a more economical and practical method of data collection.

Data collected from a census or survey are known as **primary data**. The different ways in which such data are collected and how survey samples are determined will be discussed later in this chapter.

The gathering of primary data can be very costly and time consuming, particularly in the case of a census. Because of this census data is most commonly collected by governments or specialist market research companies who then make the information more widely available to others. It is at this stage that the data become known as **secondary data**.

Secondary data

These are data, originally collected for one project, but which then can be used for another purpose.

In the UK the Government Statistical Service holds most nationally published data. There are numerous government publications which include:

- *Social Trends*: an analysis and breakdown of many aspects of British life and work;
- *Financial Statistics*: key financial and monetary statistics within the UK;
- *Economic Trends*: a compilation of the main economic indicators.

Many other government publications are based on data which have been collected from surveys. Listed below are brief descriptions of some of these surveys.

- The *Family Expenditure Survey* (*FES*) investigates the income and spending patterns of about 7000 households in the UK. The population size is approximately 22 million and the survey is conducted annually.
- The *Survey of Retail Prices*, carried out by the Department of Employment, provides around 150,000 prices which are used in the calculation of the Retail Price Index (RPI). Population size is very difficult to estimate. The survey is conducted monthly.
- The *New Earnings Survey* (*NES*) collects information on the earnings of about 180,000 people. Population size is approximately 20 million and the survey is conducted annually.

Note that in the surveys where the population size is known the sample is less than 1% of the total population. The choice of sample size will be considered later in this chapter.

5

Other useful sources of secondary data include company and bank reviews, *The Employment Gazette*, *The Economist* and so on. Nowadays computing sources of secondary data are becoming ever more popular, for example Datastream, Prestel, the Internet and even Ceefax.

Of course secondary data can also be drawn from many other sources, and some of the spreadsheet exercises in this book will demonstrate that even a simple spreadsheet file can be a secondary data source.

1.3 Primary data collection methods

Data analysis often involves manipulation or work with data which have been collected from a survey: for that reason it is important to ensure that the collection of primary data is carried out in a statistically sound way, otherwise results may be biased. In the next sections, methods of collecting primary data will be examined.

Postal questionnaires

This is where a questionnaire is sent – usually through the post – to the desired sample. It is probably the most popular data collection method as it is very easy to make contact with respondents over a wide geographical area and is inexpensive to administer. Once the questionnaire has been received the respondents generally have a period of time in which to answer. This is particularly advantageous if 'non-instant recall' information is required. However, the method often results in very low return rates and, because there is no personal contact, it is impossible to probe for further information on interesting responses or to give clarification on any questions which may be misinterpreted.

Personal interviews

This procedure usually requires a trained interviewer going out and asking a prepared set of questions, either in a public place (for example stopping people on the street to take part in a political opinion poll) or at the respondent's home or place of work. Because of the involvement of a trained individual, some of the problems of postal questionnaires can be avoided. Ambiguous questions can be explained, interesting responses can be followed up and as the interviewer can encourage participation, the response rates are generally higher. But, because of the human contact, this method is very expensive (salary, training, transport), especially if a wide geographical cover is required. Also, accurate results rely heavily on the interviewer's expertise.

6

Telephone interview

This could be considered as almost a compromise between a postal questionnaire and a personal interview. There is still personal contact, with the added bonus of being able to directly enter responses on to a computer, if such facilities are available. But, in this case, there is an immediate bias as people who do not own a phone are excluded from the sample; also one is never sure who is responding at the other end of the telephone line.

Observation

This is the main method employed when the population of interest does not consist of people or require people's responses. An example of an observational survey is a traffic survey. Again, the method relies heavily on the skills of the observer, and owing to its nature can be the most time consuming (in terms of human participation) when observation of irregular events is required.

1.4　Estimation of sample size

As mentioned previously, the sample size may be very small in relation to the overall population. In fact there is no precise way in which an optimal sample size can be calculated for any particular survey. However, there are two useful statistical facts which should be kept in mind:

- the larger the size of the sample, the more *accurate* the information on the population will be;

- above a certain size, little *extra* information about a population can be gained yet costs in time and money increase.

Without becoming too technical, common sense is used in conjunction with any information already known and details about the information sought to estimate an appropriate sample size. This will be illustrated with some scenarios and suggestions of appropriate sample sizes.

EXAMPLE 1.1

The IT resource manager of a large company wishes to do a quick market research exercise on employees' attitudes towards the printing facilities provided.

In this case, no particular specialist information is required, the results will probably have no major impact on the employees themselves and, knowing that they all use the IT facilities regularly, a sample size of, say, between 50 and 100 would be sufficient.

7

EXAMPLE 1.2

A university is considering extending the teaching week to include Saturday mornings and wishes to receive some staff and student views on this.

In this case, the outcome of the survey could bring about a major change in the university's working environment. Because of this it would be advisable to find out the population size and select between 20% and 30% of the population (staff and students) to be canvassed.

1.5 Choosing a suitable, representative sample

In the same way as selecting a suitable sample size, common sense is the most important factor in ensuring a sample is representative.

EXAMPLE 1.3

You are working for a building society and have been asked to find out the current average selling price for a three bedroom, semi-detached house in the north-east of England.

In this case you could *not* simply go into the nearest estate agent and pick up details on say 20 (or even 70) such houses and expect to have a representative sample for the whole of the area of interest.

EXAMPLE 1.4

A students' union wishes to gauge students' opinions of the catering facilities provided in the union building.

In this case it would be reasonable to assume that asking, say, 50–100 students as they leave the union building would give a sufficiently representative sample as all would probably have an interest in the catering facilities.

1.6 Sampling methods

A number of methods are available to try and achieve a representative sample of the population and these are described below.

Simple random sampling

The key to this method is that every member of the population must have an equal chance of being included in the sample. For small populations, a method such as 'drawing from a hat' would achieve this. For larger populations, each

8

member of the population is usually given a unique identification number and then random numbers are generated (often using a computer). The sample is then made up of the population members whose numbers match those generated. The method 'feels' fair, and has no bias. However, it might be difficult to contact all of the chosen sample (say if there is a wide geographical spread in the data) and (simply through chance) an unrepresentative sample may occur.

Stratified random sampling

This method is very similar to simple random sampling, but is used where it is thought that the population contains distinct groups who might have different views about the issues of interest (for example it might be thought that car owners and cyclists/pedestrians would have different views about the introduction of car control measures in a city centre). To overcome the danger of a sample accidentally being unrepresentative, the sample can be stratified according to these groups so that it has approximately the same proportions as the population (e.g., if there are 80% car owners and 20% cyclists/pedestrians in the population then the ratio of 4:1 should be reflected in the sample). For each 'stratum', the sample members are selected randomly (as above for simple random sampling). It is a comparatively unbiased sampling method and should give a representative sample. Again, however, it is necessary to have good access to the population of interest and stratification will add costs to the survey process.

Systematic sampling

Again this is similar to simple random sampling except that instead of picking a member of the sample by using a random number generator, the data are assumed to be in random order and every nth member is selected where n is given by

$$\text{(population size)} \div \text{(desired sample size)}$$

For example if a sample of 5 were required from a list of 30 people every 6th person could be chosen. Note that it is not necessary to start with the first person on the list – the start point should be chosen randomly. Thus the sample might contain the people numbered 1, 7, 13, 19 and 25 – or 2, 8, 14, 20 and 26 – or 3, 9, 15, 21 and 27 etc. It is an easy method to use, and can be useful if the exact population is not known (e.g., all users of a bank's cash machines on a particular day would be hard to define in advance, but every 15th customer could easily be questioned). Care must be taken to ensure that the sample is not biased (e.g., if every 5th item is taken from a production line with 5 machines, does that mean that the same machine is sampled each time?).

Cluster sampling

This method is frequently used when the population items of interest are widely spread and it is desirable to ensure that the sample elements are grouped together in some way (perhaps geographically or over a short period of time).

9

For example, if a retailer wanted to interview a sample of shopkeepers it would make sense to randomly select two or three sales areas first. Every shopkeeper within those areas could then be interviewed: this would avoid the selection of a number of isolated shopkeepers scattered across the country. Clearly this is a useful method for widely spread geographical data where the population is not defined exactly. Again care must be taken to ensure that bias does not occur.

Quota sampling

Quota sampling is usually used where interviewing is the main method of data collection; the aim is similar to that for stratified sampling in that it is desirable to make sure the composition of the sample matches that in the population. The interviewer is given a 'predetermined' sample profile where the numbers of interviewees in each category are chosen to match the population proportions. The interviewer then selects people from the passing population to match the required numbers in each category. For example, on the basis of Table 1.3 an interviewer for a political opinion poll is required to sample 40 people in total: two of these will be professional females (social class A/B aged between 45 and 64, etc.). This will have been chosen so that the proportion in the sample ($\frac{2}{40} = 5\%$) is similar to that in the original population.

Table 1.3 **Interview quotas for a political opinion poll**

Social class	A/B		C		D/E	
Age/Sex	M	F	M	F	M	F
18–29	0	0	3	1	2	2
30–44	1	1	2	1	4	3
45–64	2	2	3	1	2	2
65 or over	1	1	2	1	3	0

This method tends to have good response rates because the interviewer achieves the quota set – non-respondents are ignored and other people are chosen to replace them. However, it is very reliant on the interviewer, and bias could occur as it is a non-random technique.

Multistage sampling

Multistage sampling is a technique which is used for producing a representative sample from a widespread population – in similar situations to those discussed earlier for cluster sampling. However, in this case the process continues down to selection of the individual sampling units (rather than groups as for cluster sampling). This is done by splitting the sampling process into stages and using the most relevant of the sampling techniques already listed to each of these different stages. For example, a large food manufacturer wishing to conduct a national

10

survey into the lifestyle and eating habits of consumers, to provide information for the possible launch of a pre-prepared food range, might use a three-stage survey to cover the whole of the country.

- *Stage 1* (*primary sampling units*): Split the UK into a number of regions (e.g. TV regions) and then randomly select a small number of these.

- *Stage 2* (*secondary sampling units*): Taking each of the selected regions, randomly sample sub-regions (perhaps parliamentary constituencies).

- *Stage 3* (*tertiary sampling units*): Individual households could then be selected by using systematic sampling from the electoral register.

This is another technique (like cluster sampling) which is very useful for widely spread data. Careful thought is necessary at the various sample stages to avoid the risk of bias.

REVIEW ACTIVITY 2

Table 1.4 is a seminar group listing for students on the AR101 Introduction to Aromatherapy unit. With the aid of the list of random numbers below you are required to select a sample of 5 people, who will be given a free massage by the tutor, using:

(a) Simple random sampling.

(b) Stratified random sampling based on gender.

(c) Systematic random sampling.

Table 1.4 Seminar group listing for students on Aromatherapy unit

Surname	Forename	Surname	Forename
Black	Lynn	North	John
Kirk	Tim	Fox	Malcolm
Hughes	Jim	Peters	Sue
Hobson	Anne	Howe	Roy
Dixon	Patrick	Morris	Karen
Carr	Bill	Philipson	Gail
Murray	John	Plant	Vicki
Smith	Alan	Stewart	Angela
Thompson	Ivor	Ward	David
Swallow	Adam	Smith	Liz

Random numbers:

11	14	05	16	18	12	18	19	15	03	07
17	13	09	01	07	13	08	11	14	10	14
13	14	11	06	12	15	02	15	18	19	13

> **Working:**
>
>
>
>
>
>
>
> *Answers on pages 215–16.*

1.7   Questionnaire design

Most primary data collection methods make use of questionnaires. Good questionnaire design is crucial to the success of a survey. Because of this it is very important to 'pilot' the questionnaire on a small number of respondents to check for inaccuracies in wording of a question, whether all possible answers of interest will be covered, etc.

Question types

There are three basic types of question used in questionnaires: dichotomous questions, multiple choice questions and open-ended questions. Here each will be examined in turn.

Dichotomous questions

These allow for two answers only. For example, yes or no; male or female; true or false; like or dislike.

EXAMPLE 1.5

1. Are you living in halls of residence?   Yes ☐   No ☐
2. Is your personal tutor: Male ☐   Female ☐ ?
3. 7 * 3 = 20   True ☐ or   False ☐ ?
4. Do you   Like ☐ or Dislike mathematics ☐ ?

It is important that questions of the type shown in (4) above are not overused where there may be 'middle ground', that is, they must allow for don't know; no opinion etc.

In such cases it is more appropriate to use multiple choice questions.

Multiple choice questions

Respondents can choose from several indicated possibilities. Included in this category are those questions which may ask the respondent to rank choices.

12

It is important to make sure that the possibilities are both 'comprehensive' and 'mutually exclusive' (that is every respondent should, unless otherwise stated, be able to pick one and only one of the possibilities).

What type of accommodation are you living in during this year of study?

Halls of residence	☐	Own/parents' house or flat	☐
Rented house/flat	☐	Lodgings	☐

Other (please specify) _____

> You never know – someone could be living in a tent!

The *other* category provides for any types which may have been missed, but care must be taken to make sure that this category does not end up being the most popular choice.

EXAMPLE 1.7

What colour are your eyes ?

Blue ☐

Brown ☐

Other (please specify) _____

> Grey, green, violet and hazel eyes would all have to be put in the *other* category

When using questions which require a level of opinion, make sure there are the same number of potential answers 'for' as 'against'.

EXAMPLE 1.8

Do you think the students' union catering facilities overall are:

Excellent	☐	OK	☐
Very good	☐	Bad	☐
Quite good	☐		

> 3 choices on the 'for' side

> Only 1 on the 'against'

Whenever it is appropriate, remember to account for the don't knows or the don't haves.

13

EXAMPLE 1.9

How many doors does your car have?

(include the boot, if it is a hatchback)

One	☐	Four	☐
Two	☐	Five	☐
Three	☐	More than five	☐
Don't own a car	☐		

Open-ended questions

Respondents are left to answer these in any manner they choose.

The main advantage for this type of question is that it allows for an infinite number of divergent answers. This, however, is also their greatest disadvantage, as the responses to such questions are the hardest to process and analyse. Therefore, one needs to be wary not to use too many on any one questionnaire.

However, open-ended questions can be very useful in three particular areas:

1. On pilot surveys. Here they can be used to try and gauge all possible responses to a particular question so that this question can then become a well designed multiple choice question in the full survey.

EXAMPLE 1.10

How do you get to and from work on an average day?

2. Probing – to get extra information depending on a choice made by a previous response.

EXAMPLE 1.11

Was this university your first choice of place to study for your degree?

Yes ☐   No ☐   If No please briefly explain why _____

3. Used at the end of a questionnaire or section they can be a means of giving the respondent the chance to add anything they feel is important but is not covered by the questions given.

Note that open-ended questions can add weight and credibility to a final report by the use of actual responses as direct quotes.

14

In summary, when looking at the overall design of a questionnaire the following should be kept in mind:

- Questionnaires should be as short as possible.
- The questions themselves should:
  - avoid using complex words and phrases in their construction;
  - be meaningful;
  - not be too technical or involve too much calculation;
  - not be too personal or offensive;
  - not tax the memory;
  - be unambiguous.
- Questions should be arranged in a logical order.
- Questionnaires should be attractively laid out and constructed.
- How the responses will be analysed should be considered at the questionnaire design stage (i.e., appropriate coding should be considered).

1.8   Sources of error

No survey of any population can ever be 100% accurate. (One notable disaster was the predicted outcome of the 1992 general election when opinion polls stated that the Labour Party would win comfortably and, in fact, the Conservatives were returned to power.) There are several different ways in which errors can occur and there are steps which can be taken to try and avoid them.

Sampling errors

These errors arise from the sample not being representative of the population concerned. They are generally avoided by careful consideration of the sampling method to be used. With random samples, the size of these sampling errors can be usefully estimated.

Non-sampling errors

These arise from a variety of causes including:

- the incorrect recording of responses (e.g. by interviewers);
- transferring data incorrectly onto a computer for processing;
- sample members refusing to co-operate (non-respondents);
- failure to make initial contact with sample members (non-respondents);
- badly designed questions.

15

Non-sampling errors are generally avoided by good training of the individuals involved in the data collection and processing process; also, carrying out a pilot survey helps to minimize their occurrence.

1.9 Overall survey design

To summarize, here is a checklist of the main stages in survey design:

Planning

1. Define the survey aims.

2. Define the population.

3. Identify each member of the population.

4. Identify the sampling scheme (how to choose the sample and how large it should be).

5. Decide upon the method of data collection (postal questionnaire, interviews etc.).

6. Design a questionnaire (equally appropriate for personal interviews and observation).

7. Select and train any people involved in the data collection process.

Fieldwork

1. Select the sample.

2. Collect the data.

3. Follow up non-responses wherever possible.

4. Collate and code information (particularly if a computer is to be used for the analysis).

Analysis and interpretation

1. Screen data for recording errors and extreme values (known as outliers).

2. Carry out any statistical computations.

3. Identify and note any possible sources of error and/or bias.

Publication

Generally in two sections:

1. Written results and conclusions.

16

2. Detailed statistical section which includes:
   (a) details of the questionnaires used;
   (b) sampling details;
   (c) background statistical theory;
   (d) summary of data collected.

REVIEW ACTIVITY 3

The following questions are taken from a questionnaire issued to new car owners by a local car showroom:

(a) What is the colour of your new car?

   Red ☐   Blue ☐   White ☐   Other ☐

(b) Did you use cash to pay for the car?

   Yes ☐   No ☐

(c) How much did you pay for the car?

   £5000 – £7000 ☐   £7000 – £9000 ☐   £9000 – £11,000 ☐

(d) Do you feel that the service you received from our staff was

   Excellent ☐   Very good ☐   Good ☐   Poor ☐ ?

Considering each of the questions in turn state whether you think the question could be improved. If so suggest an alternative.

Working:

Answers on page 216.

Key points to remember

1. Data may be defined as categorical (qualitative) or quantitative.

2. Categorical data can be further divided into nominal data and ordinal data.

3. Quantitative data can be further divided into continuous data and discrete data.

4. Data comes from either a primary or a secondary source.

5. A census involves collecting data from a population (all items/people of interest), while a survey collects data from a sample (a carefully chosen small group).

6. Primary data may be collected through a postal questionnaire, a personal interview, a telephone interview or by observation.

7. Common sense must be used to decide on a suitable sample size.

8. Samples may be chosen through the use of simple random sampling, stratified random sampling, systematic sampling, cluster sampling, quota sampling or multistage sampling.

9. Good questionnaire design is essential to the success of a survey.

10. The basic question types used in questionnaires are dichotomous, multiple choice and open-ended.

11. The categories in multiple choice questions should be comprehensive and mutually exclusive.

12. The answers to open-ended questions are difficult to process and analyse, hence care should be taken not to overuse these sorts of questions.

13. Sampling or non-sampling errors may arise from the survey process. Non-sampling errors are generally avoidable.

ADDITIONAL EXERCISES

Question 1   The following are some commonly used sources of secondary data:

- Annual Abstract of Statistics
- Social Trends
- Economic Trends
- Regional Trends
- Family Spending
- Key Data
- Guide to Official Statistics.

Find a copy of one of these publications and prepare a summary of the information provided, giving appropriate examples. Can you think of managerial situations where such information could be valuable?

Question 2   State whether the following data are discrete, continuous, nominal or ordinal.

(a) Petrol consumption rates for a range of cars.

(b) Exam grades (A, B, C etc.) for a group of students.

(c) Corresponding percentage exam marks for the same students.

(d) Types of cheese sold in a supermarket.

Question 3   Suggest a suitable sampling method that could be used to obtain information on:

(a) The attitude of passengers to smoking on local bus services.

(b) The percentage of unsatisfactory components produced each week on a production line.

18

(c) The attitudes toward the provision of a workplace nursery in a large company.

(d) The views of car drivers to traffic calming measures on a residential road.

(e) The likely sales figures for a new type of tea bag.

Question 4 You have been commissioned, by an independent national daily newspaper, to undertake a national survey of people's reactions to a number of issues including the government's recent handling of the economy. You have been instructed that for the survey to retain any credibility, it will be necessary to survey a representative cross-section of at least 5000 people. Consider, in detail, the sampling and data collection methods you would use to carry out this survey, paying particular attention to the requirements for a large, representative group of respondents.

Question 5 A fast food company has many franchised outlets throughout the UK. An executive wants to survey the opinions of the franchise holders towards the current distribution system for raw materials. Suggest a sampling method the executive may use, giving reasons for your choice.

Question 6 Table 1.5 is a seminar group listing for students on a first year Business Studies course. With the aid of the list of random numbers below you are required to select a sample of 4 people using:

(a) Simple random sampling.

(b) Stratified random sampling based on sex.

(c) Systematic random sampling.

Table 1.5 Seminar group listing for Business Studies students

First name	Surname	First name	Surname
Steven	Adams	Andrea	Cross
Clare	Anderson	John	Davidson
Graham	Buckley	Jacqui	Hobson
Glen	Burden	Iain	McLeod
Angela	Dean	Anne	Smith
Susan	Dixon	Elizabeth	Swift
Sarah	Gray	Stuart	Trainer
Joanne	Keane	Philip	Twist
Henry	Ross	Graham	West
David	Wright	Zoe	Wilkinson

Random numbers:

12	15	06	15	17	13	17	20	14	02
18	14	10	02	09	13	07	12	16	12
15	16	10	07	13	16	01	14	19	18

19

Question 7   The deputy manager of a local department store has asked her marketing assistant to conduct a survey on the possibility of late night opening on Tuesdays and Thursdays. The deputy manager does not have a list of the store's customers but estimates there must be over 10,000 of them with 90% living locally. She does, however, have a breakdown of storecard holders based on age and gender and shown in Table 1.6.

Table 1.6 **Estimated proportion of customers by age and gender**

Age/Gender	Male	Female
Under 20	3	6
20–29	6	14
30–44	9	21
45–59	7	20
60 or over	4	10

Given that the marketing assistant only has a small budget for printing and stationery, and that the survey results are required in two weeks, suggest a suitable sample size and a sampling method. Give reasons for the choices made.

Question 8   One hundred dairy farms in four European countries have been surveyed to collect information about their size, amount of livestock and number of employees.

(a) The intention is to use this survey as a pilot study, with the eventual survey covering farms across the EEC. Suggest a suitable sampling technique that could be used to decide which farms should take part in the larger study. Give reasons for your choice.

(b) In this wider study information on the *number* of different breeds of cows kept by the farmers is also to be collected. Suggest a question to be included in the study which would allow this.

SPREADSHEET EXERCISE

This first spreadsheet exercise is designed to give an introduction to the spreadsheet package used throughout this book – Microsoft Excel. Some of the basic functions and features will be reviewed. Readers with no previous spreadsheet knowledge will find a basic guide to Excel useful if more information about the specific features of the package is required.

(a) Load up the file AROMA.XLS.
    This file contains a listing of the marks for a group of students who studied the unit AR101 'Introduction to Aromatherapy' last semester. Table 1.7 shows the marks for five students missing from the list.

20

Table 1.7 **Marks for Aromatherapy students missing from AROMA.XLS**

Name		Seminar group	Assignment 1	Assignment 2	Exam
West	Nick	B	54	42	35
Bell	Joan	B	62	64	65
Book	Iain	A	54	43	47
Philips	Tracey	B	72	72	65
Oliver	Paul	A	41	43	37

(b) *Add the details* for these five students to the spreadsheet.

(c) *Change the width* of columns D and E so that the headings fit into one cell.

(d) *Right justify* all of the column headings.

(e) Given that the final exam mark is made up as follows:

(0.8 * exam mark) + (0.1 * assignment 1 mark) + (0.1 * assignment 2 mark)

Type a formula into cell G6 to calculate the overall mark for the first student on the list. *Copy this down* to give a full column of final marks.

(f) *Format* the overall marks so that they are displayed to *one decimal place* and give column G a suitable heading.

(g) A student fails if they have less than 40% for the unit. *Enter an IF statement* in cell H6 and *copy it down* to show whether each student has passed or failed.

(h) *Save* your file onto a disk (but do not close it).

(i) *Sort* the data by seminar group and name so that group A are listed before group B and the student names are displayed alphabetically within their groups.

(j) *Copy* the headings from cells A6–G6 to a new area on your spreadsheet, then *move* the marks for group B so that there are two separate tables of marks (i.e., one table for each seminar group).

(k) Nick West (group B) has withdrawn from the course, so *delete* his name and marks.

(l) Use the *Help facility* on Excel to find a suitable *function* which would work out the average overall mark for each seminar group.

(m) Using this function, *make up a table* showing the average mark for each seminar group and add the *percentage* of students failing (*Hint*: count how many fails there are in each group first, using a *function*).

(n) *Save and close* your file, and *exit* Excel.

Unit 7:   Business Strategy

Learning hours: 60

NQF level 4:   BTEC Higher National — H2

Content Selected: Johnson and Scholes, Exploring Corporate Strategy 6th Edition, Chapter 1

Introduction from the Qualification Leader

This unit looks at evaluating and selecting strategies appropriate to business organisations. Chapter 1 has been selected as background reading to the unit, as it introduces strategy, its meaning and characteristics.

Description of unit

The aim of this unit is to develop learners' abilities to evaluate and select strategies appropriate to business organisations. This will involve an analysis of the impacts of the external operating environment and the need to plan organisational strategies to ensure effective business performance.

Summary of learning outcomes

To achieve this unit a learner must:

1   Analyse how the business environment is considered in **strategy formulation**

2   Understand the process of **strategic planning**

3   Examine approaches to **strategy evaluation and selection**

4   Analyse how **strategy implementation** is realised.

Content

---

1 **Strategy formulation**

Strategic contexts and terminology: role of strategy, missions, visions, strategic intent, objectives, goals, core competencies, strategic architecture, strategic control

Stakeholder analysis: stakeholder significance grid, stakeholder mapping

Environment auditing: political, economic, socio-cultural, technological, environmental and legal analysis (PESTEL), Porter's 5 force analysis, the threat of new entrants, the power of buyers, the power of suppliers, the threat of substitutes, competitive rivalry and collaboration

Strategic positioning: the Ansoff matrix, growth, stability, profitability, efficiency, market leadership, survival, mergers and acquisitions, expansion into the global market place

The organisational audit: benchmarking, SWOT analysis, product positions, value-chain analysis, demographic influences, scenario planning, synergy culture and values

2 **Strategic planning**

Strategic thinking: future direction of the competition, needs of customers, gaining and maintaining competitive advantage, Ansoff's growth-vector matrix, portfolio analysis

Planning systems: informal planning, top-down planning, bottom-up planning, behavioural approaches

Strategic planning issues: impact on managers, targets, when to plan, who should be involved, role of planning

Strategic planning techniques: BCG growth-share matrix, directional policy matrices, SPACE, PIMS

3 **Strategy evaluation and selection**

Market entry strategies: organic growth, growth by merger or acquisition, strategic alliances, licensing, franchising

Substantive growth strategies: horizontal and vertical integration, related and unrelated diversification

Limited growth strategies: do nothing, market penetration, market development, product development, innovation

Disinvestment strategies: retrenchment, turnaround strategies, divestment, liquidation

Strategy selection: considering the alternatives, appropriateness, feasibility, desirability

4   **Strategy implementation**

The realisation of strategic plans to operational reality: communication – selling the concepts, project teams, identification of team and individual roles, responsibilities and targets, programme of activities, benchmark targets at differing levels of the organisation

Resource allocation: finance, human resources, materials, time

Review and evaluation: an evaluation of the benchmarked outcomes in a given time period of corporate, operational and individual targets

Outcomes and assessment criteria

Outcomes	Assessment criteria for pass To achieve each outcome a learner must demonstrate the ability to:
1 Analyse how the business environment is considered in **strategy formulation**	• define the contexts of business strategy • explain the significance of stakeholder analysis • conduct an environmental and organisational audit of a given organisation • apply strategic positioning techniques to the analysis of a given organisation
2 Understand the process of **strategic planning**	• demonstrate an ability to think strategically • prepare a strategic plan for a given organisation, based on previous analysis
3 Examine approaches to **strategy evaluation and selection**	• evaluate possible alternative strategies – substantive growth, limited growth or retrenchment • identify and evaluate resource requirements to implement a new strategy for a given organisation • select an appropriate future strategy for a given organisation
4 Analyse how **strategy implementation** is realised	• compare the roles and responsibilities for strategy implementation in two different organisations • identify and evaluate resource requirements to implement a new strategy for a given organisation • propose targets and timescales for achievement in a given organisation to monitor a given strategy

Introducing Strategy

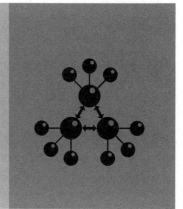

1

After reading this chapter you should be able to:

- Describe the characteristics of strategic decisions.
- Define what is meant by strategy and strategic management.
- Explain the difference between strategy as 'fit' and 'stretch'.
- Explain how strategic priorities vary by level: corporate, business and operational.
- Understand what distinguishes strategic management from operational management.
- Explain what is meant by strategic business units (SBUs) in organisations.
- Understand the vocabulary of strategy.
- Explain the elements of the *Johnson and Scholes* strategic management model.
- Understand which elements of the strategy model are likely to be most important in different contexts.

In January 2001 the Federal Communications Commission in the USA approved a $105 billion merger of AOL, the world's largest Internet service provider, with Time Warner – the multimedia empire. The intention to merge had been signalled by the two chief executives 12 months earlier. This was a defining moment for both companies. Business analysts hailed it as evidence that the previously separate sectors of computing, telecommunications and the world of media and entertainment were converging at a rapid rate. So it also had major implications for their competitors in each 'sector' and their customers and potential customers. Illustration 1.1 explains some of the background to the merger and the ways in which the new company intended to take advantage of the combined company.

The merger would clearly change the *direction* of the business, its justification was about developing a *long-term* position in the industry and it would have *far-ranging implications* for most parts of the business in terms of priorities and how the organisation would function. It also raised further challenges for the *future*. In short, this was a major *strategic* development.

All organisations are faced with the challenges of strategic development: some from a desire to grasp new opportunities, such as with AOL/Time Warner, others to overcome significant problems. This book deals with why changes in strategic direction take place in organisations, why they are important, how such decisions are taken, and some of the concepts that can be useful in understanding these issues. This chapter is an introduction and explanation of this theme, and deals with the questions of what is meant by 'strategy' and 'strategic management', why they are so important and what distinguishes them from other organisational challenges, tasks and decisions. In discussing these it will become clearer how the book deals with the subject area as a whole. The chapter draws on the AOL/Time Warner illustration for the purposes of discussion; and as the book progresses, other such illustrative examples are used to help develop discussion.

One other point should be made before proceeding. The term 'corporate strategy' is used here for two main reasons. First, because the book is concerned with strategy and strategic decisions in all types of organisation – small and large, commercial enterprises as well as public services – and the word 'corporate' embraces them all. Second, because, as the term is used in this book (discussed more fully in section 1.1.2), 'corporate strategy' denotes the most general level of strategy in an organisation and in this sense embraces other levels of strategy. Indeed Chapter 6, which looks at these higher-level issues, is entitled 'Corporate-level strategies'. Readers will undoubtedly come across other terms, such as 'strategic management', 'business policy' and 'organisational strategy', all of which are used to describe the same general topic.

1.1 THE NATURE OF STRATEGY AND STRATEGIC DECISIONS

Why are the issues facing AOL and Time Warner described as 'strategic'? What types of issues are strategic, and what distinguishes these from other types of issues in organisations – such as those that would be regarded as operational?

1.1.1 The characteristics of strategic decisions

The characteristics usually associated with the words 'strategy' and 'strategic decisions' are these:

● Strategy is likely to be concerned with the *long-term direction* of an organisation. The AOL/Time Warner merger set the new company on a path as a multimedia giant that would have lasting effects. Time Warner had already embarked on that path with its interests in film production, cable/television, music and publishing. Indeed, this empire had come together through a previous series of acquisitions and mergers. In contrast, AOL was a young company focused on Internet service provision so this was a big change in direction for them.

- Strategic decisions are normally about trying to achieve some *advantage* for the organisation over competition. For example, the AOL/Time Warner merger was justified in terms of providing 'content' (e.g. music or movies) to an Internet service provider – or (in reverse) giving a new distribution route to the content provider. It was also about moving before competitors did so and making it difficult for them to imitate. For example, the merger was expected to give major advantage in the music industry to the extent that it could transform the way in which music was sold and distributed and how artists received payments. In other situations advantage may be achieved in different ways and may also mean different things. For example, in the public sector, strategic advantage could be thought of as providing better value-for-money services than other providers, thus attracting support and funding from government. Strategic decisions are sometimes conceived of, therefore, as the search for effective *positioning* in relation to competitors so as to achieve advantage.

- Strategic decisions are likely to be concerned with the *scope of an organisation's activities*. For example, does (and should) the organisation concentrate on one area of activity, or should it have many? The issue of scope of activity is *fundamental* to strategy because it concerns the way in which those responsible for managing the organisation conceive the organisation's boundaries. It is to do with what they want the organisation to be like and to be about. This could include important decisions about product range or geographical coverage. The broadening of the scope of activities is an important reason for the AOL/Time Warner merger. This is particularly true for AOL managers who are likely to find themselves in the midst of the entertainment industry as against their previously narrower activities as an Internet service provider.

- Strategy can be seen as the *matching of the resources and activities of an organisation to the environment* in which it operates. This is sometimes known as the search for *strategic fit*.[1] The notion of **strategic fit** is developing strategy by identifying opportunities in the business environment and adapting resources and competences so as to take advantage of these. Here it would be seen as important to achieve the correct *positioning* of the organisation, for example in terms of the extent to which it meets clearly identified market needs. This might take the form of a small business trying to find a particular niche in a market, or a multinational corporation seeking to place most of its investments in businesses which have found successful market positions or have identified attractive markets. In the fast-moving world of the media and IT, customers might value providers who can provide a range of services through a set of complementary channels (e.g. Internet as well as physical retail outlets). This was certainly starting to happen in the music industry in the early 2000s. So, creating the ability to 'bundle' together services that were previously fragmented and offering new ways for customers to access products were clear priorities for the merged AOL/Time Warner. The nature of the music and entertainment markets provided opportunities not necessarily found in other markets. Customer tastes and requirements were relatively common between countries (particularly in

Strategic fit is developing strategy by identifying opportunities in the business environment and adapting resources and competences so as to take advantage of these

Illustration 1.1

AOL/Time Warner – the world's first Internet-powered media and communications company

Managing strategy requires the consideration of a wide range of factors, which shift and change over time.

On 11 January 2001 the Federal Communications Commission in the USA approved the $105 billion merger of AOL – the world's largest Internet service provider (ISP) – with Time Warner (TW) – the media and entertainment empire with interests in magazines, film studios, cable TV and news and music production. The merger created a company with annual revenue of almost $40 billion and 85,000 employees. It brought together AOL's 26 million Internet customers with TW's different customer base which included 44 million magazine and 12 million cable TV subscribers.

It was a year and a day since the intention to merge had been announced by Steve Case of AOL and Gerald Levin of TW. *Business Week* reported the planned merger as follows:

Case – who will become the chairman of AOL/TW – is making a huge bet that by melding the TW colossus with his Internet empire he will create a hybrid with unmatched advantages as the long-anticipated convergence of entertainment, information, communications and on-line services comes about in the next few years. It is a bid to define the future. By assembling more assets, audiences and advertisers for the new digital marketplace than anyone [else] . . . Case . . . sees a chance to move so far ahead that others won't catch up for years – the way that Alfred P. Sloan audaciously engineered the creation of General Motors in the 1920s – producing the corporation that dominated the auto age.

The merger brought together two quite different companies. AOL, only some 15 years old, had dominated the ISP market – being five times

bigger than the number two in the USA in terms of subscriber numbers and capturing an estimated 33 per cent of time online – three times as much as Microsoft or Yahoo!. It had become the *de facto* 'operating system' for the Internet – much to Microsoft's displeasure. It was much smaller than TW in terms of both revenue and employees (about one-fifth the size) and was an organisation that thrived on change. In contrast, TW went back to 1923 and had grown through a series of related diversifications (by mergers) and had enormous investments in movie, TV and music assets (such as best-selling TV shows (*Friends* and *ER*) and Madonna's CDs). It had a lot to lose from too much change.

AOL had a lot to gain from the merger – its stock had dropped substantially during 2000 in line with other high-tech stocks. TW might provide some solidity behind a dot.com image that was beginning to lose its initial gloss. It opened up the broadband cable network to an ISP – who were being held back technically by the slow speed of traditional telephone lines and, of course, there was all that TW content – movies, TV programmes and music. The TW customer base had not been 'exploited' in terms of selling a wider range of products and services. TW also had large advertising revenues through its magazines and TV channels.

Despite the fact that AOL made the running in the merger, there were benefits for TW too. They felt that they owned largely mature businesses with limited growth potential. TW's executives had consistently believed that technology would continue to transform the entertainment industry and that companies could not ignore major developments – like the Internet. They already had experience of how the Internet could disrupt their current businesses in publishing, music and TV. For example, they were part of the music industry lobby that eventually succeeded in 2001 in blocking the US Internet company Napster from providing music online to customers. But TW's own Internet efforts had flopped – they were simply not familiar with how to make an Internet company succeed. So they were attracted by AOL's 'Internet savvy' and proven track record in building revenue and market share. They also saw opportunities to cross-sell TW subscriptions to the younger AOL customers.

Not everyone was happy with the merger. Major rivals such as Disney, Microsoft and Yahoo! lobbied hard with the regulatory authorities to block the merger. In the end, all they achieved were some conditions. The most important was a requirement to make AOL's instant messaging service open to other providers. The regulators were trying to avoid a situation where AOL/TW customers found themselves in a 'walled garden' – benefiting from a wide range of services from AOL/TW but unable to communicate with non-AOL/TW customers or receive content from other providers. There were others who expressed concerns too – artists and composers in the music industry had campaigned in 2000 against the merging of TW and EMI music interests and they were further concerned that their interests would suffer from the stranglehold that AOL/TW would have on the music industry. For example, Roger Wallis, chairman of the Swedish Society of Popular Music composers, who claimed that Scandinavia would be particularly affected by the deal, said:

> We are concerned that [it] will put more control in the hands of the big music companies and make it difficult for all individual artists and composers to use the Internet as a great opportunity to spread music around the world. What we are pressing for is some form of . . . separation between the ownership of distribution channels and the ownership of music copyrights.

The thing that excited many observers about the merger was the creation of a platform to develop 'next-generation' services – such as interactive TV and digital music. During 2000, when the merger was still pending, the companies had worked together to launch 'AOL by Phone' (telephone access to the Internet) and 'AOL TV' (Internet by cable TV).

Those journalists who had experienced previous mega-mergers that had failed to deliver their promise were also cautious about AOL/TW. They reminded readers that more than 70 per cent of mergers fail and the 1990 merger that created TW had itself got off to a rocky start. AOL had a corporate culture that was speedy and collaborative whilst TW was slow and decentralised. Its reward structure emphasised performance at business-unit level and (by implication) discouraged collaborative efforts. Each of the TW business units was a multi-billion dollar business headed by a CEO and usually a leader in its own markets. So the trick would be to gain advantage from the synergies that the merger promised without undermining those qualities that had created leadership in publishing, film, cable TV and music. Delivering next-generation products – digital music and interactive TV – were what these synergies were about. This was a tough agenda.

Main sources: Adapted from *Business Week*, 8 May 2000, p. 65; *The Times*, 7 September 2000, p. 27; *Fortune*, 8 January 2001, p. 72.

Questions

1. Why were the issues facing AOL/TW described as strategic?

2. Identify examples of issues that fit each of the circles of the model in Exhibit 1.4 on page 17.

3. To what extent would you describe the strategy for AOL/TW in its various markets as 'fit' or 'stretch' as described in Exhibit 1.1 on page 8?

Exhibit 1.1	The leading edge of strategy: fit or stretch	
ASPECT OF STRATEGY	**ENVIRONMENT-LED 'FIT'**	**RESOURCE-LED 'STRETCH'**
Underlying basis of strategy	Strategic fit between market opportunities and organisation's resources	Leverage of resources to improve value for money
Competitive advantage through . . .	'Correct' positioning Differentiation directed by market need	Differentiation based on competences suited to or creating market need
How small players survive . . .	Find and defend a niche	Change the 'rules of the game'
Risk-reduction through . . .	Portfolio of products/businesses	Portfolio of competences
Corporate centre invests in . . .	Strategies of business units or subsidiaries	Core competences

Source: Adapted from G. Hamel and C.K. Prahalad, *Competing for the Future*, Harvard Business School Press, 1994.

the Internet where universal standards had been adopted – but also in the media), allowing for rapid globalisation.

- However, strategy can also be seen as *building on or 'stretching' an organisation's resources and competences* to create opportunities or to capitalise on them.[2] Strategy development by **stretch** is the leverage of the resources and competences of an organisation to provide competitive advantage and/or yield new opportunities. For example, a small business might try to change the 'rules of the game' in its market to suit its own competences – which was the basis on which many 'dot.com' companies entered established sectors. A large multinational corporation may focus its strategies on those businesses with development potential. Here the emphasis is not just on ensuring that resources are available (or can be made available) to take advantage of some new opportunity in the marketplace, but also on identifying existing resources and competences that might be a basis for creating new opportunities in the marketplace. So the AOL/Time Warner merger should be viewed in terms not only of improved competitiveness in current 'arenas' – such as in the distribution of music – but also of exploiting strengths to create new offerings or to compete in new arenas. For example, the combined company could offer new subscription packages covering TV, movies, telephone and Internet services. It could then exploit this customer base to generate income from advertisers or other providers of complementary products or services. Of course, in practice, organisations develop strategies on the bases of both 'fit' and 'stretch'. Exhibit 1.1 contrasts the two approaches.

- Strategies may require *major resource* changes for an organisation. For example, decisions to expand geographically have significant implications in terms of the need to build and support a new customer base. Sometimes this

> **'Stretch'** is the leverage of the resources and competences of an organisation to provide competitive advantage and/or yield new opportunities

might be seen as high risk – for example for AOL/Time Warner, entering markets where there is no tradition of subscription and where 'piracy' is prevalent. Strategies, then, need to be considered not only in terms of the extent to which the existing resource capability of the organisation is suited to opportunities, but also in terms of the extent to which resources can be obtained and controlled to develop a strategy for the future.

● Strategic decisions are likely to *affect operational decisions*: for example, the AOL/Time Warner strategy required a whole series of decisions at the operational level – even to get the merger approved by the regulatory authorities. After the merger, new structures and management controls would be needed to deal with the much more diverse set of activities. Human resource policies and practices would also have to be reviewed. This link between overall strategy and operational aspects of the organisation is important for two other reasons. First, if the operational aspects of the organisation are not in line with the strategy, then, no matter how well considered the strategy is, it will not succeed. Second, it is at the operational level that real strategic advantage can be achieved. AOL was successful as an Internet service provider not only because of a good strategic concept, but also because of the detail of how the concept was put into effect in terms of the logistics of accessing and servicing customers, generating advertising revenue etc. Indeed, competence in particular operational activities might determine which strategic developments might make most sense. For example, AOL's knowledge of how to provide service to the younger consumer was seen as particularly attractive to Time Warner as a major provider of popular music.

● The strategy of an organisation is affected not only by environmental forces and resource availability, but also by the *values and expectations* of those who have *power* in and around the organisation. In some respects, strategy can be thought of as a reflection of the attitudes and beliefs of those who have most influence on the organisation. Whether a company is expansionist or more concerned with consolidation, and where the boundaries are drawn for a company's activities, may say much about the values and attitudes of those who influence strategy – the *stakeholders* of the organisation. In the merger the running was set by AOL, reflecting the influence of the AOL chief executive Steve Case. But he was constrained by regulatory authorities and lobby groups (including performers) – not only in the USA but also in other major markets such as Europe – and the ability to persuade both sets of shareholders that the deal made commercial sense and would increase the long-term value of the company.

  In general, of course, there are other stakeholders who have influence: financial institutions, the workforce, buyers and perhaps suppliers and the local community. The beliefs and values of these stakeholders will have a more or less direct influence on the strategy development of an organisation.

Overall, if a *definition* of a strategy is required, the most basic might be 'the long-term direction of an organisation'. However, the characteristics described above can provide the basis for a fuller definition:

Strategy is the *direction* and *scope* of an organisation over the *long term*, which achieves *advantage* for the organisation through its configuration of *resources* within a changing *environment* and to fulfil *stakeholder* expectations

Strategy is the *direction* and *scope* of an organisation over the *long term*, which achieves *advantage* for the organisation through its configuration of *resources* within a changing *environment* and to fulfil *stakeholder* expectations.

There are a number of consequences of these characteristics:

● Strategic decisions are likely to be *complex in nature*. It will be emphasised that this complexity is a defining feature of strategy and strategic decisions. This is especially so in organisations with wide geographical scope, such as multinational firms, or wide ranges of products or services. AOL/Time Warner needed to coordinate their activities over a wide geographical area.

● Strategic decisions may also have to be made in situations of *uncertainty*: they may involve taking decisions with views of the future about which it is impossible for managers to be sure. No one can really predict with much clarity where the industry convergence that AOL/Time Warner represent will lead or pace of change. This applies to the various sectors in which they are involved, such as music, cable TV and Internet service provision – the impact may not be the same or move at the same pace in each of these sectors.

● Strategic decisions are also likely to demand an *integrated* approach to managing the organisation. Unlike functional problems, there is no one area of expertise, or one perspective, that can define or resolve the problems. Managers, therefore, have to cross-functional and operational boundaries to deal with strategic problems and come to agreements with other managers who, inevitably, have different interests and perhaps different priorities. If AOL/Time Warner are to gain benefit from the merger then TW managers have to see the Internet as a major new distribution opportunity whilst AOL managers need to be more strategic as to how they might extend the portfolio of content offered to AOL customers.

● They may also have to manage and perhaps change *relationships and networks* outside the organisation, for example with suppliers, distributors and customers. AOL/Time Warner needed to decide to what extent their new internal relationship as content provider to Internet service provider should be exclusive. For example, should Time Warner customers be offered an alternative Internet service provider other than AOL and should AOL be able to source from other content providers such as Disney?

● Strategic decisions will very often involve *change* in organisations which may prove difficult because of the heritage of resources and because of culture. These cultural issues are heightened following mergers as two very different cultures need to be brought closer together – or at least learn how to tolerate each other. Indeed, this often proves difficult to achieve – up to 70 per cent of mergers fail to deliver their 'promise' for these reasons.

1.1.2 Levels of strategy

Strategies exist at a number of levels in an organisation. Individuals may say they have a strategy – to do with their career, for example. This may be relevant when considering influences on strategies adopted by organisations, but it is not the subject of this book. Taking AOL/Time Warner as an example, it is possible to distinguish at least three different levels of organisational strategy. **Corporate-level strategy** is concerned with the overall purpose and scope of an organisation and how value will be added to the different parts (business units) of the organisation. This could include issues of geographical coverage, diversity of products/services or business units, and how resources are to be allocated between the different parts of the organisation. For AOL/Time Warner, the most important corporate issues were about how new opportunities could be created by the merged company. This was the fundamental rationale for the merger. The corporate centre needed to play a crucial role in determining how the organisation should be structured, how resources should be allocated in setting targets and reviewing performance. The corporate centre should also be asking whether there are other ways in which they can add value to the separate business units within the company. It might be argued, for example, that a new corporate brand should be created. Corporate-level strategy is also likely to be concerned with the expectations of owners – the shareholders and the stock market. Being clear about corporate-level strategy is important: it is a *basis* of other strategic decisions. It may well take form in an explicit or implicit statement of 'mission' that reflects such expectations.

> **Corporate-level strategy** is concerned with the overall purpose and scope of an organisation and how value will be added to the different parts (business units) of the organisation

The second level can be thought of in terms of **business unit strategy**,[3] which is about how to compete successfully in particular markets. The concerns are therefore about how advantage over competitors can be achieved; what new opportunities can be identified or created in markets; which products or services should be developed in which markets; and the extent to which these meet customer needs in such a way as to achieve the objectives of the organisation – perhaps long-term profitability or market share growth. So, whereas corporate strategy involves decisions about the organisation as a whole, strategic decisions here need to be related to a strategic business unit (SBU). A **strategic business unit** is a part of an organisation for which there is a distinct external market for goods or services that is different from another SBU. In public sector organisations a corresponding definition of a SBU might be a part of the organisation or service for which there is a distinct client group. For example, ICI has a paints business that sells paints to various different types of customers, including industrial buyers and retail buyers. ICI Paints might choose to organise itself with an industrial division and a retail division. However, within those structural divisions there will be a need for different strategies according to different markets. Retailers could include huge multiple chain stores buying direct from ICI and small retailers buying through distributors. These are distinct markets that require different strategies, and are therefore different SBUs.

> **Business unit strategy** is about how to compete successfully in particular markets

> A **strategic business unit** is a part of an organisation for which there is a distinct external market for goods or services that is different from another SBU

Confusion can often arise because an SBU may not be defined in terms of an organisational structure. It may not be a separate structural part of an organisation. For example, AOL/Time Warner had inherited separate companies structured around particular products (cable/TV, publishing, Internet service provision). Also, the customer bases of the two companies were different – particularly in terms of age profile. But the logic of the merger dictated that 'bundling' these services in different ways for different customer groups should be the basis of competitive advantage. So SBUs needed to be thought about in these terms – for example, businesses vs. households and by different demographic characteristics – such as age. The specific products that might be bundled into an attractive package for younger consumers and the extent to which the Internet is the dominant access and distribution channel will be very different from customers in older age groups. This emphasises the difference between an SBU and a division or a business within an organisation. An SBU is a unit of an organisation for strategy-making purposes. It may or may not be a separate structural part of the organisation.

The third level of strategy is at the operating end of an organisation. Here there are **operational strategies**, which are concerned with how the component parts of an organisation deliver effectively the corporate- and business-level strategies in terms of resources, processes and people. For example, in AOL/Time Warner it was important that film production, TV scheduling, publishing titles and subscriber recruitment efforts dovetailed into higher-level decisions about service bundling and market entry. For example, it was important that the acquisition and distribution of content was planned to match the needs of the various customer groups that they were targeting. Indeed, in most businesses, successful business strategies depend to a large extent on decisions that are taken, or activities that occur, at the operational level. The integration of operational decisions and strategy is therefore of great importance.

Operational strategies are concerned with how the component parts of an organisation deliver effectively the corporate- and business-level strategies in terms of resources, processes and people

1.1.3 The vocabulary of strategy

At the end of section 1.1.1, a definition of strategy was given. It can be dangerous to offer a definition, because lengthy semantic discussions can follow about whether or not it is precise enough, and whether everyone would agree with it. In fact, there are different definitions according to different authors. There are also a variety of terms used in relation to strategy, so it is worth devoting a little space to clarifying some of these.

Exhibit 1.2 and Illustration 1.2 employ some of the terms that readers will come across in this and other books on strategy. Exhibit 1.2 explains these in relation to a personal strategy readers may have followed themselves – becoming fit. Illustration 1.2 shows how these relate to an organisation – British Airways.

Not all these terms are always used in organisations or in strategy books: indeed, in this book the word 'goal' is rarely used. Moreover, it may or may not be that mission, goals, objectives, strategies and so on are written down precisely. In some organisations this is done very formally; in others it is not. As is shown in Chapter 2, a mission or strategy might sometimes more sensibly be conceived of as that which is implicit or can be deduced about an organisation from what it is doing. However, as a general guideline the following terms are often used.

● A *mission* is a general expression of the overall purpose of the organisation, which, ideally, is in line with the values and expectations of major

Exhibit 1.2	The vocabulary of strategy	
TERM	**DEFINITION**	**A PERSONAL EXAMPLE**
Mission	Overriding purpose in line with the values or expectations of stakeholders	Be healthy and fit
Vision or strategic intent	Desired future state: the aspiration of the organisation	To run the London Marathon
Goal	General statement of aim or purpose	Lose weight and strengthen muscles
Objective	Quantification (if possible) or more precise statement of the goal	Lose 5 kilos by 1 September and run the Marathon next year
Unique resources and core competences	Resources, processes or skills which provide 'competitive advantage'	Proximity to a fitness centre, supportive family and friends and past experience of successful diet
Strategies	Long-term direction	Associate with a collaborative network (e.g. join running club), exercise regularly, compete in marathons locally, stick to appropriate diet
Control	The monitoring of action steps to: ● assess effectiveness of strategies and actions ● modify strategies and/or actions as necessary	Monitor weight, kilometres run and measure times: if progress satisfactory, do nothing; if not, consider other strategies and actions

stakeholders and concerned with the scope and boundaries of the organisation. It is sometimes referred to in terms of the apparently simple, but actually challenging question: *'What business are we in?'*

● A *vision* or *strategic intent* is the desired future state of the organisation. It is an aspiration around which a strategist, perhaps a chief executive, might seek to focus the attention and energies of members of the organisation.

● If the word *goal* is used, it usually means a general aim in line with the mission. It may well be qualitative in nature.

● On the other hand, an *objective* is more likely to be quantified, or at least to be a more precise aim in line with the goal. However, in this book the word 'objective' is used whether or not there is quantification.

● *Unique resources* and *core competences* are the bases upon which an organisation achieves strategic advantage in terms of activities, skills or know-how which distinguish it from competitors and provide value to customers or clients.

● The concept of *strategy* has already been defined. It is the long-term direction of the organisation. It is likely to be expressed in fairly broad statements of the direction that the organisation should be taking and the types of

Illustration 1.2

STRATEGY IN ACTION

British Airways and the vocabulary of strategy

Annual reports and public statements contain much of the vocabulary of this book.

Mission

To be the undisputed leader in world travel.

We are passionately committed to excellence and to the highest levels of customer service.

Goals

- *The customers' choice* – the airline of first choice in our key markets.
- *Strong profitability* – meeting investors' expectations and securing the future.
- *Truly global* – global network, global outlook: recognised everywhere for superior value in world travel.
- *Inspired people* – inspired teams of people, building and benefiting from the company's success.

Values

- Safe and secure
- Honest and responsible
- Innovative and team-spirited
- Global and caring
- A good neighbour

Competitive strategy

The airline's strategy is focused on a revised fleet strategy, aimed at targeting profitable passenger segments and on product developments for all its brands.

Elements of strategy

- Reducing aircraft size to reduce dependence on unprofitable transfer passengers and other low-yielding business.
- Product and network improvements to maintain share of key business markets.

- Cost cutting and efficiency programmes.
- Developing alliance relationships to strengthen the global network.
- Establishing the airline's low-cost subsidiary GO, which can serve a segment of the market that the mainline airline is not designed to meet.

Strategic initiatives

There are eight focus areas:

1. People: Employee numbers will reduce to reflect the reduction in capacity.
2. Distribution costs: Exploiting the opportunities offered by e-business and working with travel agents to manage the costs of distribution.
3. Gatwick: Review the destinations served from Gatwick and reduce costs.
4. Domestic routes: Select appropriate-sized aircraft; focus on point-to-point traffic and review of further product specification.
5. Product costs: Aim product offerings at customer needs to ensure value for money for the customer.
6. Aircraft utilisation: Improvements in aircraft use through changes to schedules, standby aircraft and maintenance downtime.
7. Subsidiaries: Review the role of subsidiary operations and their contribution to network revenue margin and group profitability.
8. Procurement: Work with suppliers to achieve cost savings through lower prices, more efficient methods of payment and optimum specification of items.

Prepared by Urmilla Lawson, University of Strathclyde.

Source: Adapted from *BA Fact Book 2000* (from website).

Question

Find websites for other companies (including airlines) and compare their use of strategic vocabulary. What conclusions do you draw from the similarities and differences?

action required to achieve objectives: for example, in terms of market entry, new products or services, or ways of operating.

- It is, then, important to exercise some degree of *strategic control* so as to monitor the extent to which the action is achieving the objectives and goals.

As the book develops, many other terms will be introduced and explained. These are the basics with which to begin.

1.2 STRATEGIC MANAGEMENT

What, then, is *strategic management*? It is not enough to say that it is the management of the process of strategic decision making. This fails to take into account a number of points important both in the management of an organisation and in the area of study with which this book is concerned.

Strategic management is different in nature from other aspects of management. Exhibit 1.3 summarises some of these differences. An individual manager is most often required to deal with problems of operational control, such as the efficient production of goods, the management of a salesforce, the monitoring of financial performance or the design of some new system that will improve the level of customer service. These are all very important tasks, but they are essentially concerned with effectively managing resources already deployed, often in a limited part of the organisation within the context of an existing strategy. Operational control is what managers are involved in for most of their time. It is vital to the effective implementation of strategy, but it is not the same as strategic management.

Exhibit 1.3	**Characteristics of strategic management and operational management**	
STRATEGIC MANAGEMENT	**OPERATIONAL MANAGEMENT**	
• Ambiguous/uncertain	• Routinised	
• Complex		
• Organisation-wide	• Operationally specific	
• Fundamental		
• Long-term implications	• Short-term implications	

The scope of strategic management is greater than that of any one area of operational management. Strategic management is concerned with complexity arising out of ambiguous and non-routine situations with organisation-wide rather than operation-specific implications. This is a major challenge for managers who are used to managing on a day-to-day basis the resources they control. It can be a particular problem because of the background of managers who may typically have been trained, perhaps over many years, to undertake operational tasks and to take operational responsibility. Accountants find that they still tend to see problems in financial terms, IT managers in IT terms, marketing managers in marketing terms, and so on. Each aspect in itself is important, of course, but none is adequate alone. The manager who aspires to manage, or influence, strategy needs to develop a capability to take an overview, to conceive of the whole rather than just the parts of the situation facing an organisation. Because strategic management is characterised by its complexity, it is also necessary to make decisions and judgements based on the *conceptualisation* of difficult issues. Yet the early training and experience of managers is often about taking action, or about detailed *planning* or *analysis*. This book explains many analytical approaches to strategy, and it is concerned too with action related to the management of strategy. There is also, however, an emphasis on understanding concepts of relevance to the complexity of strategy which informs this analysis and action.

Nor is strategic management concerned only with taking decisions about major issues facing the organisation. It is also concerned with ensuring that the strategy is put into effect. It can be thought of as having three main elements within it, and it is these that provide the framework for the book. **Strategic management** includes *understanding the strategic position* of an organisation, *strategic choices* for the future and turning *strategy into action*.

The next sections of this chapter discuss each of these aspects of strategic management and identifies elements that make up each aspect. Exhibit 1.4 shows these elements and defines the broad coverage of this book. It is important to understand why the exhibit has been drawn in this particular way. It could have shown the three aspects of strategic management in a linear form – understanding the strategic position preceding strategic choices, which in turn precede strategy into action. Indeed, many texts on the subject do just this. However, in practice, the elements of strategic management do not take this linear form – they are interlinked. One way of understanding a strategy better is to begin to implement it, so strategic choices and strategy into action may overlap. Similarly, an understanding of the strategic position may be built up from the experience of strategies in action. It is for structural convenience only that the subject has been divided into sections in this book; it is not meant to suggest that the process of strategic management must follow a neat and tidy path. Indeed, the evidence provided in Chapter 2 on how strategic management occurs in practice suggests that it usually does not.

Strategic management includes *understanding the strategic position* of an organisation, *strategic choices* for the future and turning *strategy into action*

1.2.1 The strategic position

The **strategic position** is concerned with the impact on strategy of the external environment, internal resources and competences, and the expectations and influence of stakeholders

Understanding the **strategic position** is concerned with impact on strategy of the external environment, internal resources and competences, and the expectations and influence of stakeholders. The sorts of questions this raises are central to future strategy. What changes are going on in the environment, and how will they affect the organisation and its activities? What are the resources and competences of the organisation and can these provide special advantages or yield new opportunities? What is it that those people and groups associated with the organisation – managers, shareholders or owners,

Exhibit 1.4 A model of the elements of strategic management

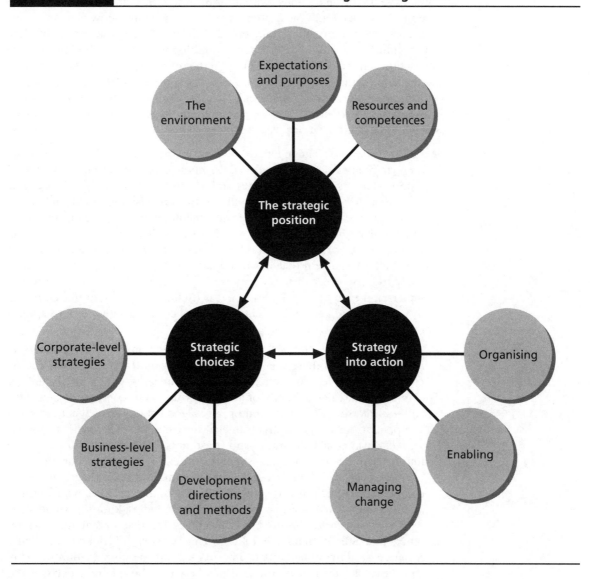

unions and others who are stakeholders in the organisation – aspire to, and how do these affect what is expected for the future development of the organisation?

These are clearly all important issues for AOL/Time Warner. Decisions to forge the merger no doubt required careful consideration about the convergence of technologies and consumer behaviour leading to views about future demand for new services in the market. An equally important issue was how the particular competences of the merged organisation might be configured to provide competitive advantage – perhaps by developing new services such as interactive TV or digital music online. Also, the expectations of stakeholders need to be understood, for example the concerns being shown by musicians and composers about the stranglehold that AOL/Time Warner might have on the music industry. These groups could lobby regulatory bodies to place restrictions on the company's activities in the music industry. So the reason for understanding the strategic position is to form a view of the key influences on the present and future well-being of an organisation, and what opportunities and threats are created by the environment, the competences of the organisation and the expectations of stakeholders. These are discussed briefly below.

- The *environment*. The organisation exists in the context of a complex commercial, political, economic, social, technological, environmental and legal world. This environment changes and is more complex for some organisations than for others. How this affects the organisation could include an understanding of historical and environmental effects, as well as expected or potential changes in environmental variables. Many of those variables will give rise to *opportunities* and others will exert *threats* on the organisation – or both. A problem that has to be faced is that the range of variables is likely to be so great that it may not be possible or realistic to identify and understand each one; and therefore it is useful to distil out of this complexity a view of the key environmental impacts on the organisation. Chapter 3 examines how this might be possible.

- The *resources and competences* of the organisation make up its *strategic capability*. Just as there are outside influences on the organisation and its choice of strategies, so there are internal influences. One way of thinking about the strategic capability of an organisation is to consider its *strengths* and *weaknesses* (what it is good or not so good at doing, or where it is at a competitive advantage or disadvantage, for example). The aim is to form a view of the internal influences – and constraints – on strategic choices for the future. On occasions, specific resources – for example, the particular location of an organisation – could provide it with competitive advantage. However, competences which provide real advantage – in this book we refer to these as *core competences* – are more likely to be activities, know-how and skills which *in combination* provide advantages for that organisation which others find difficult to imitate. In AOL/Time Warner, it is not one particular resource or activity that was of importance but the combination of many and the ability to manage the linkages between the different parts of the enlarged business that might provide the company with its competitive advantage. Chapter 4 examines resources and competences in detail.

- There are a number of influences on an organisation's *purpose*. Chapter 5 explores these. Formally, the issue of *corporate governance* is important. Here the question is: who *should* the organisation primarily serve and how should managers be held responsible for this? The *expectations* of different *stakeholders* affect purpose and what will be seen as acceptable in terms of strategies advocated by management. Which views prevail will depend on which group has the greatest *power*, and understanding this can be of great importance in recognising why an organisation follows the strategy it does. *Cultural influences* from within the organisation and from the world around it also influence the strategy an organisation follows, not least because the environmental and resource influences on the organisation are likely to be interpreted in terms of the assumptions inherent in that culture. Chapter 5 builds on the discussion in Chapter 2 to show how cultural influences on strategy can be examined. All of this raises *ethical* issues about what managers and organisations do and why. This array of influences also takes form in statements of *objectives*. These are also discussed in Chapter 5.

Together, a consideration of the *environment*, *strategic capability*, the *expectations* and the *purposes* within the *cultural* and *political* framework of the organisation provides a basis for understanding the strategic position of an organisation. Such an understanding needs to take the future into account. Is the current strategy capable of dealing with the changes taking place in the organisation's environment? Is it likely to deliver the results expected by influential stakeholders? If so, in what respects, and if not, why not? It is unlikely that there will be a complete match between current strategy and the picture which emerges from answering these questions. It may be that the mismatch is marginal, or it may be that there is a need for a fundamental realignment of strategy. Assessing the magnitude of required strategic changes and the ability of the organisation to effect such changes is another important aspect of the organisation's strategic position.

1.2.2 Strategic choices

Strategic choices involve understanding the underlying bases for future strategy at both the corporate and business unit levels (discussed above) and the options for developing strategy in terms of both the directions in which strategy might move and the methods of development.

Strategic choices involve understanding the underlying bases for future strategy at both the corporate and business unit levels and the options for developing strategy in terms of both the directions and methods of development

- At the highest level in an organisation there are issues of *corporate-level strategy*, which are concerned with the scope of an organisation's strategies, the relationship between the separate parts of the business and how the corporate centre adds value to these various parts. For example, the corporate centre, as a parent to the business units, could add value by looking for synergies between business units, by channelling resources – such as finance – or through particular competences – such as marketing or brand building. There is a danger, of course, that the centre does not add value and is merely a cost upon the business units and is therefore destroying value. There are very different ways in which these issues might be resolved. For example, AOL/Time Warner could continue to operate as separate businesses with a very slim corporate centre simply 'policing' a market-like relationship between AOL and the separate business units within Time Warner as its content provider. In contrast, the corporate centre could integrate the businesses into a new single organisation and create divisions around target markets (e.g. geographically) or customer groups (e.g. by age group). These issues about the role of the centre and how it adds value are *parenting* issues and will be discussed in Chapter 6.

- There are strategic choices in terms of how the organisation seeks to compete at *business level.* This requires an identification of *bases of competitive advantage* arising from an understanding of both markets and customers, and special competences that the organisation has; for example, whether AOL/Time Warner will take advantage of the reduced costs that should result from the merger to reduce prices in its separate business units such as music, cable TV and Internet service provision or whether it will focus on investing in ways of differentiating itself from competitors through innovative new services, such as interactive TV, that others cannot match. Or perhaps they will choose to do both of these. These issues of business-level strategies will be discussed in Chapter 7.

- Strategy may develop in the future in different *directions.* For example, historically Time Warner had developed through diversification into related fields (publishing, film, music and television). Indeed, the merger with AOL is just the latest example of the dominance of this particular development direction. This would contrast with other organisations that might concentrate in a narrower field and seek to grow market share and/or progressively develop the product features and enter new geographical markets. AOL had developed through such a combination of directions.

- Organisations also have choices of the *method* of strategy development. The development *method* used by Time Warner had been merger or acquisition (as against internal development or strategic alliances, which are favoured by many other organisations). These options for development directions and methods are important and need careful consideration: indeed, in developing strategies, a potential danger is that managers do not consider any but the most obvious course of action – and the most obvious is not necessarily the best. These issues are discussed in Chapter 8 together with a discussion of the success criteria that determine why some strategic choices are likely to be better than others. These include the *suitability* of the strategy – whether it addresses the strategic position of the organisation; whether the strategy is *feasible* in terms of resources and competences required to implement it; and, finally, whether the strategy would be *acceptable* to the stakeholders. For example, in considering strategic choices for AOL/Time Warner further mergers might seem attractive in terms of further securing their ability to offer a differentiated portfolio of services. But this might not be feasible in terms of the further resources required or, indeed, there may not be a suitable partner. It may not be acceptable to shareholders for the reason of raised financial risk nor to regulators because of monopoly considerations or concerns over the types of services. It could be argued that they would be better advised to concentrate on consolidating the merger and allowing the separate business units to compete strongly and gain market share in their own sectors.

1.2.3 Strategy into action

Translating **strategy into action** is concerned with ensuring that strategies are working in practice. A strategy is not just a good idea, a statement or a plan. It is only meaningful when it is actually being carried out. How this occurs is typically thought of in terms of:

Strategy into action is concerned with ensuring that strategies are working in practice

- *Structuring* an organisation to support successful performance. This includes structures, organisational processes, boundaries and relationships (and the interaction between these elements). These issues will be discussed in Chapter 9. For example, if AOL/Time Warner remains structured around its current business units (music, film/TV, publishing, Internet) it will need to establish new roles and processes to facilitate those separate business units in working together to create new services like online digital music. This is the rationale for the merger. It will have the difficult problem of building relationships between separate groups of people (for example, music and Internet specialists) that have different cultures and who are used to working in different ways.

- *Enabling* success through the way in which the separate resource areas of an organisation support strategies; and also the reverse of this – the extent to which new strategies are built on the particular resource and competence strengths of an organisation. Chapter 10 will consider this two-way relationship between strategy and four important resource areas (people, information, money and technology). Clearly a central issue for AOL/Time Warner is how they can continue to get market advantage in publishing, music and TV through the exploitation of IT – particularly the Internet. But this will have implications for the people and financial resources of the organisation too.

- Strategy very often involves *change*, and Chapter 11 looks at how organisations might manage change processes. This will include the need to change day-to-day routines and cultural aspects of the organisation, and overcoming political blockages to change. Following mergers, such as AOL and Time Warner, an inability to manage one or more of these change issues results in the performance expectations of the merger not being met. This is a very common outcome of mergers and acquisitions.

1.3 STRATEGY AS A SUBJECT OF STUDY

An explanation of the history of strategy as a subject of study is helpful in understanding how it will be presented in this book. It will also introduce the important idea of the different *lenses* through which strategy might be viewed – an issue that will be explained in depth in Chapter 2 and will run through all the parts of the book.

The origins of the study and teaching of strategy can be traced to a number of major influences:

- The first is to do with the *task of the general manager* and, perhaps most obviously, took form in the *business policy*[4] courses run at universities such as Harvard going back to the 1960s. The continual question posed here was 'what would you do if you took over as chief executive of such and such an organisation?' It positioned strategy as the responsibility of the general manager (typically a CEO) and was based on the common-sense experience of executives and not so much on theory or research. Teaching was dominated by attempts to replicate real business situations in the classroom by the saturation exposure to case studies.

- In parallel there developed in the 1960s and 1970s the influence of books on *corporate planning*.[5] Here the emphasis was on trying to analyse the various influences on an organisation's well-being in such a way as to identify opportunities or threats to future development. It took the form of highly systematised approaches to planning. This analytic approach is a dominant legacy in the study of the subject. It assumes that managers can and should understand all they possibly can about their organisational world; and that by so doing they can make optimal decisions about the organisation's future. It was a highly influential approach and, for example, gave rise to specialist corporate planning departments in organisations in the private and public sectors, especially in the 1970s.

In the 1980s both of these approaches came in for considerable criticism. There developed a growing body of research addressing many key strategic questions which started to become influential in how the subject was seen and how students and managers should learn about strategy:

- Typically this took the form of examining *evidence* about the links between financial performance and the strategies followed by organisations on, for example, product development, market entry, diversification and associated decisions about organisational structure.[6] It was argued that managers benefit from lessons drawn from such research in order to make wiser strategic decisions. The continuing assumption was, of course, that strategic decisions should be driven by analysis and evaluation so as to make optimal decisions; but that an accumulation of research findings could provide evidence by which to do this.

- Others[7] argued that the world was simply not that straightforward. Its complexity and uncertainty meant that it was impossible to analyse everything up front, predict the future; and that the search for optimal decisions was futile. It was necessary to accept the messiness of organisational life, that managers made decisions which were as much to do with collective and individual experience, organisational politics and the substantial influence of organisational history and culture as they were to do with strategy. As evidence of this, they pointed to the adaptive nature of how strategies developed in organisations.[8] They argued that it would be fruitful to spend more time understanding *managerial processes* of decision making in dealing with the complexity of strategic management in the reality of their social, political and cultural contexts.

- The orthodox view has been that such social and political and cultural constraints on managers result in sub-optimal decisions, inertia and perhaps underperformance. In other words, that managers do need to be better at analysis and planning and can take optimal decisions but that their personal biases and the culture of their organisation get in the way. More recently, others have questioned this.[9] They suggest that organisations are not so very different from living organisms. These organisms do not just plan and analyse, they live, they experience, they interpret and between them and within them there is sufficient diversity and variety for them to be able to change and innovate to deal with their changing environments. There has grown up an argument that organisations and managers are better understood not so much as living in the world of planning and analysis, but as using their skills and senses within the more complex world of *social interaction* in their organisation and, more widely, in the world around them. Moreover, that this will better explain how organisations cope with fast-changing environments, how new ideas and innovation come about and therefore how more significant strategic transformations come about.

This book argues that it is useful to draw on all of these views. The sort of analysis, conceptual models, research evidence, and planning systems and tools employed by those who seek to *design* strategies are useful. They help strategists think through problems and issues so as to challenge and question and, indeed, inform decision making. No doubt such an approach played a large part in the partners in the AOL/TW merger thinking through its benefits and its problems. However, it is also important to understand how the *experience* of managers and the culture of organisations inform and constrain the development of strategies; and how differences between people and groups are resolved. Moreover, by understanding such phenomena, important insights can be gained into the management of strategic change. It would be unwise of the top management of AOL/TW to believe that the sorts of change they have in mind are likely to happen without addressing such issues in the businesses that comprise the new portfolio of the merged corporation. There is also much to be learned from understanding how new *ideas* might emerge in organisations from the variety of experience and behaviours that are to be found across a huge corporation such as AOL/TW. It is unrealistic to believe that all such ideas can be planned from the top. Given the purpose of the merger – to search for new opportunities by bringing the different businesses together – thinking about how such potential innovation can be encouraged and tapped would be important. So all three ways of looking at strategy development are useful. They will be referred to in this book as the *lenses* through which strategy in organisations can be viewed:

- *Strategy as design*: the view that strategy development can be a logical process in which economic forces and constraints on the organisation are weighed carefully through analytic and evaluative techniques to establish clear strategic direction and in turn carefully planned in its implementation is perhaps the most commonly held view about how strategy is developed and what managing strategy is about. It is usually associated with the notion that it is top management's responsibility to do this and that top management leads the development of strategy in organisations.

- *Strategy as experience*: here the view is that future strategies of organisations are based on the *adaptation* of past strategies influenced by the experience of managers and others in the organisation, and are taken-for-granted assumptions and ways of doing things embedded in the cultural processes of organisations. In so far as different views and expectations exist, they will be resolved not just through rational analytic processes, but also through processes of bargaining and negotiation. Here, then, the view is that there is a tendency for the strategy of the organisation to build on and be a continuation of what has gone before.

- *Strategy as ideas*: neither of the above lenses is especially helpful in explaining innovation. So how do new ideas come about? This lens emphasises the potential variety and diversity which exist in organisations and which can potentially generate novelty. If we are to understand how innovations and innovative strategies come about, it is necessary to understand how this potential diversity contributes to it. Here strategy is seen not so much as planned from the top but as *emergent* from within and around the organisation as people cope with an uncertain and changing environment in their day-to-day activities. New ideas will emerge, but they are likely to have to battle for survival against the forces for conformity to past strategies that the experience lens explains. Drawing on explanations from evolutionary and complexity theories, the ideas lens provides insights into how this might take place.

These 'lenses' will be introduced more fully in Chapter 2 and referred to regularly throughout the book – particularly in the commentaries, which are at the end of each part of the book. It is important to understand these different explanations because all three provide insights into the challenges that are faced in managing the complexity of strategy.

Illustration 1.3 shows an example of the three lenses as it might apply to decisions of individuals.

1.4 STRATEGIC MANAGEMENT IN DIFFERENT CONTEXTS[10]

The AOL/Time Warner merger has been used in this chapter to illustrate different aspects of strategic management. To a greater or lesser extent, all these aspects are relevant for most organisations. However, it is likely that different aspects will be more important in some contexts and in some organisations than in others. For example, the need to understand the convergence of previously separate industries (such as media and the Internet), to develop new 'routes to market' and to maintain a dominant market share in its various markets was of particular importance to AOL/Time Warner. This is a different emphasis from that of a steel or glass manufacturer supplying commodity-like materials into mature markets or a public sector service provider tailoring services to the needs of a local community within statutory requirements.

Illustration 1.3

Choosing a new car

The strategy lenses also apply to the personal strategies followed by individuals.

A manager was considering buying a new car. He had driven Jaguars for some time. However, he thought it would be a good idea to review the options systematically (*the design lens*). He obtained the brochures for a range of luxury car makes, identified the major factors that were important to him and considered all the performance indicators for each of the cars against these. He even allocated a weighted score to the factors that meant most to him. The analysis told him that a BMW or a Mercedes might be a better choice than a Jaguar.

This surprised him; and he didn't much like the answer. He had always driven a Jaguar, he was used to it, felt it had an especially English character and that it suited his personality (*the experience lens*). He was also looking forward to having the new model. So his inclination was to buy another Jaguar.

Actually he ended up buying an open-top Mercedes sports. This was because his wife thought he needed to liven up his image and liked the idea of driving it on holidays (*the ideas lens*). With some reluctance he bought the new Mercedes. This proved to be a good decision. They both liked the car and it depreciated in value much more slowly than a Jaguar.

So what are the lessons? The planning and analysis was there; and if it didn't end up informing the decision directly, it did indirectly. His wife justified the purchase of the Mercedes in part on the basis of that analysis. He would have ended up with another Jaguar; a continuity of what he was used to. He actually chose what (to him) was a novel, innovative option that, in the long run, significantly changed his approach to car buying. Of course, if his wife had not intervened, his inclination to the Jaguar based on past experience would probably have prevailed. This depended on him and his circumstances – the context. Some ideas get through, some do not, depending how attractive the ideas were to him. Or it could have been that the power of analysis had been such as to overcome this. So it is with organisations. All these three lenses are likely to be there. The nature and context of the organisation are likely to determine which one prevails.

It is also difficult to say which lens was best. Who is to say that the analysis actually provided the optimal result? Maybe it was important that he should feel comfortable with his past.

Question

Choose a decision from your own personal life and consider how the three lenses impacted on the final choice that you made.

However, in AOL/Time Warner these current priorities are likely to shift over time as the industry convergence progresses and more parts of the market mature. Even within the one company, different business units may face quite different market conditions – Internet service provision and publishing are in different phases of technological and market development. It would, then, be wrong to assume that all aspects of strategic management are equally important in all circumstances. This section reviews some of the ways in which aspects differ in different contexts.

1.4.1 The small business context[11]

Small businesses are likely to be operating in a single market or a limited number of markets, probably with a limited range of products or services. The scope of the operation is therefore likely to be less of a strategic issue than it is in larger organisations. It is unlikely that small businesses will have central service departments to undertake complex analysis and market research; rather, it may be senior managers themselves, perhaps even the founder of the firm, who has direct contact with the marketplace and whose experience is therefore very influential. Indeed, in small firms the values and expectations of senior executives, who may themselves be in an ownership position, are likely to be very important, and even when current management are not owners, it may be that the values and expectations of the founders persist. It is also likely that, unless the firm is specialising in some particular market segment, it will be subject to significant competitive pressures; so issues of competitive strategy are likely to be especially important for the small firm. However, decisions on competitive strategies are likely to be strongly influenced by the experience of those running the business, so the questions posed and concepts discussed about the nature of competition in Chapter 3 and bases of competitive strategy in Chapter 6 are likely to be especially relevant.

Small firms are also likely to be private companies. This significantly affects their ability to raise capital. Combined with the legacy of the founder's influence on choice of product and market, this may mean that choices of strategy are limited. The firm may see its role as consolidating its position within a particular market. If it does not, and is seeking growth, then the raising of finance is crucial, so building or maintaining relationships with funding bodies such as banks becomes a key strategic issue.

1.4.2 The multinational corporation[12]

The key strategic issues facing multinationals such as AOL/Time Warner are substantially different from those facing the small business. Here the organisation is likely to be diverse in terms of both products and geographical markets. It may be that they have a range of different types of business in the form of subsidiary companies within a holding company structure, or divisions within a multidivisional structure. Therefore, issues of structure and control at the corporate level and relationships between businesses and the corporate centre are usually a major strategic issue for multinational companies. Indeed, a central concern is the extent to which the corporate centre adds to or detracts from the value of its businesses (see Chapters 6 and 9). At the business unit level, many of the competitive strategic issues will, perhaps, be similar to those faced by smaller firms – though the strength of the multinational within a given geographical area may be greater than for any small firm. However, for the multinational parent company, a significant issue will be how corporate business units should be allocated resources given their different, and often competing, demands and how this is to be coordinated. The coordination of operational logistics across different business units and different countries may become especially important. For example, a multinational manufacturing company such as Toyota or General Motors has to decide on the most sensible configuration of plants for the manufacture of cars. Most have moved from manufacturing a particular car at a particular location, and now manufacture different parts of cars in different locations, bringing together such components for the assembly of a given model in a given location. The logistics problems of coordinating such operations are immense, requiring sophisticated control systems and management skills far removed from those in the smaller firm. An important choice that a major multinational has to make is the extent to which it controls such logistics centrally, or devolves autonomy to operating units. It is, again, an issue of structure, management processes and relationships – the subject of Chapter 9 of this book.

1.4.3 Manufacturing and service organisations

Whilst differences exist between organisations providing services and those providing products, there is also an increasing awareness of similarities. For an organisation that competes on the basis of the services it provides – for example, insurance, management consultancy and professional services – there is no physical product. Here competitive advantage is likely to be much more related to the extent to which customers value less tangible aspects of the firm. This could be, for example, the soundness of advice given, the attitude of staff, the ambience of offices, the swiftness of service and so on. For manufacturing organisations the physical product itself has been regarded as central to competitive strategy and services are needed simply to support the product (such as product information, back-up service and so on). Managers in manufacturing organisations may therefore believe they exercise more direct control over competitive strategy than can be exercised in a service organisation. However, the computer hardware industry demonstrates that in a competitive commodity-like world the physical products of competitors are very similar, and competing by providing more functionality (storage and processor speed) fails to win new customers. Increasingly it is service that determines the winners – speed to market with new products, simplicity of the ordering process and effective helpline support make the difference. So, most have come to understand that, since physical products are often perceived by customers as very similar, other features such as service or brand image are just as important in achieving competitive advantage. Bases of competitive advantage related to resources, organisational competences and value to customers are discussed in Chapters 4 and 6.

1.4.4 The innovatory organisation[13]

There are an increasing number of organisations that claim to depend substantially on innovation for their strategic success, and still others that argue the importance of becoming more innovatory. Certainly businesses in the field of high technology products or those dependent on research and development, for example in the pharmaceutical industry, have long experienced the extent to which innovation is important. Innovation is seen as the ability to 'change the rules of the game'. The rapid developments in information technology have thrown up opportunities for organisations that can do business in new ways – the dot.com companies of the e-commerce revolution. The success of all these innovatory organisations is likely to be built on a willingness to challenge the status quo in an industry or a market and an awareness of how the organisation's resources and competences can be 'stretched' to create new opportunities. The need to see and act strategically against very short time horizons is another key feature of the innovatory context. Although the same strategic issues exist as with other companies, it is unlikely to be the formal procedures that matter so much as the type and quality of the people, the sources of knowledge in the organisation and the extent to which the prevailing culture encourages the transfer of knowledge and the questioning of what is taken for granted. Innovation will also be influenced by how people are managed and how they interact. For example, organisational structures that encourage interaction and integration, rather than formal divisions of responsibility, may encourage innovation.

Although the ideas lens is especially important in understanding strategy in innovatory organisations, there has been evidence that some of the difficulties of the dot.coms has been a failure to look at their development in other ways – particularly through the design lens – for example, to understand some of the basic ideas about competition and strategic capability.

1.4.5 Strategy in the public sector[14]

The concepts of strategy and strategic management are just as important in the public sector as in commercial firms. However, like the private sector, the public sector is diverse, as some examples show.

● *Nationalised companies* may be similar in many respects to commercial organisations; the differences are associated with the nature of ownership and control. Postal services in many countries are in, or moving towards, this position. There is likely to be a good deal of direct or indirect control or influence exercised from outside the organisation, by government in particular. A commercial enterprise that is state controlled may find not only planning horizons determined more by political than by market conditions, but also constraints on investment capital and therefore on bases of financing, and on the latitude that managers have to change strategies. It is for these reasons that there has been large-scale privatisation of previously state-run enterprises over the past 20 years – steel, telecommunications, rail services, airlines and many more. Understanding the power of different stakeholders (Chapter 5) and constraints on change (see Chapters 2 and 11) may be especially important here.

● A *government agency* has a labour market, and a money market of sorts; it also has suppliers and users or customers. However, at its heart lies a political market that approves budgets and provides subsidies. It is the explicit nature of this political dimension which managers – or officers – have to cope with which particularly distinguishes government bodies, be they national or local, from commercial enterprises. This may in turn change the horizons of decisions, since they may be heavily influenced by political considerations, and may mean that analysis of strategies requires the norms of political dogma to be considered explicitly. However, although the magnitude of the political dimension is greater, the model of strategic management discussed here still holds.

● *Public service* organisations – for example, health services and many of the amenities run by local government – face difficulties from a strategic point of view because they may not be allowed to specialise, and may not be able to generate surpluses from their services to invest in development. This can lead to a mediocrity of service where strategic decisions mainly take the form of striving for more and more efficiency so as to retain or improve services on limited budgets. Careful deployment and appropriate development of resources becomes very important (see Chapters 4 and 10).

● In the public sector, the notion of competition is usually concerned with competition for *resource inputs*, typically within a political arena. The need to demonstrate *best value* in *outputs* has become increasingly important. Many of the developments in management practices in the public sector, such as internal markets, performance indicators, competitive tendering and so on, were attempts to introduce elements of competition in order to encourage improvements in value for money. More recently there has been a shift of emphasis to cooperation and inter-agency working in an attempt to address *outcomes* of social importance. Examples would be tackling the drugs problem, crime and disorder or mental health, all of which require cooperative efforts to improve outcomes. This means that being able to build and sustain strategic alliances is a priority – as discussed in Chapter 8.

● Overall, the role of ideology in the development of strategy in the public sector is probably greater than that in commercial organisations. Putting it in the terminology of this book, the criterion of *acceptability to stakeholders* of strategic choices is probably of greater significance in the public sector than in the commercial sector.

1.4.6 The voluntary and not-for-profit sectors[15]

In the voluntary sector it is likely that underlying values and ideology will be of central strategic significance and play an important part in the development of strategy. This is particularly the case where the *raison d'être* of the organisation is rooted in such values, as is the case with organisations providing services traditionally not for profit, such as charities.

In not-for-profit organisations such as charities, churches, private schools, foundations and so on, the sources of funds may be diverse and are quite likely not to be direct beneficiaries of the services offered. Moreover, they may provide funds in advance of the services being offered – in the form of grants, for example. There are several implications. Influence from funding bodies may be high in terms of the formulation of organisational strategies. Competition may be high for funds from such bodies; but the principles of competitive strategy (see Chapter 7) nonetheless hold. However, since such organisations are dependent on funds which emanate not from users but from sponsors, there is a danger that they may become concerned more with resource efficiency than with service effectiveness (see Chapter 4). The fact that multiple sources of funding are likely to exist, linked to the different objectives and expectations of the funding bodies, might also lead to a high incidence of political lobbying, difficulties in clear strategic planning, and a requirement to hold decision making and responsibility at the centre, where it is answerable to external influences, rather than delegate it within the organisation.

1.4.7 Professional service organisations

Traditionally based values are often of particular importance in professional services such as medicine, accountancy, law and other professions. Private sector professional firms may also have a partnership structure. Partners may be owners and perhaps bear legal responsibility for advice and opinion offered by the firm; they may therefore carry considerable power; and there may be many of them – each of the top four accountancy firms now aspires to global strategies, but each may have thousands of partners. Traditionally, although interacting with clients and exercising actual or potential control over resources, these partners may not have regarded themselves as managers at all. As a partner in a major accountancy firm put it: 'We see ourselves as the largest network of sole traders in the world.' The problems of developing and implementing strategy within such a context are, therefore, heavily linked to the management of internal political influences (see Chapter 5) and the ability to take account of, and where necessary to change, organisational culture (see Chapters 5 and 11). Another factor is the pressure that those in the professions find themselves under to be more 'commercial' in their approach. Such pressure may come from government, as in the case of doctors; or it may be a function of size, as has been found in the growing accountancy and law firms. This has meant that

Illustration 1.4

Strategic issues in different contexts

The strategic issues faced by managers in different organisations depend on their business context.

Global organisations

Many companies today are struggling to achieve a globally integrated organisation that retains the capability for local flexibility and responsiveness. Virtually no company has achieved a totally satisfactory solution. . . . The task is achievable if managers break it down into digestible pieces and if they relate changes in organisation to the specific changes in global strategy.

G. Yip, *Total Global Strategy*,
Prentice Hall, 1995, pp. 161–162

A multi-business company

The business units of multi-business companies create value through direct contact with customers. They compete in their markets to satisfy customer needs and to generate revenues and profits. In contrast the parent [company] . . . acts as an intermediary influencing the decisions and strategies pursued by the businesses and standing between the businesses and those who provide capital for their use.

M. Goold, A. Campbell and M. Alexander,
Corporate Level Strategy, Wiley, 1994, p. 12

Professional services

The players [in accountancy] are broadly similar in size and in their range of resources, consequently there is no natural leader to direct and structure the market. Even where the professional offerings are similar . . . the ability to co-ordinate and integrate people to create a real benefit for the client can be a distinguishing factor. The result is that teamwork, relationship management and integration are the competences that may distinguish one firm from the pack.

Colin Sharman, Senior Partner,
KPMG, 1998

Not-for-profit sector

If your mission is, say, to eliminate poverty or save the planet, then almost anything you do can be justified. If management is weak and without legitimacy (which is too often the case), this means staff often set their own personal agendas. To a greater extent than most private organisations, there are also multiple stakeholders, and managers can find themselves buffeted by warring factions both outside and inside the organisation. Young staff often join with a view that they are going to change the world, and find out that many jobs are pretty routine. There is a great danger that they then invest their energy in trying to create their vision of the world within the organisation.

Sheila McKechnie, Director of
Shelter until 1995

Public sector

Efficient and effective public services are an essential part of a healthy democratic society. Many local authorities recognise this and successfully achieve high standards, often in difficult circumstances. Others are less successful, and provide services that fall well short of the best that can be achieved within the resources that are available. The Government's proposals for best value . . . will require councils to meet the aspirations of local people for the highest quality and most efficient services at a price that people are willing to pay.

'Modernising Local Government',
DETR, 1998, p. 5

Question

Refer to Exhibit 1.4 and answer the following question separately *in relation to each of the contexts*:

Which element of the strategy model is being emphasised? Why?

such organisations have had to be concerned with competitive strategy (see Chapter 7).

Illustration 1.4 shows some examples of the different emphasis of strategy in different contexts.

SUMMARY

- Strategy is the *direction* and *scope* of an organisation over the *long term*, which achieves *advantage* for the organisation through its configuration of *resources* within a changing *environment* and to fulfil *stakeholder* expectations. So all organisations are faced with the challenge of managing strategy.

- Strategic decisions may be about a search for strategic 'fit' – trying to find ways to match the organisation's resources and activities to the environment in which it operates. Strategic decisions could also be based on trying to 'stretch' the resources and competences of the organisation to create new opportunities.

- Strategies will also be influenced by the values and expectations of stakeholders in and around the organisation, and the extent of the power they exert. The culture within and around an organisation will also influence its strategy.

- Strategic decisions are made at a number of levels in organisations. Corporate-level strategy is concerned with an organisation's overall purpose and scope; business level (or competitive) strategy with how to compete successfully in a market; and operational strategies with how resources, processes and people can effectively deliver corporate- and business-level strategies.

- The formulation of business-level strategies is best thought of in terms of strategic business units (SBUs) which are parts of organisations for which there are distinct external markets for goods or services. However, these may not represent formal structural divisions in an organisation.

- Strategic management is distinguished from day-to-day operational management by the complexity of influences on decisions, the fundamental, organisation-wide implications that strategic decisions have for the organisation, and their long-term implications. It can be problematic for managers not least because their strategic horizons are likely to be limited by their experience and organisational culture and most of their training may have been in operational management.

- Strategic management can be conceived of in terms of understanding the *strategic position*, *strategic choices* for the future and translating *strategy into action*. The strategic position of an organisation is influenced by the external environment, internal resources and competences, and the expectations and influence of stakeholders. Strategic choices include the underlying bases of choices at both the corporate and business levels and the directions and methods of development. Strategic management is also concerned with understanding which choices are likely to succeed or fail. Translating strategy into action is concerned with issues of structuring, resourcing to enable future strategies and managing change.

- How organisations develop strategies can be explained in different ways. A design view sees the process as planned from the top. An experience view sees it as the product of individual experience and organisational culture. The ideas view sees strategy as emerging from ideas within and around an organisation.

- Organisations in different contexts are likely to emphasise different aspects of the strategic management process. For some organisations the major challenge will be developing competitive strategy; for others it will be building organisational structures capable of integrating complex global operations; for yet others it will be understanding their competences so as to focus on what they are especially good at; and for still others it will be developing a culture of innovation. Strategic priorities need to be understood in terms of the particular context of an organisation.

RECOMMENDED KEY READINGS

It is useful to read about how strategies are managed in practice and some of the lessons that can be drawn from this which inform key themes in this book. For example:

- For readings on the concepts of strategy in organisations, John Kay's book, *Foundations for Corporate Success: How business strategies add value*, Oxford University Press, 1993, is a helpful explanation from an economics point of view. For a wider theoretical perspective, see R. Whittington, *What is Strategy and Does it Matter?*, 2nd edition, Routledge, 2001.

- It is also useful to read accounts of where the management of strategy in organisations has made an

impact on organisational performance. Reference is also often made in this book to G. Hamel and C.K. Prahalad, *Competing for the Future*, Harvard Business School Press, 1994, which draws extensively on examples of successful strategies in organisations. Readers are encouraged to keep up to date with developments and strategies in organisations through newspapers, business magazines and dedicated business websites (such as FT.com).

- For a discussion of strategy in different types of organisations, see H. Mintzberg, J. Quinn and S. Ghoshal (eds), *The Strategy Process: Concepts, contexts and cases*, 4th edition, Prentice Hall, 1998.

REFERENCES

1. In the 1980s much of the writing and practice of strategic management was influenced by the writings of industrial organisations economists. One of the most influential books was Michael Porter, *Competitive Strategy*, Free Press, first published 1980. In essence, the book describes means of analysing the competitive nature of industries so that managers might be able to select among attractive and less attractive industries and choose strategies most suited to the organisation in terms of these forces. This approach, which assumes the dominant influence of industry forces and the over-riding need to tailor strategies to address those forces, has become known as a 'fit' view of strategy.

2. The notion of strategy as 'stretch' is perhaps best explained in G. Hamel and C.K. Prahalad, *Competing for the Future*, Harvard Business School Press, 1994.

3. The term 'SBU' can be traced back to the development of corporate-level strategic planning in General Electric in the USA in the early 1970s. For an early account of its uses, see W.K. Hall, 'SBUs: hot, new topic in the management of diversification', *Business Horizons*, vol. 21, no. 1 (1978), pp. 17–25.

4. See for example: C. Christensen, K. Andrews and J. Bower, *Business Policy: Text and cases*, 4th edition, Irwin, 1978.

5. For example, J. Argenti, *Systematic Corporate Planning*, Nelson, 1974 or H. Ansoff, *Corporate Strategy*, Penguin, 1975.

6. One of the important books that marked this shift was: D. Schendel and C. Hofer, *Strategic Management: A new view of business policy and planning*, Little, Brown, 1979.

7. See: C. Lindblom, 'The science of muddling through', *Public Administration Review*, vol. 19 (Spring 1959), pp. 79-88; J. Quinn, *Strategies for Change*, Irwin, 1980; A. Pettigrew, *The Awakening Giant*, Blackwell, 1985; H. Mintzberg, 'Crafting strategy', *Harvard Business Review*, vol. 65, no. 4 (1987), pp. 66-75.

8. See Quinn (reference 7 above).

9. See: R. Stacey, *Managing Chaos: Dynamic business strategies in an unpredictable world*, Kogan Page, 1992; S. Brown and K. Eisenhardt, *Competing on the Edge: Strategy as structured chaos*, HBR Press, 1998.

10. For an extensive discussion of strategy in different types of organisations, see H. Mintzberg, J. Quinn and S. Ghoshal (eds), *The Strategy Process: Concepts, contexts and cases*, 4th edition, Prentice Hall, 1998.

11. For strategy development in small businesses, see C. Barrow, R. Brown and L. Clarke, *The Business Growth Handbook*, Kogan Page, 1995.

12. There are now many books on managing strategy in multinationals. In this book we will refer often to C. Bartlett and S. Ghoshall, *Managing Across Borders: The transnational solution*, 2nd edition, Random House, 1998; and G. Yip, *Total Global Strategy*, Prentice Hall, 1995.

13. A good review of aspects of innovation and their organisational implications can be found in J. Tidd, J. Bessant and K. Pavitt, *Managing Innovations: Integrating technological, marketing and organisational change*, 2nd edition, Wiley, 2001.

14. See: G. Johnson and K. Scholes (eds.), *Exploring Public Sector Strategy*, FT/Prentice Hall, 2001, in particular J. Alford, 'The implications of publicness for strategic management theory' (Chapter 1) and N. Collier, F. Fisnwick and G. Johnson, 'The processes of strategy development in the public sector' (Chapter 2). Also: D. McKevitt and A. Lawton, *Public Sector Management: Theory, critique and practice*, Sage, 1994.

15. See J.M. Bryson, *Strategic Planning for Public and Nonprofit Organizations*, Prentice Hall, 1995.

WORK ASSIGNMENTS

* Refers to a case study in the Text and Cases edition. ✸ Denotes more advanced work assignments.

1.1 Using the characteristics discussed in section 1.1.1, write out a statement of strategy for Corus* or an organisation with which you are familiar.

1.2 Note down the characteristics of strategy development at AOL/Time Warner, or Microsoft/Netscape which would be explained by the notion of (a) strategic management as 'environmental fit', and (b) strategic management as the 'stretching' of capabilities.

1.3 Using Exhibit 1.2 and Illustration 1.2 as a guide, note down and explain examples of the vocabulary of strategy used in the annual report of a company of your choosing.

1.4✸ Using annual reports, press articles and the Internet, write a brief case study (similar to the AOL/Time Warner illustration or the Corus* case), which shows the strategic development and current strategic position of an organisation.

1.5 Using Exhibit 1.4 as a guide, note down the elements of strategic management discernible in the Corus* case or an organisation of your choice.

1.6✸ Using Exhibit 1.4 as a guide, show how the different elements of strategic management differ in:

(a) a multinational business (e.g. AOL/Time Warner, The News Corporation*)
(b) a professional services firm (e.g. KPMG*)
(c) a public sector organisation (e.g. CSA*)
(d) a small business (e.g. Coopers Creek*)
(e) a high technology business (e.g. Microsoft, Netscape, Amazon* or Freeserve*).

CASE EXAMPLE

Battle of the browsers: rounds one and two

In June 2000 a federal court judge upheld the US Justice Department's contention that the Microsoft Corporation was guilty of breaking the law by using its monopoly to stifle competition and crush its rivals. The court stated that Microsoft had violated anti-trust laws by using its position to monopolise the web browser market. They were accused of imposing 'technological shackles' on other software companies. The company was ordered to be split into two separate businesses – one owning the 'Windows' operating system and the other owning software applications and Internet browser developments. The company's shares had fallen by 50 per cent during the court hearings and Bill Gates, the Microsoft chairman, warned that this ruling would lead to disaster for Microsoft and America and immediately indicated that the company would appeal against the decision.

The seeds of the court case started some six years earlier in 1994 when Marc Andreesen, a 24-year-old from Silicon Valley, launched a new way to search and retrieve information from the Internet. His company Netscape invented the Navigator Internet browser. The world's press hailed the arrival of a cyber-genius, and predicted he would create a new computer standard that could make him as powerful as Bill Gates. Netscape grabbed 80 per cent of the booming browser market. It began building intranets, providing systems for companies to create their own web-like networks. It became the platform and promoter of Sun Microsystem's Java, a new software language that challenged Microsoft's Windows operating system for personal computers (PCs). When Netscape was listed on the stock market in August 1995 its shares took off like a rocket. Before the company had made a net profit it was valued at $2.7 billion (£1.7 billion).

Gates initially dismissed the Internet and Netscape as unimportant. But Netscape's surging sales, and the phenomenal growth and popularity of the Internet, quickly forced him to change his tune. Marshalling the vast resources of Microsoft, and spending hundreds of millions of dollars on research and development, he had 2,000 of his best programmers rush out a browser of his own, the Explorer, and then bombarded the public with free copies. Microsoft's share of the browser market soared from 2.9 per cent at the end of 1995 to more than 40 per cent by the end of 1997, while Netscape's share fell to 54 per cent. Netscape's financial performance suffered badly too. Some analysts believed that the company might be in terminal decline and might not be able to survive – at least as an independent company.

So Netscape looked for help from the US Justice Department, which in October 1997 charged Microsoft with using its monopolistic 90 per cent control of all PC operating systems to force computer manufacturers to install its browser on their machines. In December, Judge Thomas Jackson issued a preliminary injunction to force Microsoft to make available two versions of Windows to PC manufacturers, one including the browser and one without. The Justice Department wanted Microsoft to remove the Explorer icon that automatically appeared on the computer screen when a user started the Windows programme. Microsoft denied it used unfair business practices, and claimed that it was simply exercising its right to enhance its operating system. It said that an Internet browser was an integral part of its Windows software.

But Microsoft realised they were playing for big stakes. In May 1995, Bill Gates wrote: 'The Internet is the most important single development to come along since the IBM PC was introduced in 1981. It has enough users that it is benefiting from the positive feedback loop of the more users it gets, the more content it gets; and the more content it gets, the more users it gets.' He went on to say that it presented a huge threat to Microsoft, because rival companies, such as Netscape and Sun, were trying to use it to 'commoditise the underlying operating system'. In other words, Netscape might gain control of the desktop with its browser becoming an alternative to Windows.

This first battle of the browsers also brought to the surface some fundamental policy issues for governments about the fostering of technological development. It was a reminder that free-market forces do not necessarily guarantee the success of the best product in high-technology fields, as they usually do in other areas of commerce. Whenever a company gets ahead (in high technology) it had an increasing advantage over its rivals, made increasing returns, and was able to use its position to dominate other markets. So many 'inferior products' had beaten superior ones, such as the VHS video beating Betamax and Dos beating Apple's operating system. So the critical issue was to establish a user base more quickly than competitors. The more people that used a given technology, the more likely that technology was to beat its competitors. In the computer industry the first company to establish an industry standard and a large installed base of products invariably dominated its market, as Microsoft dominated PC operating systems. Moreover, it puts it in a position to expand into other markets and dominate them in the same way.

Microsoft was dismissive of such theories, which they claimed missed the realities in the computer industry. In particular the fact that life cycles were short and leaders vulnerable to their products being made obsolete by superior products from competitors. They argued that there were many examples of great successes that became failures, such as Word Perfect, dBase, Lotus 1-2-3, and it was simply to do with people taking their eye off the ball.

As the legal proceedings rolled on through 1999 and 2000 developments in browsers moved on at a rapid pace – in ways that perhaps made the court hearings look like 'yesterday's battle'. A new browser war was under way as software firms started to compete to provide browsers for 'information devices' such as set-top boxes (e.g. for digital cable or satellite TV), handheld computers and third-generation ('smart') mobile phones. These devices were widely expected to eventually outnumber PCs. This second browser battle was shaping up very differently from the first one. The main difference being that Microsoft's ability to include browser software as part of the device's operating

systems (as it could do with Windows on PCs) was no longer the case. Their cut-down version of Windows for these devices had failed. In the meantime Netscape had become part of AOL and was strongly in the running – but alongside dozens of new rivals such as Opera, OpenTV, Lineo, QNX and Plixo. Also, with these new devices the choice of browser was made by the appliance manufacturer and the service provider (such as the cable company) rather than, in the case of PCs, by the operating system supplier (Microsoft) or the individual user (downloading from the Internet). So the new rivals were courting the appliance manufacturers and service providers rather than targeting consumers. With so many potential suppliers it seemed much less likely that just one browser would dominate. Also, this resulting diversity meant that an important selling point for a browser was its conformity to the technical standards agreed by the World Wide Web Consortium. The existence of these standards would also reduce the switching costs for appliance makers if they decided to change browsers – a very difficult thing to achieve with the old browsers on PCs. Netscape seemed to have learnt lessons from its bruising encounter with Microsoft in the first browser battle. It was actively supporting these standardisation measures as a means of preventing a re-run – even though it left Netscape's new software (Gecko) facing more competitors.

Sources: Adapted from *The Sunday Times*, 11 January 1998; *The Economist*, 16 December 2000.

Questions

1. Refer to section 1.1 and explain why the issues facing Netscape and Microsoft were strategic.
2. List the main factors that you would identify in the strategic position of Netscape and Microsoft (separately and under the three headings of environment, resources and expectations).
3. Think about the strategic choices for the future for each company in relation to the issues raised in section 1.2.2.
4. This case example concerns global competition in an innovative industry. Refer to section 1.4 and decide how this particular context 'shapes' the relative importance of the elements of strategy – as shown in Exhibit 1.4.

Unit 8:   Research Project

Learning hours: 60

NQF level 4:   BTEC Higher National — H2

Content Selected: Lewis, Saunders and Thornhill, Research Methods for Business Students 3rd Edition, Chapter 2

Introduction from the Qualification Leader

This unit is designed to introduce learners to the techniques and methods of research, which will then enable them to produce a project report. Chapter 2 has been selected as it deals with generating ideas for the choice of a suitable project, what makes a good project and how to draft a research proposal.

Description of unit

This unit is designed to introduce learners to the techniques and methods of research. The unit addresses a variety of research methodologies, including the opportunity to carry out interventionist or action research.

Learners will be required to produce a project report based on independent research into an area of professional business practice that interests them and will add to their professional development.

The study should use both primary and secondary sources of information, and should be an exploration of a current major issue. The study undertaken should build on knowledge, skills and understanding that have been achieved in other units. Tutor approval should be sought before commencing study.

Summary of learning outcomes

To achieve this unit a learner must:

1   Prepare a **research proposal** relating to a specified area of business

2   Conduct research using **primary and secondary sources** of information

3   Carry out the **research project** into a specified area of business

4   **Present and evaluate** the findings with regard to the initial proposal.

Content

1 **Research proposal**

Research methodologies: intervention, non-intervention, action research

Hypothesis: definition, suitability, skills and knowledge to be gained, aims, objectives, terms of reference, duration, ethical issues

Action plan: rationale for research question or hypothesis, task dates, review dates, monitoring/reviewing process, strategy

2 **Primary and secondary sources**

Primary: questionnaires – type, layout, distribution, original research data gathered by the learner; interviews, selecting interviewees, bias, verification of data, time, place, style

Secondary: eg books, journals, library search, use of IT, internet, media

3 **Research project**

Preparation: identifying ideas/topics/areas of investigation, research question(s), scope and feasibility, hypothesis, literature search, agreeing the process, targets, milestones, action plan, timetable and procedure, monitoring and revision

Methodology: literature search, eg library, internet, sector data sources; pure and applied research, developmental, longitudinal, survey, case study, research and development, concepts and theories, terminology, validity and reliability

Qualitative data analysis: interpreting transcripts, coding techniques, categorisation, relationships, trends, use of computers; presentation of data

Quantitative data analysis: coding/values, manual/electronic methods, specialist software; presentation of data, eg bar/pie charts, graphs, statistical tables; comparison of variables, trends, forecasting

4 **Present and evaluate**

Presentation: eg formal written format, by viva voce or oral presentation, diagrammatic or graphical figures

Methodology: presentation, eg IT, audio, visual aids, time, pace; delivery critique of the methods used in the study, recommendations, eg using the findings, recommendations for the future, areas for future research

Evaluation: planning, objectives, focus, benefits, difficulties

Criteria: purpose, editing, format, sequencing success, critical analysis, discussion of evidence and findings

Outcomes and assessment criteria

Outcomes	Assessment criteria for pass **To achieve each outcome a learner must demonstrate the ability to:**
1 Prepare a **research proposal** relating to a specified area of business	• identify a research question or hypothesis and justify choice • justify the chosen methodology in terms of the research question • prepare an action plan with target dates and methods for monitoring and updating • devise a code of ethics for the conduct of the study
2 Conduct research using **primary and secondary sources** of information	• undertake primary and secondary research relating to the proposal • describe and justify the chosen methodology
3 Carry out the **research project** into a specified area of business	• prepare for the research project and agree process and action plan with supervisor • monitor and revise schedule when required • collect and review data using appropriate methods, including primary and secondary research techniques • analyse and interpret appropriate qualitative and quantitative data
4 **Present and evaluate** the findings with regard to the initial proposal	• record findings in an accepted format • present and summarise the findings using suitable methods • evaluate the methodology used and critically analyse the findings • propose recommendations based on the findings which identify and justify areas for future research

Chapter 2

Formulating and clarifying the research topic

By the end of this chapter you should be able:

■ to generate ideas that will help in the choice of a suitable research topic;

■ to identify the attributes of a good research topic;

■ to turn research ideas into a research project that has clear research question(s) and objectives;

■ to draft a research proposal.

2.1 Introduction

Before you start your research you need to have at least some idea of what you want to do. This is probably the most difficult, and yet the most important, part of your research project. Up until now most of your studies have been concerned with answering questions that other people have set. This chapter is concerned with how to formulate and clarify your research topic and your research question. Without being clear about what you are going to research it is difficult to plan how you are going to research it. This reminds us of a favourite quote in *Alice's Adventures in Wonderland*. This is part of Alice's conversation with the Cheshire Cat. In this Alice asks the Cat (Carroll, 1989:63–4):

'Would you tell me, please, which way I ought to walk from here?'
'That depends a good deal on where you want to get to,' said the Cat.
'I don't much care where,' said Alice.
'Then it doesn't matter which way you walk,' said the Cat.

Formulating and clarifying the research topic is the starting point of your research project (Ghauri and Grønhaug, 2002; Smith and Dainty, 1991). Once you are clear about this you will be able to choose the most appropriate research strategy and data collection and analysis techniques. The formulating and clarifying process is time consuming and will probably take you up blind alleys (Saunders and Lewis, 1997). However, without spending time on this stage you are far less likely to achieve a successful project (Raimond, 1993).

In the initial stages of the formulating and clarifying process you will be generating and refining research ideas (Section 2.3). It may be that you have already been given a research idea, perhaps by an organisation or tutor. Even if this has happened you will still need to refine the idea into one that is feasible. Once you have done this you will need to turn the idea into research questions and objectives (Section 2.4) and to write the research proposal for your project (Section 2.5).

However, before you start the formulating and clarifying process we believe that you need to understand what makes a good research topic. For this reason we begin this chapter (Section 2.2) with a discussion of the attributes required for a good research topic.

2.2   Attributes of a good research topic

The attributes of a business and management research topic do not vary a great deal between universities (Raimond, 1993), although there will be differences in the emphasis placed on different attributes. If you are undertaking your research project as part of a course of study the most important attribute will be that it meets the examining body's requirements and, in particular, that it is at the correct level. This means that you must choose your topic with care. For example, some universities require students to collect their own data as part of their research project whereas others allow them to base their project on data that have already been collected. You therefore need to check the assessment criteria for your project and ensure that your choice of topic will enable you to meet these criteria. If you are unsure, you should discuss any uncertainties with your project tutor.

In addition, your research topic must be something you are capable of undertaking and one that excites your imagination. Capability can be considered in a variety of ways. At the personal level you need to feel comfortable that you have, or can develop, the skills that will be required to research the topic. We hope that you will develop your research skills as part of undertaking your project. However, some skills, for example foreign languages, may be impossible to acquire in the time you have available. As well as having the necessary skills we believe that you also need to have a genuine interest in the topic. Most research projects are undertaken over at least a six-month period. A topic in which you are only vaguely interested at the start is likely to become a topic in which you have no interest and with which you will fail to produce your best work.

Your ability to find the financial and time resources to undertake research on the topic will also affect your capability. Some topics are unlikely to be possible to complete in the time allowed by your course of study. This may be because they require you to measure the impact of an intervention over a long time period. Similarly, topics that are likely to require you to travel widely or need expensive equipment should also be disregarded unless financial resources permit.

Capability also means you must be reasonably certain of gaining access to any data you might need to collect. Gill and Johnson (1997) argue that this is usually relatively straightforward to assess. They point out that many people start with ideas where access to data will prove difficult. Certain, more sensitive topics, such as financial performance or decision-making by senior managers, are potentially fascinating.

However, they may present considerable access problems. You should therefore discuss this with your project tutor after reading Chapter 5.

For most topics it is important that the issues within the research are capable of being linked to theory (Raimond, 1993). Initially, theory may be based just on the reading you have undertaken as part of your study to date. However, as part of your assessment criteria you are almost certain to be asked to set your topic in context (Section 3.2). As a consequence you will need to have a knowledge of the literature and to undertake further reading as part of defining your research questions and objectives (Section 2.4).

Most project tutors will argue that one of the attributes of a good topic is clearly defined research questions and objectives (Section 2.4). These will, along with a good knowledge of the literature, enable you to assess the extent to which your research is likely to provide fresh insights into the topic. Many students believe this is going to be difficult. Fortunately, as pointed out by Phillips and Pugh (2000), there are many ways in which such insight can be defined as 'fresh' (Section 2.5).

If you have already been given a research idea (perhaps by an organisation) you will need to ensure that your questions and objectives relate clearly to the idea (Kervin, 1992). It is also important that your topic will have a *symmetry of potential outcomes*: that is, your results will be of similar value whatever you find out (Gill and Johnson, 1997). Without this symmetry you may spend a considerable amount of time researching your topic only to find an answer of little importance. Whatever the outcome, you need to ensure you have the scope to write an interesting project report.

---

worked example   ## Ensuring symmetry of potential outcomes

Karmen was a part-time student. Her initial research topic was concerned with finding out whether there was any relationship between the levels of stress experienced by social workers and the number of years they had been employed as social workers. If she established that there was a link between these factors this would be an interesting finding; if, however, she discovered no relationship the finding would be less interesting and would have no real practical relevance to her organisation.

She therefore decided to amend her topic to exploring and understanding the impact of a forthcoming stress management course on the relative levels of stress experienced by social workers before the course. The results of this research would be interesting and important whether or not the course had an impact.

Finally, it is important to consider your career goals (Creswell, 1994). If you wish to become an expert in a particular subject area or industry sector, it is sensible to use the opportunity to develop this expertise.

It is almost inevitable that the extent to which these attributes apply to your research topic will depend on your topic and the reasons for which you are undertaking the research. However, most of these attributes will apply. For this reason it is important that you check and continue to check any potential research topic against the summary checklist contained in Box 2.1.

Box 2.1	Checklist of attributes of a good research topic

☑ Does the topic fit the specifications and meet the standards set by the examining institution?

☑ Is the topic something with which you are really fascinated?

☑ Does your research topic contain issues that have a clear link to theory?

☑ Do you have, or can you develop within the project time frame, the necessary research skills to undertake the topic?

☑ Is the research topic achievable within the available time?

☑ Is the research topic achievable within the financial resources that are likely to be available?

☑ Are you reasonably certain of being able to gain access to data you are likely to require for this topic?

☑ Are you able to state your research question(s) and objectives clearly?

☑ Will your proposed research be able to provide fresh insights into this topic?

☑ Does your research topic relate clearly to the idea you have been given (perhaps by an organisation)?

☑ Are the findings for this research topic likely to be symmetrical: that is, of similar value whatever the outcome?

☑ Does the research topic match your career goals?

2.3   Generating and refining research ideas

Some business and management students are expected both to generate and to refine their own research ideas. Others, particularly those on professional and post-experience courses, are provided with a research idea by an organisation or their university. In the initial stages of their research they are expected to refine this to a clear and feasible idea that meets the requirements of the examining organisation. If you have already been given a research idea we believe you will still find it useful to read the next subsection, which deals with generating research ideas. Many of the techniques which can be used for generating research ideas can be used for the refining process.

■ Generating research ideas

If you have not been given an initial *research idea* there is a range of techniques that can be used to find and select a topic that you would like to research. They can be thought of as those that are predominantly *rational thinking* and those that involve more *creative thinking* (Box 2.2). The precise techniques that you choose to use and the order in which you use them are entirely up to you. However, like Raimond (1993), we believe you should use both rational and creative techniques, choosing those that you believe are going to be of most use to you and which you will enjoy using. By using one or more creative techniques you are more likely to ensure that your heart as well as your head is in your research project. In our experience, it is usually better to use a variety of techniques. In order to do this you will need to have some understanding of the techniques and the ways in which they work. We therefore outline the techniques in Box 2.2 and suggest possible ways they might be used to generate research ideas. These techniques will generate one of two outcomes:

- one or more possible project ideas that you might undertake;
- absolute panic because nothing in which you are interested or which seems suitable has come to mind (Jankowicz, 2000).

In either instance, but especially the latter, we suggest that you talk to your project tutor.

Box 2.2	More frequently used techniques for generating and refining research ideas

Rational thinking	*Creative thinking*
■ Examining your own strengths and interests	■ Keeping a notebook of ideas
■ Looking at past project titles	■ Exploring personal preferences using past projects
■ Discussion	■ Relevance trees
■ Searching the literature	■ Brainstorming

Examining own strengths and interests

It is important that you choose a topic in which you are likely to do well and, if possible, already have some academic knowledge. Jankowicz (2000) suggests that one way of doing this is to look at those assignments for which you have received good grades. For most of these assignments they are also likely to be the topics in which you were interested (Box 2.1). They will provide you with an area in which to search for and find a research idea. In addition you may, as part of your reading, be able to focus more precisely on the sort of ideas about which you wish to conduct your research.

As noted in Section 2.2, there is the need to think about your future. If you plan to work in financial management it would be sensible to choose a research project in the financial management field. One part of your course that will inevitably be discussed at any job interview is your research project. A project in the same field will provide you with the opportunity to display clearly your depth of knowledge and your enthusiasm.

Looking at past project titles

Many of our students have found looking at *past projects* a useful way of generating research ideas. For undergraduate and taught masters degrees these are often called *dissertations*. For research degrees they are termed *theses*. A common way of doing this is to scan a list of past project titles (such as those in Appendix 1) for anything that captures your imagination. Titles that look interesting or which grab your attention should be noted down, as should any thoughts you have about the title in relation to your own research idea. In this process the fact that the title is poorly worded or the project report received a low mark is immaterial. What matters is the fact that you have found a topic that interests you. Based on this you can think of new ideas in the same general area that will enable you to provide fresh insights.

Scanning actual research projects may also produce research ideas. However, you need to beware. The fact that a project is in your library is no guarantee of the quality of the arguments and observations it contains. In many universities all projects are placed in the library whether they are bare passes or distinctions.

Discussion

Colleagues, friends and university tutors are all good sources of possible project ideas. Often project tutors will have ideas for possible student projects, which they will be pleased to discuss with you. In addition, ideas can be obtained by talking to practitioners and professional groups (Gill and Johnson, 1997). It is important that as well as discussing possible ideas you also make a note of them. What seemed like a good idea in the coffee shop may not be remembered quite so clearly after the following lecture!

Searching the literature

As part of your discussions, relevant literature may also be suggested. Sharp and Howard (1996) discuss types of literature that are of particular use for generating research ideas. These include:

- articles in academic and professional journals;
- reports;
- books.

Of particular use are academic *review articles*. These articles contain both a considered review of the state of knowledge in that topic area and pointers towards areas where further research needs to be undertaken. In addition you can browse recent publications, in particular journals, for possible research ideas (Section 3.5). For many subject areas your project tutor will be able to suggest possible recent review articles, or articles that contain recommendations for further work. *Reports* may also be of use. The most recently published are usually up to date and, again, often contain recommendations that may form the basis of your research idea. *Books* by contrast are less up to date than other written sources. They do, however, often contain a good overview of research that has been undertaken, which may suggest ideas to you.

Searching for publications is only possible when you have at least some idea of the area in which you wish to undertake your research. One way of obtaining this is to re-examine your lecture notes and course textbooks and to note those subjects that appear most interesting (discussed earlier in this section) and the names of relevant authors. This will give you a basis on which to undertake a *preliminary search* (using techniques outlined in Sections 3.4 and 3.5). When the articles, reports and other items have been obtained it is often helpful to look for unfounded assertions and statements on the absence of research (Raimond, 1993), as these are likely to contain ideas that will enable you to provide fresh insights.

Keeping a notebook of ideas

One of the more creative techniques that we all use is to keep a *notebook of ideas*. All this involves is simply noting down any interesting research ideas as you think of them and, of equal importance, what sparked off your thought. You can then pursue the idea using more rational thinking techniques later. Mark keeps a notebook by his bed so he can jot down any flashes of inspiration that occur to him in the middle of the night!

Exploring personal preferences using past projects

Another way of generating possible project ideas is to explore your *personal preferences* using past project reports from your university. To do this Raimond (1993) suggests that you:

1 Select six projects that you like.
2 For each of these six projects note down your first thoughts in response to three questions (if responses for different projects are the same this does not matter):
   a What appeals to you about the project?
   b What is good about the project?
   c Why is the project good?
3 Select three projects that you do not like.
4 For each of these three projects note down your first thoughts in response to three questions (if responses for different projects are the same, or cannot be clearly expressed, this does not matter; note them down anyway):
   a What do you dislike about the project?
   b What is bad about the project?
   c Why is the project bad?

You now have a list of what you consider to be excellent and what you consider to be poor in projects. This will not be the same as a list generated by anyone else. It is also very unlikely to match the attributes of a good research project (Box 2.1). However, by examining this list you will begin to understand those project characteristics that are important to you and with which you feel comfortable. Of equal importance is that you will have identified those that you are uncomfortable with and should avoid. These can be used as the parameters against which to evaluate possible research ideas.

Relevance trees

Relevance trees may also prove useful in generating research topics. In this instance, their use is similar to that of mind mapping (Buzan with Buzan, 2000), in which you start with a broad concept from which you generate further (usually more specific) topics. Each of these topics forms a separate branch from which you can generate further more detailed sub-branches. As you proceed down the sub-branches more ideas are generated and recorded. These can then be examined and a number selected and combined to provide a research idea (Sharp and Howard, 1996).*

* This technique is discussed in more detail in Section 3.4, which also includes a worked example in which a relevance tree is used to help generate key words for a literature search.

Brainstorming

The technique of *brainstorming*, taught as a problem-solving technique on many business and management courses, can also be used to generate and refine research ideas. It is best undertaken with a group of people, although you can brainstorm on your own. To brainstorm, Moody (1983) suggests that you:

1 Define your problem – that is, the sorts of ideas you are interested in – as precisely as possible. In the early stages of formulating a topic this may be as vague as 'I am interested in marketing but don't know what to do for my research topic.'
2 Ask for suggestions relating to the problem.
3 Record all suggestions observing the following rules:
   – No suggestion should be criticised or evaluated in any way before all ideas have been considered.
   – All suggestions, however wild, should be recorded and considered.
   – As many suggestions as possible should be recorded.
4 Review all the suggestions and explore what is meant by each.
5 Analyse the list of suggestions and decide which appeal to you most as research ideas and why.

---

worked example **Brainstorming**

George's main interest was football. When he finished university he wanted to work in marketing, preferably for a sports goods manufacturer. He had examined his own strengths and discovered that his best marks were in marketing. He wanted to do his research project on some aspect of marketing, preferably linked to football, but had no real research idea. He asked three friends, all taking business studies degrees, to help him brainstorm the problem.

George began by explaining the problem in some detail. At first the suggestions emerged slowly. He noted them down on the whiteboard. Soon the board was covered with suggestions. George counted these and discovered there were over 100.

Reviewing individual suggestions produced nothing that any of the group felt to be of sufficient merit for a research project. However, one of George's friends pointed out that combining the suggestions of Premier League football, television rights and sponsorship might provide an idea which satisfied the assessment requirements of the project.

They discussed the suggestion further, and George noted the research idea as 'something about how confining the rights to show live Premiership football to Sky TV would impact upon the sale of Premiership club-specific merchandise'.

George arranged to see his project tutor to discuss how to refine the idea they had just generated.

■ Refining research ideas

The Delphi technique

An additional approach that our students have found particularly useful in refining their research ideas is the *Delphi technique*. This involves using a group of people who are either involved or interested in the research idea to generate and choose a more specific research idea (Robson, 2002). To use this technique you need:

1 to brief the members of the group about the research idea (they can make notes if they wish);
2 at the end of the briefing to encourage group members to seek clarification and more information as appropriate;
3 to ask each member of the group, including the originator of the research idea, to generate independently up to three specific research ideas based on the idea that has been described (they can also be asked to provide a justification for their specific ideas);
4 to collect the research ideas in an unedited and non-attributable form and to distribute them to all members of the group;
5 a second cycle of the process (steps 2 to 4) in which individuals comment on the research ideas and revise their own contributions in the light of what others have said;
6 subsequent cycles of the process until a consensus is reached. These either follow a similar pattern (steps 2 to 4) or use discussion, voting or some other method.

This process works well, not least because people enjoy trying to help one another. In addition it is very useful in moulding groups into a cohesive whole.

---

worked example

Using a Delphi group

Tim explained to the group that his research idea was concerned with understanding the decision-making processes associated with mortgage applications and loan advances. His briefing to the three other group members, and the questions that they asked him, considered aspects such as:

- the influences on a potential first-time buyer to approach a specific financial institution;
- the influence of face-to-face contact between potential borrower and potential lender on decision-making.

The group then moved on to generate a number of more specific research ideas, among which were the following:

- the factors that influenced potential first-time house purchasers to deal with particular financial institutions;
- the effect of interpersonal contact on mortgage decisions;
- the qualities that potential applicants look for in mortgage advisers.

These were considered and commented on by all the group members. At the end of the second cycle Tim had, with the other students' agreement, refined his research idea to:

- the way in which a range of factors influenced potential first-time buyers' choice of lending institution.

He now needed to pursue these ideas by undertaking a preliminary search of the literature.

The preliminary study

Even if you have been given a research idea, it is still necessary to refine it in order to turn it into a research project. Some authors, for example Bennett (1991), refer to this process as a *preliminary study*. For some research ideas this will be no more than a review of some of the literature. This can be thought of as the first iteration of your critical literature review (Figure 3.1). For others it may include revisiting the techniques discussed earlier in this section as well as informal discussions with people who have personal experience of and knowledge about your research ideas. In some cases *shadowing* employees who are likely to be important in your research may also provide insights. If you are planning on undertaking your research within an organisation it is important to gain a good understanding of your host organisation (Kervin, 1992). However, whatever techniques you choose the underlying purpose is to gain a greater understanding so that your research question can be refined.

At this stage you need to be testing your research ideas against the checklist in Box 2.1 and where necessary changing them. It may be that after a preliminary study, or discussing your ideas with colleagues, you decide that the research idea is no longer feasible in the form in which you first envisaged it. If this is the case do not be too downhearted. It is far better to revise your research ideas at this stage than to have to do it later, when you have undertaken far more work.

Integrating ideas

The integration of ideas from these techniques is essential if your research is to have a clear direction and not contain a mismatch between objectives and your final research report. Jankowicz (2000:46–9) suggests an integrative process that our students have found most useful. This he terms 'working up and narrowing down'. It involves classifying each research idea first into its area, then its field, and finally the precise aspect in which you are interested. These represent an increasingly more detailed description of the research idea. Thus your initial area, based on examining your course work, might be accountancy. After browsing some recent journals and discussion with colleagues this becomes more focused on the field of financial accounting methods. With further reading, the use of the Delphi technique and discussion with your project tutor you decide to focus on the aspect of activity-based costing.

You will know when the process of generating and refining ideas is complete as you will be able to say 'I'd like to do some research on ...'. Obviously there will still be a big gap between this and the point when you are ready to start serious work on your research. Sections 2.4 and 2.5 will ensure that you are ready to bridge that gap.

Refining topics given by your employing organisation

If, as a part-time student, your manager gives you a topic, this may present particular problems. It may be something in which you are not particularly interested. In this case you will have to weigh the advantage of doing something useful to the organisation against the disadvantage of a potential lack of personal motivation. You therefore need to achieve a balance. Often the project your manager wishes you to undertake is larger than that which is appropriate for your course project. In such cases, it may be possible to complete both by isolating an element of the larger organisational project that you find interesting and treating this as the project for your course.

One of our students was asked to do a preliminary investigation of the strengths and weaknesses of her organisation's pay system and then to recommend consultants to design and implement a new system. She was not particularly interested in this project. However, she was considering becoming a freelance personnel consultant. Therefore, for her course project she decided to study the decision-making process in relation to the appointment of personnel consultants. Her organisation's decision on which consultant to appoint, and why this decision was taken, proved to be a useful case study against which to compare management decision-making theory.

In this event you would write a larger report for your organisation and a part of it for your project report. Section 13.4 offers some guidance on writing two separate reports for different audiences.

2.4   Turning research ideas into research projects

▓ Writing research questions

Much is made in this book of the importance of defining clear *research questions* at the beginning of the research process. The importance of this cannot be overemphasised. One of the key criteria of your research success will be whether you have a set of clear conclusions drawn from the data you have collected. The extent to which you can do that will be determined largely by the clarity with which you have posed your initial research questions.

worked example	**Defining the research question**

> Imran was studying for a BA in Business Studies and doing his placement year in an advanced consumer electronics company. When he first joined the company he was surprised to note that the company's business strategy, which was announced in the company newsletter, seemed to be inconsistent with what Imran knew of the product market.
>
> Imran had become particularly interested in corporate strategy in his degree. He was familiar with some of the literature that suggested that corporate strategy should be linked to the general external environment in which the organisation operated. He wanted to do some research on corporate strategy in his organisation for his degree dissertation.
>
> After talking this over with his project tutor Imran decided on the following research question: 'Why does my organisation's corporate strategy not seem to reflect the major factors in the external operating environment?'

Defining research questions, rather like generating research ideas (Section 2.3), is not a straightforward matter. It is important that the question is sufficiently involved to generate the sort of project that is consistent with the standards expected of you (Box 2.1). A question that prompts a descriptive answer, for example 'What is the proportion of graduates entering the civil service who attended the old-established UK universities?' is far easier to answer than: 'Why are graduates from old-established UK universities more likely to enter the civil service than graduates from other universities?' More will be said about the importance of theory in defining the research question later in this section. However, beware of research questions that are too easy.

It is perhaps more likely that you fall into the trap of asking research questions that are too difficult. The question cited above, 'Why are graduates from old-established UK universities more likely to enter the civil service than graduates from other universities?' is a case in point. It would probably be very difficult to gain sufficient access to the inner portals of the civil service to get a good grasp of the subtle 'unofficial' processes that go on at staff selection which may favour one type of candidate over another. Over-reaching yourself in the definition of research questions is a danger.

The pitfall that you must avoid at all costs is asking research questions that will not generate new insights (Box 2.1). This raises the question of the extent to which you have consulted the relevant literature. It is perfectly legitimate to replicate research because you have a genuine concern about its applicability to your research setting (for example, your organisation). However, it certainly is not legitimate to display your ignorance of the literature.

It is often a useful starting point in the writing of research questions to begin with one *general focus research question* that flows from your research idea. This may lead to several more detailed questions or the definition of research objectives. Table 2.1 has some examples of general focus research questions.

Writing your research questions will be, in most cases, your individual concern but it is useful to get other people to help you. An obvious source of guidance is your project tutor. Consulting your project tutor will avoid the pitfalls of the questions that are too easy or too difficult or have been answered before. Discussing your area of interest with your project tutor will lead to your research questions becoming much clearer.

Prior to discussion with your project tutor you may wish to conduct a brainstorming session with your peers or use the Delphi technique (Section 2.3). Your research questions may flow from your initial examination of the relevant literature. As outlined in Section 2.3, journal articles reporting primary research will often end with a conclusion that includes the consideration of the author of the implications for future research of the work in the article. This may be phrased in the form of research questions. However, even if it is not, it may suggest pertinent research questions to you.

Writing research objectives

Your research may begin with a general focus research question that then generates more detailed research questions, or you may use your general focus research ques-

Table 2.1 **Examples of research ideas and their derived focus research questions**

Research idea	General focus research question
Job recruitment via the Internet	How effective is recruiting for new staff via the Internet in comparison with traditional methods?
Advertising and share prices	How does the running of a TV advertising campaign designed to boost the image of a company affect its share price?
The use of aromas as a marketing device	In what ways does the use of specific aromas in supermarkets affect buyer behaviour?
The future of trade unions	What are the strategies that trade unions should adopt to ensure their future viability?

tion as a base from which you write a set of *research objectives*. Objectives are more generally acceptable to the research community as evidence of the researcher's clear sense of purpose and direction. It may be that either is satisfactory. Do check whether your examining body has a preference.

We contend that research objectives are likely to lead to greater specificity than research or investigative questions. Table 2.2 illustrates this point. It summarises the objectives of some research conducted by one of our students. Expression of the first research question as an objective prompted a consideration of the objectives of the organisations. This was useful because it led to the finding that there often were no clear objectives. This in itself was an interesting theoretical discovery.

The second and third objectives operationalise the matching research questions by introducing the notion of explicit effectiveness criteria. In a similar way the fourth objective (parts a and b) and the fifth objective are specific about factors that lead to effectiveness in question 4. The biggest difference between the questions and objectives is illustrated by the way in which the fifth question becomes the sixth objective. They are similar but differ in the way that the objective makes clear that a theory will be developed that will make a causal link between two sets of variables: effectiveness factors and team briefing success.

This is not to say that the research questions could not have been written with a similar amount of specificity. They could. Indeed, you may find it easier to write specific research questions than objectives. However, we doubt whether the same level of precision could be achieved through the writing of research questions alone. Research objectives require more rigorous thinking, which derives from the use of more formal language.

◼ The importance of theory in writing research questions and objectives

Section 4.1 outlines the role of theory in helping you to decide your approach to research design. However, your consideration of theory should begin earlier than this. It should inform your definition of research questions and objectives.

Table 2.2 Phrasing research questions as research objectives

Research question	Research objective
1 Why have organisations introduced team briefing?	1 To identify organisations' objectives for team briefing schemes.
2 How can the effectiveness of team briefing schemes be measured?	2 To establish suitable effectiveness criteria for team briefing schemes.
3 Has team briefing been effective?	3 To describe the extent to which the effectiveness criteria for team briefing have been met.
4 How can the effectiveness of team briefing be explained?	4a To determine the factors associated with the effectiveness criteria for team briefing being met. b To estimate whether some of those factors are more influential than other factors.
5 Can the explanation be generalised?	5 To develop an explanatory theory that associates certain factors with the effectiveness of team briefing schemes.

Theory is defined by Gill and Johnson (1997:178) as 'a formulation regarding the cause and effect relationships between two or more variables, which may or may not have been tested'.

There is probably no word that is more misused and misunderstood in education than the word 'theory'. It is thought that material included in textbooks is 'theory' whereas what is happening in the 'real world' is practice. The citing of references in students' written work is often referred to by them as 'theory'. Students who saw earlier drafts of this book remarked that they were pleased that the book was not too 'theoretical'. What they meant was that the book concentrated on giving lots of practical advice. Yet the book is full of theory. Advising you to carry out research in a particular way (variable A) is based on the theory that this will yield effective results (variable B). This is the cause and effect relationship referred to in the definition of theory cited above.

The definition demonstrates that 'theory' has a specific meaning. It refers to situations where if A is introduced B will be the consequence. Therefore the marketing manager may theorise that the introduction of loyalty cards by a supermarket will lead to customers being less likely to shop regularly at a competitor supermarket. That is a theory. Yet the marketing manager would probably not recognise it as such. He or she is still less likely to refer to it as a theory, particularly in the company of fellow managers. Many managers are very dismissive of any talk that smacks of 'theory'. It is thought of as something that is all very well to learn about at business school but bears little relation to what goes on in everyday organisational life. Yet the loyalty card example shows that it has everything to do with what goes on in everyday organisational life.

Section 4.1 notes that every purposive decision we take is based on theory: that certain consequences will flow from the decision. It follows from this that every managers' meeting that features a number of decisions will be a meeting that is highly *theory dependent* (Gill and Johnson, 1997). All that will be missing is a realisation of this fact. So, if theory is something that is so rooted in our everyday lives it certainly is something that we need not be apprehensive about. If it is implicit in all our decisions and actions then recognising its importance means making it explicit. In research the importance of theory must be recognised: therefore it must be made explicit.

Kerlinger and Lee (2000) reinforce Gill and Johnson's definition by noting that the purpose of examining relationships between two or more variables is to explain and predict these relationships. Gill and Johnson (1997:27) neatly tie these purposes of theory to their definition:

> ... it is also evident that if we have the expectation that by doing A, B will happen, then by manipulating the occurrence of A we can begin to predict and influence the occurrence of B. In other words, theory is clearly enmeshed in practice since explanation enables prediction which in turn enables control.

In our example, the marketing manager theorised that the introduction of loyalty cards by a supermarket would lead to customers being less likely to shop regularly at a competitor supermarket. Following Gill and Johnson's (1997:27) point that 'explanation enables prediction which in turn enables control', the supermarket would be well advised to conduct research that yielded an explanation of why loyalty cards encourage loyalty. Is it a purely economic rationale? Does it foster the 'collector' instinct in all of us? Does it appeal to a sense of thrift in us that helps us cope with an ever more wasteful world? These explanations are probably complex and interrelated. Reaching a better understanding of them would help the marketing manager to predict the outcome of any changes to the scheme. Increasing the amount of points per item would be effective if the economic explanation was valid. Increasing the range of products on which extra points were offered might appeal to the 'collector' instinct. More accurate prediction would offer the marketing manager increased opportunities for control.

Phillips and Pugh (2000) distinguish between research and what they call *intelligence gathering*. The latter is the gathering of facts. For example, what is the relative proportion of undergraduates to postgraduates reading this book? What is the current spend per employee on training in the UK? What provision do small businesses make for bad debts? This is often called descriptive research (Section 4.2) and may form part of your research project. Descriptive research would be the first step in our example of supermarket loyalty card marketing. Establishing that there had been a change in customer behaviour following the introduction of supermarket loyalty cards would be the first step prior to any attempt at explanation.

Phillips and Pugh contrast such 'what' questions with 'why' questions. Examples of these 'why' questions are as follows: Why do British organisations spend less per head on training than German organisations? Why are new car purchasers reluctant to take out extended warranties on their vehicles? Why do some travellers still prefer to use cross-channel ferries as opposed to the Channel Tunnel? Such questions go 'beyond description and require analysis'. They look for 'explanations, relationships, comparisons, predictions, generalisations and theories' (Phillips and Pugh, 2000:47–8).

It is a short step from the 'why' research question to the testing of an existing theory in a new situation or the development of your own theory. This may be expressed as a hypothesis that is to be tested (Section 4.1), or the eventual answer to your research question may be the development or amendment of a theory.

worked example

Writing a research question based on theory

David was a senior manager studying part time. He was worried that the many changes that had taken place in his organisation, including large-scale redundancies at all levels, meant that the nature of the relationship between the organisation and its employees was changing.

His reading led him to become fascinated by the idea of the psychological contract between the organisation and the employee: what each will give the other (e.g. security, loyalty, ambition, career progression) in return for work and employment over and above the normal terms and conditions that are part of the legal employment contract.

David's research question was: 'How are the structural changes in my organisation affecting the way in which employees think about the psychological contract they have with the organisation?'

David was asked to clarify the theory underpinning his research. He did so by explaining that redundancies created in employees feelings of insecurity such that they saw the employment relationship simply as a short-term 'wage–work bargain'. This meant that they were unprepared to put in the extra commitment normally associated with building a career.

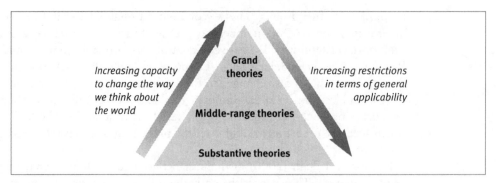

Figure 2.1 **Grand, middle-range and substantive theories**

Although intelligence gathering will play a part in your research, it is unlikely to be enough. You should be seeking to explain phenomena, to analyse relationships, to compare what is going on in different research settings, to predict outcomes and to generalise; then you will be working at the theoretical level. This is a necessary requirement for most assessed research projects.

You may still be concerned that the necessity to be theory dependent in your research project means that you will have to develop a ground-breaking theory that will lead to a whole new way of thinking about management. If this is the case you should take heart from the threefold typology of theories summarised by Creswell (1994) (see Figure 2.1). He talks of 'grand theories', usually thought to be the province of the natural scientists (e.g. Darwin and Newton). He contrasts these with 'middle-range theories', which lack the capacity to change the way in which we think about the world but are nonetheless of significance. Some of the theories of human motivation well known to managers would be in this category. However, most of us are concerned with 'substantive theories' that are 'restricted to a particular setting, group, time population or problem' (Creswell, 1994:83). For example, studying the reasons why a total quality initiative in a particular organisation failed would be an example of a substantive theory. Restricted they may be, but a host of 'substantive theories' that present similar propositions may lead to 'middle-range theories'. By developing 'substantive theories', however modest, we are doing our bit as researchers to enhance our understanding of the world about us. A grand claim, but a valid one!

This discussion of theory does assume that a clear theoretical position is developed prior to the collection of data (the *deductive* approach). This will not always be the case. It may be that your study is based on the principle of developing theory after the data have been collected (the *inductive* approach). This is a fundamental difference in research approach, and will be discussed in detail in Section 4.1.

2.5   Writing your research proposal

At the start of all courses or modules we give our students a plan of the work they will be doing. It includes the learning objectives, the content, the assessment strategy and the recommended reading. This is our statement of our side of the learning contract. Our students have a right to expect this.

However, when we insist on a proposal for a dissertation that is often the equivalent of at least two other modules, there is often a marked reluctance to produce anything other than what is strictly necessary. This is unsatisfactory. It is unfair to your project tutor because you are not making entirely clear what it is you intend to do in your research. You are also being unfair to yourself because you are not giving yourself the maximum opportunity to have your ideas and plans scrutinised and subjected to rigorous questioning.

Writing a research proposal is a crucial part of the research process. If you are applying for research funding, or if your proposal is going before an academic research committee, then you will know that you will need to put a great deal of time into the preparation of your proposal. However, even if the official need for a proposal is not so vital it is still a process that will repay very careful attention.

The purposes of the research proposal

Organising your ideas

Section 13.1 notes that writing can be the best way of clarifying our thoughts. This is a valuable purpose of the proposal. Not only will it clarify your thoughts but it will help you to organise your ideas into a coherent statement of your research intent. Your reader will be looking for this.

Convincing your audience

However coherent your ideas and exciting your research plan, it counts for little if the proposal reveals that what you are planning to do is simply not possible. As part of our research methods course for taught postgraduate students we have a three-stage assignment, the first stage of which is to write a proposal. This is then discussed with a project tutor. What usually happens is that this discussion is about how the plans can be amended so that something more modest in scope is attempted. Often work that is not achievable in the given timescale is proposed. If your proposal has not convinced your audience that the research you have proposed is achievable, then you will have saved yourself a great deal of time and frustration.

Contracting with your 'client'

If you were asked to carry out a research project for a commercial client or your own organisation it is unthinkable that you would go ahead without a clear proposal that you would submit for approval. Acceptance of your proposal by the client would be part of the contract that existed between you. So it is with your proposal to your project tutor or academic committee. Acceptance implies that your proposal is satisfactory. While this is obviously no guarantee of subsequent success, it is something of comfort to you to know that at least you started your research journey with an appropriate destination and journey plan. It is for you to ensure that you are not derailed!

The content of the research proposal

Title

This may be your first attempt at the title. It may change as your work progresses. At this stage it should closely mirror the content of your proposal.

Background

This is an important part of the proposal. It should tell the reader why you feel the research that you are planning is worth the effort. This may be expressed in the form of a problem that needs solving or something that you find exciting and has aroused your curiosity. The reader will be looking for evidence here that there is sufficient interest from you to sustain you over the long months (or years) ahead.

This is also the section where you will demonstrate your knowledge of the relevant literature. Moreover, it will clarify where your proposal fits into the debate in the literature. You will be expected to show a clear link between the previous work that has been done in your field of research interest and the content of your proposal. In short, the literature should be your point of departure. This is not the same as the critical literature review (Section 3.2) you will present in your final project report. It will just provide an overview of the key literature sources from which you intend to draw.

Research questions and objectives

The background section should lead smoothly into a statement of your research question(s) and objectives. These should leave the reader in no doubt as to precisely what it is that your research seeks to achieve. Be careful here to ensure that your objectives are precisely written and will lead to observable outcomes (look again at Table 2.2, e.g., 'to describe the extent to which the effectiveness criteria specified for the team briefing scheme have been met'). Do not fall into the trap of stating general research aims that are little more than statements of intent (e.g. 'to discover the level of effectiveness of the team briefing scheme').

Method

This and the background sections will be the longest sections of the proposal. It will detail precisely how you intend to go about achieving your research objectives. It will also justify your choice of method in the light of those objectives. These two aims may be met by dividing your method section into two parts: research design and data collection.

In the part on research design you will explain where you intend to carry out the research. If your earlier coverage has pointed out that your research is a single-organisation issue, then this will be self-evident. However, if your research topic is more generic you will wish to explain, for example, which sector(s) of the economy you have chosen to research and why you chose these sectors. You will also need to explain the identity of your research population (for example, managers or trade union officials) and why you chose this population.

This section should also include an explanation of the general way in which you intend to carry out the research. Will it be based on a survey, interviews, examination of secondary data or a combination of methods? Here again it is essential to explain why you have chosen your approach. Your explanation should be based on the most effective way of meeting your research objectives.

The research design section gives an overall view of the method chosen and the reason for that choice. The data collection section goes into much more detail about how specifically the data are to be collected. For example, if you are using a survey approach you should specify your population and sample size. You should also clarify how the questionnaires will be distributed and how they will be analysed. If you are using interviews you should explain how many interviews will be conducted, their intended duration, whether they will be tape recorded, and how they will be analysed. In short, you should demonstrate to your reader that you have thought carefully about all the issues regarding your method and their relationship to your research objectives. However, it is normally not necessary in the proposal to include precise detail of the method you will employ, for example the content of the observation schedule or questionnaire questions.

In addition, it may also be necessary to include a statement about how you are going to adhere to any ethical guidelines. This is particularly important in some research settings, e.g. the National Health Service.

Timescale

This will help you and your reader to decide on the viability of your research proposal. It will be helpful if you divide your research plan into stages. This will give you a clear idea as to what is possible in the given timescale. Experience has shown that however well the researcher's time is organised the whole process seems to take longer than anticipated.

worked example	**A research timescale**

As part of the final year of their undergraduate business studies degree all our students have to undertake an 8000–10 000-word research project. In order to assist them with their time management we discuss the following outline timescale with them.

Target date	Month number	Task to be achieved
Start October	1	Start thinking about research ideas (latest start date)
End November	2	Literature read Objectives clearly defined with reference to literature
End December	3	Literature review written Methodology literature read for dissertations involving secondary/primary date
End January	4	Secondary/primary data collected and analysed (analysis techniques linked to methodology/research literature) Literature review extended further
Mid-February	5	Further writing up and analysis
End March	6	Draft completed including formatting bibliography etc.
Mid-May	8	Draft revised as necessary
End May	8	Submission

As part of this section of their proposal, many researchers find it useful to produce a schedule for their research using a *Gannt chart*. Developed by Henry Gannt in 1917, this provides a simple visual representation of the tasks or activities that make up your research project, each being plotted against a time line. The time we estimate each task will take is represented by the length of an associated horizontal bar, whilst the task's start and finish times are represented by its position on the time line. Figure 2.2 shows a Gannt chart for a student's research project. As we can see from the first bar on this chart, the student has decided to schedule in two weeks of holiday. The first of these occurs over the Christmas and New Year period, and the second occurs while her tutor is reading a draft copy of the completed project in April. We can also see from the second and fourth bar that, like many of our students, she intends to begin to draft her literature review while she is still reading new articles and books. However, she has also recognised that some activities must be undertaken sequentially. For example, bars 9 and 10 highlight that before she can administer her questionnaire (bar 10) she must complete all the revisions highlighted as necessary by the pilot testing (bar 9).

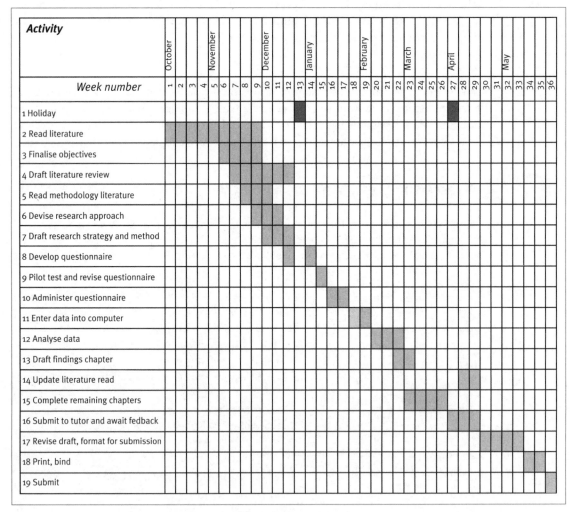

Figure 2.2 **Gantt chart for a student's research project**

Resources

This is another facet of viability (Box 2.1). It will allow you and the reader to assess whether what you are proposing can be resourced. Resource considerations may be categorised as finance, data access and equipment.

Conducting research costs money. This may be for travel, subsistence, help with data analysis, or postage for questionnaires. Think through the expenses involved and ensure that you can meet these expenses.

Assessors of your proposal will need to be convinced that you have access to the data you need to conduct your research. This may be unproblematic if you are carrying out research in your own organisation. Many academic committees wish to see written approval from host organisations in which researchers are planning to conduct research. You will also need to convince your reader of the possibility of obtaining a reasonable response to any questionnaire that you send.

It is surprising how many research proposals have ambitious plans for large-scale surveys with no thought given to how the data will be analysed. It is important that you convince the reader of your proposal that you have access to the necessary computer hardware and software to analyse your data. Moreover, it is necessary for you to demonstrate that you have either the necessary skills to perform the analysis or can learn the skills in an appropriate time, or you have access to help.

References

It is not necessary to try and impress your proposal reader with an enormous list of references (Robson, 2002). A few literature sources to which you have referred in the background section and which relate to the previous work that is directly informing your own proposal should be all that is necessary.

■ Criteria for evaluating research proposals

The extent to which the components of the proposal fit together

Your rationale for conducting the research should include a study of the previous published research, including relevant theories in the topic area. This study should inform your research question(s) and objectives. Your proposed methodology should flow directly from these research question(s) and objectives. The time that you have allocated should be a direct reflection of the methods you employ, as should the resources that you need.

worked example	Fitting together the various components of the research proposal

Jenny was a middle manager in a large insurance company. She was very interested in the fact that electronic forms of communication meant that organisations could move information-based administrative work round different locations. Her company was scanning paper applications for insurance policies onto their computer system and delivering these into a central electronic bank of work. The company had employees in three different locations in the UK, and work was drawn from the bank on the basis of workload existing in each particular location. Recently senior management had been considering developing work locations in

South Asian cities, where it felt the standard of English meant that such functions could be fulfilled effectively. Jenny anticipated that this would pose certain logistical problems, for example staff training and communications. Knowledge of these problems would give her a clear picture of the limit of complexity of the work that could be done. This was particularly important since the complexity range went from the simple to the technically complex. Research into the literature on cross-cultural training justified Jenny's concern. As a consequence of her thought and reading she developed her research question as: 'What cross-cultural problems may be posed by international electronic work transfer in the insurance industry, and how may these problems limit the complexity of the work that may be transferred?'

Through her reading of the practitioner journals Jenny was aware that some other financial services organisations had been sending their work to Asia for some time. She decided that approaching these companies and interviewing their key personnel would be a fruitful approach. The main problem that Jenny would have with this research would be the time that the interview work would take, given that such companies were located all over the UK and North America. She was unsure how many interviews would be necessary. This would become clearer as she progressed in the research. However, it was unlikely that less than 10 companies would yield sufficient valuable data. She thought that she could collect the necessary data in a four-month period, which fitted in with her university deadline. There were no specific resources that Jenny needed other than finance and time. Since her research would be of immediate benefit to her employer she though that neither would pose a problem.

The viability of the proposal

This is the answer to the question: 'Can this research be carried out satisfactorily within the timescale and with available resources?'

The absence of preconceived ideas

Your research should be an exciting journey into the unknown. Do not be like the student who came to Phil to talk over a research proposal and said 'Of course, I know what the answer will be'. When asked to explain the purpose of doing the research if he already knew the answer he became rather defensive and eventually looked for another supervisor and, probably, another topic.

---

worked example | **A written research proposal**

Puvadol was a student from Thailand who returned home from the UK to complete his MA dissertation. His proposed dissertation concerned the applicability of Western methods of involving employees in decision-making in Thai organisations.

An abbreviated version of Puvadol's proposal follows:

Title

The influences of Thai culture on employee involvement.

Background

Involving employees in the decision-making of their employing organisations has been increasingly popular in Europe and North America in recent years. The influx of American organisations into Thailand has meant that similar approaches are being adopted. However, this assumes that Thai employees will respond to these techniques as readily as their European and American counterparts.

Doubts about the validity of these assumptions derive from studies of Thai national culture (Komin, 1990). Using Rokeach's (1979) conceptual framework, Komin characterised Thai culture in a number of ways. I have isolated those that relate to employee involvement. These are that Thais wish to:

a save face, to avoid criticism and to show consideration to others;
b exhibit gratitude to those who have shown kindness and consideration;
c promote smooth, conflict-free interpersonal relations;
d interpret 'rules' in a flexible way with little concern for principles;
e promote interdependent social relations;
f be seen to be achieving success through good social relations rather than individual success.

I intend to demonstrate in this section that these six cultural values contradict the values of employee involvement (e.g. employee involvement may involve employees in openly criticising managers, which directly contradicts **a** above).

Research objectives

1 To examine the assumptions behind the management technique of employee involvement.
2 To establish the characteristics of the Thai national culture.
3 To identify the opinions of Thai employees and their managers, working in American-owned organisations in Thailand, towards values underpinning employee involvement.
4 To draw conclusions about the applicability of employee involvement to Thai employees.

Method

1 Conduct a review of the literatures on employee involvement and Thai national culture in order to develop research hypotheses.
2 Carry out primary research in three American-owned petrochemical and manufacturing organisations in Thailand to assess the opinions of Thai employees and their managers towards values underpinning employee involvement. Informal approval has been gained from three organisations. American-owned organisations are relevant because it is in these that employee involvement is most likely to be found and values underpinning employee involvement exhibited. Petrochemical and manufacturing organisations are chosen because the occupations carried out in these organisations are likely to be similar, thus ensuring that any differences are a function of Thai national culture rather than of occupational culture.

A questionnaire will be developed with questions based on the Thai values a–f in the Background section above. Each value will lead to a hypothesis (e.g. employee involvement may not be appropriate to Thai culture because it may mean that employees openly criticise their managers). The questions in the questionnaire will seek to test these hypotheses. The questionnaire will be distributed to a sample (size to be agreed) of employees and of managers across all three organisations.

Data analysis will use the SPSS software. Statistical tests will be run to ensure that results are a function of Thai cultural values rather than of values that relate to the individual organisations. ▶

Timescale

January–March 2002: review of literature
April 2002: draft literature review
May 2002: review research methods literature and agree research strategy
June 2002: agree formal access to three organisations for collection of primary data
July–August 2002: compile, pilot and revise questionnaire
September 2002: administer questionnaire
October–November 2002: final collection of questionnaires and analysis of data
November 2002–February 2003: completion of first draft of project report
March–May 2003: final writing of project report

Resources

I have access to computer hardware and software. Access to three organisations has been negotiated, subject to confirmation. My employer has agreed to pay all incidental costs as part of my course expenses.

References

Komin, S. (1990) *Psychology of the Thai People: Values and Behavioral Patterns*, Thailand, National Institute of Development Administration (in Thai).
Rokeach, M. (1979) *Understanding Human Values: Individual and Society*, New York, The Free Press.

If it is absolutely crucial that your proposal is of the highest quality then you may wish to use an *expert system* such as Peer Review Emulator. This software is available either on its own or as part of the Methodologist's Toolchest suite of programs. It asks you a series of questions about your proposed research. The program then critiques these answers to ensure that common research standards are achieved (Scolari Sage, 2002).

2.6   Summary

- The process of formulating and clarifying your research topic is the most important part of your research topic.

- Attributes of a research topic do not vary a great deal between universities. The most important of these is that your research topic will meet the requirements of the examining body.

- Generating and refining research ideas makes use of a variety of techniques. It is important that you use a variety of techniques including those that involve rational thinking and those that involve creative thinking.

- The ideas generated can be integrated subsequently using a technique such as working up and narrowing down.

- Clear research questions, based on the relevant literature, will act as a focus for the research that follows.

- Research can be distinguished from intelligence gathering. Research is theory dependent.

- Writing a research proposal helps you to organise your ideas, and can be thought of as a contract between you and the reader.

- The content of the research proposal should tell the reader what you want to do, why you want to do it, what you are trying to achieve, and how you to plan to achieve it.

self-check Questions

2.1 Why is it important to spend time formulating and clarifying your research topic?

2.2 You have decided to search the literature to 'try and come up with some research ideas in the area of Operations Management'. How will you go about this?

2.3 A colleague of yours wishes to generate a research idea in the area of accounting. He has examined his own strengths and interests on the basis of his assignments and has read some review articles, but has failed to find an idea about which he is excited. He comes and asks you for advice. Suggest two techniques that your colleague could use, and justify your choice.

2.4 You are interested in doing some research on the interface between business organisations and schools. Write three research questions that may be appropriate.

2.5 What may be the theory underpinning the decision by organisations sponsoring schools?

2.6 How would you demonstrate the influence of relevant theory in your research proposal?

progressing your research project

From research ideas to a research proposal

☐ If you have not been given a research idea consider the techniques available for generating and refining research ideas. Choose a selection of those with which you feel most comfortable, making sure to include both rational and creative thinking techniques. Use these to try to generate a research idea or ideas. Once you have got some research ideas, or if you have been unable to find an idea, talk to your project tutor.

☐ Evaluate your research ideas against the checklist of attributes of a good research project (Box 2.1).

☐ Refine your research ideas using a selection of the techniques available for generating and refining research ideas. Re-evaluate your research ideas against the checklist of attributes of a good research project (Box 2.1). Remember that it is better to revise (and in some situations to discard) ideas that do not appear to be feasible at this stage. Integrate your ideas using the process of working up and narrowing down to form one research idea.

☐ Use your research idea to write a general focus research question. Where possible this should be a 'why?' or a 'how?' rather than a 'what?' question.

☐ Use the general focus research question to write more detailed research questions and your research objectives.

☐ Write your research proposal making sure it includes a clear title and sections on:

☐ the background to your research;

☐ your research questions and objectives;

☐ the method you intend to use;

☐ the timescale for your research;

☐ the resources you require;

☐ references to any literature to which you have referred.

References

Bennett, R. (1991) 'What is management research?', in Smith, N.C. and Dainty, P. (eds) *The Management Research Handbook*, London, Routledge, pp. 67–77.

Buzan, T. with Buzan, B. (2000) *The Mind Map Book* (Millennium edn), London, BBC Books.

Carroll, L. (1989) *Alice's Adventures in Wonderland*, London, Hutchinson.

Creswell, J. (1994) *Research Design: Quantitative and Qualitative Approaches*, Thousand Oaks, CA, Sage.

Ghauri. P. and Grønhaug, K. (2002) *Research Methods in Business Studies: A Practical Guide* (2nd edn), Harlow, Financial Times Prentice Hall.

Gill, J. and Johnson, P. (1997) *Research Methods for Managers* (2nd edn), London, Paul Chapman.

Jankowicz, A.D. (2000) *Business Research Projects* (3rd edn), London, Thomson Learning.

Kerlinger, F. and Lee, H. (2000) *Foundations of Behavioral Research* (4th edn), Fort Worth, Harcourt College Publishers.

Kervin, J.B. (1992) *Methods for Business Research*, New York, HarperCollins.

Moody, P.E. (1983) *Decision Making: Proven Methods for Better Decisions*, Maidenhead, McGraw-Hill.

Phillips, E.M. and Pugh, D.S. (2000) *How to get a PhD* (3rd edn), Buckingham, Open University Press.

Raimond, P. (1993) *Management Projects*, London, Chapman & Hall.

Robson, C. (2002) *Real World Research* (2nd edn), Oxford, Blackwell.

Saunders, M.N.K. and Lewis, P. (1997) 'Great ideas and blind alleys? A review of the literature on starting research', *Management Learning*, 28:3, 283–99.

Scolari Sage (2002) Methodologist's Toolchest (online) (cited 24th February 2002). Available from <URL:http://www.scolari.co.uk>.

Sharp, J. and Howard, K. (1996) *The Management of a Student Research Project* (2nd edn), Aldershot, Gower.

Smith, N.C. and Dainty, P. (1991) *The Management Research Handbook*, London, Routledge.

Further reading

Gill, J. and Johnson, P. (1997) *Research Methods for Managers* (2nd edn), London, Paul Chapman. Chapter 3 is a particularly clear account of the role of theory in research methods and is worth reading to gain a better understanding of this often-misunderstood area.

Raimond, P. (1993) *Management Projects*, London, Chapman & Hall. Chapter 4 contains a useful discussion of techniques for helping to identify project ideas. It is particularly good for those techniques that we have classified as creative rather than rational.

Robson, C. (2002) *Real World Research* (2nd edn), Oxford, Blackwell. Appendix A is devoted to the writing of research proposals and is a very useful source of further information.

CASE 2	Strategic issues in the UK brewing industry

Steve was thinking about how to write his research proposal. A few weeks earlier he had been allocated a project tutor on the basis of his wanting to do something in the area of strategic management. Now his project tutor had emailed him and suggested they meet early next week to discuss Steve's ideas for the research topic. He asked Steve to bring along his research proposal. Steve started to look through his lecture notes from the Strategic Management module, and the following extract caught his eye:

> As companies reach maturity in their product's life cycle a number of occurrences tend to become commonplace. Competition increases, international competitors achieve market entry, overcapacity within the industry increases, profit margins in gross profit terms generally begin to fall, and acquisitions and mergers take place. Certainly within the UK marketplace these trends have recently occurred in a number of industries: banking and brewing would be two good examples.

Steve decided that he would look at these ideas by undertaking 'in-depth' research on the UK brewing industry. Steve used the *Financial Times* CD-ROMs available in his university library to produce a time line of what had happened in the industry since 1989 and added a few notes regarding what he intended to do for his research project. This was what he produced:

Changes in the United Kingdom brewing industry
A research proposal by Steve Smith

There have been numerous changes to the UK brewing industry since the Monopolies and Mergers Commission Report of 1989:

Year	What happened
1989	Monopolies & Mergers Commission restricted brewers to 2000 public houses plus 50% of their original holdings. This ruling was modified in 1997; however, the commencement of dismantling of vertical integration within the industry had commenced by that date. This dramatically changed the distribution system, brewers having sold off many of their public houses.
1995	Scottish & Newcastle purchases Courage; now known as Scottish Courage it becomes the largest brewer in the UK.
1996	Allied Domecq decides to sell its 50% share of Carlsberg-Tetley to Bass; merger not allowed by Monopolies & Mergers Commission as it is considered to be anti-competitive. This decision appears to be instrumental to a change of strategy at Bass plc. It sells its brewing interests in 1999 unconditionally to Belgian brewer Interbrew. Bass plc is renamed Six Continents and refocuses its operations in the hotel business.
1999–2002	Interbrew grows further by the acquisition of Whitbread's brewing division and Becks lager. The UK Monopolies & Mergers Commission orders Interbrew to sell Bass brewing. After appeal this is reduced, allowing Interbrew to retain some of the Bass brands including Tennents Scottish Lager. However, it is ordered to reduce its monopoly in the lager market, resulting in the Carling division of Bass brewers being sold to the American brewers Coors, with completion in February 2002.

Notes

The major growth trends within the industry are:

- increased sales of brewery products by supermarkets;
- growth of personal imports;
- traditional town and country style public houses closing rapidly;
- a massive growth in dining out, with town centre theme pub chains growing in popularity.

However, this is no more than a change of buying and lifestyle habits. The brewing production part of the industry currently reflects overcapacity, is experiencing low profit margins, and is in the mature part of its life cycle.

There is a wealth of material on UK brewing, particularly on the Web.

Approach

I am thinking of using the Competitive Advantage model developed by M. E. Porter (*Competitive Strategy*, Free Press, 1980) to help explain the competitive situation.

Convinced he had a solid proposal, Steve attended the appointment with his project tutor. The project tutor was obviously interested in Steve's ideas but was concerned about Steve's lack of clear thought and the fact that he had still to develop a project proposal. The project tutor suggested that Steve's perspective of the industry appeared to be extremely vague, and asked him to define his intended project area more clearly, thinking not only in terms of the industry but also in relation to academic theories and research in the area of company consolidation. He also said that Steve must think carefully about the research strategy and data collection techniques he was going to use, keeping in mind that it was a course requirement to collect some primary data for the project. They then spent 15 minutes discussing what Steve's research proposal should look like. At the end of the meeting Steve's project tutor asked him to produce a clearly thought proposal prior to their next tutorial, arguing that, until this was done, there was little point in their meeting again.

Questions

1 From the information collected by Steve on the brewing industry, suggest at least two possible research questions.

2 What criteria would you use to assess whether or not these research questions form the basis of a good research topic?

3 How do you think Steve should address the requirement for collecting at least some primary data?

4 Outline the structure that Steve's research proposal should take, indicating:
   a those areas where Steve will need to do more work;
   b how the content will be formulated to address one of the titles you have chosen at question 1.

5 Outline a possible research timescale for Steve's project, taking into account your answers to question 4.

6 What lessons can you learn from Steve's first meeting with his project tutor?

self-check Answers

2.1 There are numerous reasons you could include in your answer. Some of the more important include:

- without being clear what you are going to do it is difficult to plan your research;
- to enable you to choose the most appropriate research strategy and data collection and analysis techniques;
- to ensure that your topic meets the examining body's requirements;
- to ensure that your topic is one that you are capable of doing and excites your imagination;
- to ensure that you will have sufficient time and money resources to undertake your topic;
- to ensure that you will be able to gain access to the data you require;
- to ensure that the issues in your topic are capable of being linked to theory.

2.2 One starting point would be to ask your project tutor for suggestions of possible recent review articles or articles containing recommendations for further work that he or she has read. Another would be to browse recent editions of operations management journals such as the *International Journal of Operations & Production Management* for possible research ideas. These would include both statements of the absence of research and unfounded assertions. Recent reports held in your library may also be of use here. You could also scan one or two recently published operations management textbooks for overviews of research that has been undertaken.

2.3 From the description given it would appear that your colleague has considered only rational thinking techniques. It would therefore seem sensible to suggest two creative thinking techniques, as these would hopefully generate an idea that would appeal to his heart. One technique that you could suggest is brainstorming, perhaps emphasising the need to do it with other colleagues. Exploring past projects in the accountancy area would be another possibility. You might also suggest that he keeps a notebook of ideas.

2.4 Your answer will probably differ from that below. However, the sorts of things you could be considering include:
1 How do business organisations benefit from their liaison with schools?
2 Why do business organisations undertake school liaison activities?
3 To what degree do business organisations receive value for money in their schools liaison activities?

2.5 Undoubtedly organisations would be looking for a 'pay-off'. This may be left undefined: that it is bound to be a 'good thing' or it may be linked to a specific theory that it will create an image of the organisation as one that is community minded. This is a particularly important concept if the product or service is one that has community values, for example water or electricity.

2.6 Try including a subsection in the background section that is headed 'how the previous published research has informed my research questions and objectives'. Then show how, say, a gap in the previous research that is there because nobody has pursued a particular approach before has led to you filling that gap.

Notes

Notes

Notes

Notes